Can you recognize 'the personal' in a man's work?

Selection from "Louis I. Kahn: Berkeley Lecture, 1966" page 5, line 29

foreword

What we say is often less telling than how we say. A turn of phrase — a pause —
a hesitation — a nervous flurry of words, all reveal a state of mind, a sensibility, a
personal position in the world. *What we see* is often more potent than what we are told.
An atmosphere or attitude — an object or landscape — can convey a powerful visual
message about the way things are in the world. *What we learn* is often not a matter of
fact, but a manner of being, a way of thinking.

It is this less articulate message which carries clues to "the personal" to which Kahn
refers. "Can you recognize the personal in a man's work?" implies an ability to note or
care for something subtle, something singular in a person's work. In this book, we have
asked architects to contribute statements and visual work which document their inspirations and attitudes toward making architecture.

Their response arrived to us over the past few years in two parts: as typed notes, brief
statements, tapes, and interviews — simple candid thoughts about themselves; and as
photographs, colorful drawings, and video — images which carried some heartfelt meaning outside of words. Happily, it was a collection of material as diverse as the personalities that shaped it. Given our interest in the design process, as a personal activity, it was
precisely the diversity of the written and visual responses of the contributors that was so
encouraging. It was in this spirit that the book took shape; that our understanding of
process was not about a broad interest in intuition or method but about the singularity
of every person.

The essays are presented as a collection of discrete installations. The final form of each
contributor's essay grew, quite naturally, from its particular written and visual message —
and it was the "installation" or act of locating this message, exploring how we read and
see within the silent structure of the page, that began to note, or reveal, the "personal"
in each contributor's work.

These essays believe in the power of personal vision and the singularity of that vision in
the process of perceiving, transforming, and building a world outside of oneself. They are
words and images which explore and listen to the values and energies in the human
person — and *per sonare* means precisely a "sounding" or "saying through" — which
cannot be revealed through analytic means. These essay-installations hope to provide
access to such intimations — intimations which, if outside reason, are nonetheless
instinctual to us all.

Robert Joyce, co-editor

Editors:
Robert Joyce
Rossana Santos
Laura Turlington

Graphic Designer:
Andrea Wollensak

Book Design Concept:
Robert Joyce
Andrea Wollensak

Proofreader:
Barbara Bergeron

Additional thanks to:
Generous funding for digital image manipulation and electronic
pre-press production was provided by a grant from the Graham
Foundation, Inc.

ISBN: 0-262-66102-0
Library of Congress Catalog Card Number: 96-77824

Send editorial and business correspondence to:
Perspecta: The Yale Architectural Journal
The Yale School of Architecture
180 York Street
New Haven, Connecticut 06510

Printed and bound in Hong Kong by
South China Printing Company (1988) Limited

Perspecta 28 The Yale Architectural Journal

ARCHITECTS

PROCESS

INSPIRATION

Robert Joyce, Rossana Santos, and Laura Turlington, editors
Andrea Wollensak and Robert Joyce, visual concept

The MIT Press
Cambridge, Massachusetts
London, England

contents

vision; intention

"The architect makes a work which inspires society to take a different turn ...

"That's true of a poem — it's true of a painting. It's true of a painting: it gives you a different sense of point of view about things. You certainly realize that a painter can really paint a red dress when he sees a blue one. You wonder why he does it, but still, you see: well, he really can — you see, he *does* it. Is he inhuman? Of course not. Terribly human — in fact, more so than those who are so amazed by it." *5; 13*

Whether or not architecture can inspire society to take a different turn, it *is* true that we, as architects, often envision the world in very personal ways — that it is precisely the architect's will to bring something "new" into the world that defines his or her desire to build.

The following transcript of Louis Kahn's lecture to students at Berkeley represents one person's position on architecture and its making, a position firmly rooted in Kahn's belief in the human spirit and creative will. Tapes from this lecture have been carefully presented to reflect Kahn's voice; his ... halting delivery, his *childlike emphasis,* or his — reverent pause. For reference, the lecture is noted by both line and page number: page 4, line 5, or *(4; 5)*. All quotes or concepts from the talk are cross-referenced in this fashion to related critical essays within the journal.

A folio of full- or near-full-scale charcoal study drawings for Salk Institute and the Assembly Building at Dacca accompany Kahn's comments on these projects. It is the exchange between Kahn's voice and hand, between his words and marks, and the heartfelt thoughts of his critics which, taken together, begin to construct the spirit of Kahn's vision.

contributing architect:

Louis I. Kahn

Louis I. Kahn: Berkeley Lecture, 1966

A Note on the Transcript   Ellen Morris

The transcript of this lecture by Louis I. Kahn, given at the University of California, Berkeley, is published here in *Perspecta 28* for the first time. Transcription from the original tapes of the lecture was undertaken by Edward Levin, with my assistance. The poor quality of the original reel-to-reel recording, together with Kahn's staccato delivery, freewheeling grammar, and strong Philadelphia-by-way-of-Brooklyn accent, all impeded the process of transcribing the lecture. In the end, however, with the exception of a break in continuity when one reel was replaced by another, plus no more than a few scattered instances which ultimately proved impossible to decipher with certainty, both of us are confident of the accuracy of the results. Sophisticated audio technology may someday clarify the few omissions in the lecture (noted in brackets), although none of these gaps is serious enough to impede the flow of ideas.

To the best of my recollection, Louis Kahn delivered his lecture wholly extemporaneously. No one can say what Kahn himself might have added, deleted, or otherwise modified in this transcript had he himself been given the opportunity to do so. We have therefore sought to transcribe the full delivery, replete with Kahn's half-sentences and false starts, although we have chosen to eliminate his occasional struggle for words, when such words are merely repetitions, and we have chosen to delete from the final transcript passages involving fumbling with microphones or slides. Although these deletions have no bearing on intended meaning and, instead, facilitate a much smoother reading of the lecture, they are admittedly made at some expense to the sound of the lecture; that is, to the sense of Kahn attempting to clearly formulate his thoughts extemporaneously. However, whenever pertinent to intended meaning, the many nuances in Kahn's spoken delivery are conveyed by liberal editorial use of single quotes, wordspacing, and italics, meant to approximate the impact of the actual lecture.

The original tapes of the lecture have been placed on permanent deposit with The Getty Center for the History of Art and the Humanities, in Santa Monica, California, and a cassette copy has been furnished to the Kahn archive at the University of Pennsylvania, in Philadelphia. Also placed on deposit at The Getty Center are tapes of a lengthy seminar given by Kahn to students at Berkeley. The date and nature of these seminar tapes have not yet been determined, and a complete and accurate transcript has not yet been produced. This seminar may or may not be associated with Kahn's visit to Berkeley on the occasion of this present lecture. It may result from a visit by Kahn to Berkeley subsequent to this lecture, for Kahn visited and spoke at Berkeley in April and again in November 1968 (these tapes may relate to one of these visits). Future scholarly inquiry is necessary to clarify this matter.

I wish to note here my gratitude to the editors of *Perspecta 28* for the opportunity to publish the transcript of this important lecture. It is my hope that it will add yet another dimension to Kahn scholarship as it becomes assimilated into the corpus of literature on or by Kahn that has already been published. It is equally my hope that this lecture will help shed some light on a significant debate in the history of twentieth-century American architectural education, illustrated in the ideological foment of Berkeley at the time, and in particular upon Louis Kahn's position relative to these issues.

Los Angeles, 1992

[a round of applause greets Professor Kahn on entering the lecture hall]

Berkeley Faculty: **I think your applause is ample demonstration of the fact that no introduction is needed, and that we would only like to say to Professor Kahn, to welcome you here and hope that you come back and visit us often.** 10

Professor Kahn: Well, I feel peculiar in front of this chemistry desk because I flunked chemistry consistently, but I don't know how I'll do this time.

I understand that you have a *great* student body ... and that there's much concern about the way the architect ... is to exercise ... his work through life. I can't talk for everybody ... I can only talk for myself. On coming to this – I guess it's called an auditorium, right? I heard there were many directions that people are taking in the thinking about our profession. All I can say is this; that architecture does not exist. 20

Architecture, per se, does not exist.

Architecture is a spirit.

Architecture knows no style, knows no method.

Out of the blue, you might say, which can be, in more specific terms, said to be out of the *enclosures*, warm enclosures: as though ... a man behind a wall, who felt very secure, and loved the wall 30 because ... it protected him. But he was many years behind the wall, and he wanted to look out, since, no, he did not feel that the wall had to continue its protection, and broke a hole through it, and the wall cried. It said, 'What are you doing to me? I'm a wall. I helped you so much during the ages, and now you defile me with your axe.' And the man tried to apologize, as to say, 'But I want to look out. I think you did me a service, I do admit, but I do want to see the *sun*. I want to see somebody else.' And soon the opening became an *ordained* thing – something that belonged to the order of the making of the wall. A lintel was put over the opening, the stones were smooth ... at the opening so that the sun and the light would come in more evenly, and the wall became very proud ... that it could be part of such elegance.

And from it grew ... the wonder of the column, which was – the rhythmic – position- 40
ing of support and opening.   And we're still living on the wonders of this revelation.
It is ... so remarkable, in my mind,   *that a temple – like the Parthenon – could come to man without any indication of its shape, in nature.*

1

That's a *marvel* of architecture to me; the fact that these wonderful things exist, and they existed when knowledge was almost nothing. And we still refer to the wonder of St. Mark's: that is to say – the square, San Marco. There isn't a city planner who, with all the statistics and everything else, who doesn't refer to *it*, you see, as a kind of example from which ... one must refer. It's *that spirit* which I think is the most important thing to serve if you're an architect.

But there are other aspects of architecture. There is the *profession* of architecture, which is quite different from being an architect. The profession has definite demands: of service to the client, technologies (as distinguished from sciences), strength of materials, knowledge of all kinds that must enter the consideration of the making of the building. But all of it is really very minor.

10

The most minor consideration is the professional consideration.

I said that architecture does not exist, and I really mean that.

But what *does* exist is *a work of architecture* – yes, which a man makes (which, by the way, I don't think very many *can* make). If it *is* made by many people, it is hardly a work of architecture. It probably is a very good and competent *instruction* for building, but can never be a work of architecture.

This, then, is made: a work is made, which, if done by a truly great man, he would in all modesty offer this to architecture, hoping that it would become part of the 'Treasury of Architecture'   something in the spirit to which the Pantheon belongs, to which the Parthenon belongs, to which the great works of the past belong, and many of the works of today's outstanding architects.

20

I hear much about *machines* taking the place of men. I think it's the greatest nonsense in the world! – the most colossal nonsense to think that anyone would believe that a machine could be anything but a 'brain' – never a *mind*!   But maybe a superior brain,   yes,   I do admit that could be, but never a mind.

A mind is a singularity.

30

There isn't one mind like the other mind ...

If you would get the most competent program from a machine, of instructions, I am *positive*, giving this to ten architects, you'd get ten different solutions. That can't be anything else, unless you were mesmerized by some kind of foreign influence, like 'LSD' or something like that.

[audience laughter]

I think it must be *assumed* that a building, when made, is a 'solution of the problem': and not   40 to think that you are doing so marvelous a job in doing *that*. Because it's probably the most easy thing to do – if you have the predilection for it. The reason why some deviate from this is because the program *itself,* is not worthy ...   to be extended ...   in the form of a building.

Very simple examples: you get a program of a school, and can you tell me that a teacher says the same thing in a room in which thirty are, as he would when he had but four near him, close to a fireplace, let us say, – and just a nice, intimate room, smoking a pipe ... and a dog nearby? He just don't [sic] say the same things.

A school is an environment of spaces where it is good to learn, where even the corridor must be changed into galleries, because galleries then become the only classroom the student has. There he meets other classmates. There the boy who didn't know exactly what was said in the classroom can ask his fellow students what was said – something psychologically very important to a man: to know that he can speak on a level of the student who is like his own age, and those who are teaching.   10
It's an 'environment.'
Can you put this in a machine and get an answer?   No,   you can't do that.

A man has to realize that suddenly one element of architecture, 'the gallery,' is an important part of 'School' – something which is not in the program at all. Do you find a gallery in a program? No. You will find a *lobby*, but you'll never find a 'Place of Entrance.'
Will you find written into it ...   that every space must have natural light, and every space must be in light, like the shape that's chosen? *Can you say that a square room is in the proper light when it*   20
only has one direction of light?   No.   That's Architecture.
But if you want to include all building in architecture, then you haven't got Architecture at all.

A work of architecture is an offering,

... as a painting is an offering. To understand the prerogative, the nature of a living work is terribly important. I must use examples which I've always used, because I don't think up ones every day, nor do I talk every day. (That'd be pretty bad, if I did.)   30
As I tried to say, Giotto, as a painter, painted skies black in the daytime,   and dogs that couldn't run,   and birds that couldn't fly,   and made doorways smaller than people. And the sculptor can make square wheels on a cannon to express the futility of war. But an architect has to use round wheels, and he has to make doors bigger than people.   Does it make him less of an artist?   No ...
His prerogatives ...   are different.

A space ...   'architectural,' as is indicated by the columns of our early architecture,
                    40
the structure ...   is the maker of light

... the opening, you might say, for light. This, if you think in terms of the times when this was almost miraculously discovered, or not even, let's say, consciously in the mind of the architect (who, like Icthinus, would think in terms of the columns as being beautiful supports for a temple, that merge out of the wall never conscious, maybe, of the fact that *light* is what he actually got with his columns) – a rhythmic composition ...

of light ...   and no light,   light ...   no light,   light ... no light,

... and as the columns spread apart, he had an *immense* amount of light. And then your problem is, what do   10
you do with all this?

If you consider it [light] even more immensely as being that which is three hundred feet away, you see, in which these, say, supports become events in the building of a different nature than the column entirely, a kind of station. Is there any reason why you can't build a Renaissance facade that covers the thing as a facade? Or even draw a building, you see, which encloses such a large opening, and build it of stone, if you like?

There's no reason why not. The great advantage was the making of the span, which was required, and the enclosure could be actually an *office* building that supports the large span. The tremendous   20
openings [one has], architecturally, if only you think of it *architecturally* – and *not* think of it in terms of solving problems.
Because if you were to do this, you would end up with nothing but curtain-wall architecture, or some other damn thing. I don't know what it would be – but it wouldn't, certainly, be architecture. You'd be satisfying just very, very meager, cursory things.

The reason why I speak to you about this (because I didn't intend to speak to you about it at all; I just heard this only riding up [to the campus]) ...   I heard the problems of the school. And I think it's exciting, really, that you have a kind of revolutionary atmosphere, you see, in the school. *I think there's nothing more important to a college than to feel the revolutionary spirit that exists everywhere.* But if the revo-   30
lutionary spirit is, let's say, if you're revolutionizing in Spain for America, then I believe it's misguided.
I believe that it's really [important that]   –   you're revolutionary about *Architecture*, you see, and not about some other thing which is *not* architecture.
I'm so mad!; you have no idea!
I can't express – *anywhere near* express   –   what I really *feel* about any kind of thinking in the direction of machines that would apply to architecture, *except* ...   in the feeding of an architect with imagination ...   and with a sense of composition ...   of new elements, and to know what they are. And you need to know what they are, so the clearest mind, or, rather, even the clearest *brain* (which a machine could be)

... but as soon as it enters the *mind*, then something else happens.   40

I don't believe you can design for 'environments.'
It's *another* thing – I dislike the word very much: 'environmental architecture,' or 'environmental design.'

I think, clearly, you can't design *an environment.*

You can't do that!

Did Mozart ask society what he should compose? ... Of course not. He composed, and society became a different thing.

10

The architect makes a work which inspires society to take a different turn ...

That's true of a poem – it's true of a painting. It's true of a painting: it gives you a different sense of point of view about things. You certainly realize that a painter can really paint a red dress when he sees a blue one. You wonder why he does it, but still, you see: well, he really can – you see, he *does* it. Is he inhuman? Of course not.   *Terribly human* – in fact, more so than those who are so amazed by it.

20

I believe that you could – if *I* were, let's say, on a jury, I would like to *not* talk about the functional aspect of the problem, whatsoever. I would assume *that*, in time – it will become a known thing to you, because you will – through the process of getting a building approved –   find that you will be hit on every side if you do not make a building work. It just comes quite ... as a matter of the course of the design of the building.
If a jury could speak about the spirit of architecture, does it have the spirit of architecture? ...

Can you recognize 'the personal' in a man's work? ...

30

And *that* is, his *'offering'* to Architecture ...   And can you recognize its responsibilities as a professional work?   I believe it *should* be responsible. It *shouldn't* be something that's just helter-skelter, 'made' without consideration of the problems that's [sic] involved.

But it must be considered, however, as the *least important* of all, because it takes your lifetime to know that aspect of it. Because a man is born with 'what to do,' but not 'how to do it.' 'How to do it' takes a   long,   long, long time.

40

And man is always greater than his works.

And you want to recognize *that* aspect of the man, rather than that which has to be shown only later through the luck he may have, or the choice he makes in choosing the right office to work in, or if he gets the right kind of work, or he learns more quickly than others, is given more opportunity. All these things become 'food for how to make things.' After a while you make them with a kind of knowledge and rest and repose. You're not worried about *that* aspect, and [instead] you begin to worry about the other. The 'what to make,' you see, is always the big concern. And you're *born* with that, but you may never, ever, bring it out because you may not have the technical knowledge to do it. So, it's important, on all sides, to have all the tools for the opportunity to make that which really presents *you* in the end.

A man finds himself out through his work.

I just read recently, a little piece that Corbusier wrote in a little book that came out on Roman architecture – a new one – published here in this country. It had a statement which I liked very much. It was written in 1929, when most of us were – I know all of *you* weren't born yet, and ...   I was pretty wet behind the ears, too.

He wrote that: "People accuse me of being a revolutionary, but I confess that I have only one master; the past. And I have only one discipline; the study of the past."

It is true today as it will be true thousands of years from now.
He wasn't speaking about the technical advances; he wasn't speaking about those things ... He was speaking about the '*spirit of architecture*': ... that which, by some miraculous thing about man, can make that which nature cannot make. Don't you think Chartres is fabulous? [unclear: In that sunlight?] Is it just the design?
No.   It's a tremendous outburst of human spirit ... *What else do you want?*

Is there a man alive, is there an architect alive who wouldn't trade all his richness, all his wealth, for being acclaimed for the littlest house?   There is no such animal.

Well, again, I told you that I didn't have any intention of saying what I just said.

[audience laughter]

I just get this from thinking that you're a great group of people. And I really care for students. I mean, I really think that school is my chapel, you see. It's a place where I – if I have any purification, it comes from there; it comes from such a place as this. So that's why I think it's so important.

Hi, Pat: just looking at you.

10

20

30

40

[Professor Kahn noticing Professor Patrick Quinn, a former student, in the audience]

Projectionist: **The slides are ready, Mr. Kahn.**

Professor Kahn: The slides are ready? Good. It's good to be reminded that I have things to do.
I want to make one remark about building in general, just introducing the slides, pretty much:

In planning, I feel that what stands in my mind as the most important consideration is not
the sociological findings – the thing will *change*, like great streams ... But it is a sense of 'the institutions
of man' – what, you want to ... 'support' ... *as a way of life* – that's what I mean by 'institutions.' They
are deep-seated, this desire – these desires.

Everything that nature makes it records in what it makes, how it was made.

In the rock is a record of the making of the rock.   Every grain of sand on a mountain is completely valid.
There is no such thing as chaos;   that's only in the mind ...   but never in nature.
The record of how we were made is also evident. The fetus is a perfect record, a complete
record, of how we were made – right from the very start. I believe it to be one of the most occupying of
studies – [that] of human existence. We, as *conscious* beings, made our desire as well as the means.

The means is 'Nature.'

It's the tools. It is the way – it is the tool house of God: the desire *to be*, *to express*. To
express, I believe, is the *raison d'être* for living: to express hate ...   love ...   nobility ...   integrity. 'How
we were made' ... we have access to, which probably the rose does not, though I believe the rose has consciousness of a certain type; every living thing has.
And we, through our high degree of consciousness, can sense something, or, rather, we are
enthralled by how we were made. And I think all knowledge, all will to learn is only to learn how we were
made, because if you knew it, you'd know all the laws of the universe. Out of this comes the inspiration to
learn. Just think of it. How could you avoid it? If someone feels something ... that you don't, don't you want
to know it? It's so natural. See, you're really here, assembled, as a place of learning, out of the inspirations
of how you were made. Now, when you are given, entrusted, with a building, you are sure you are entrusted
with one of the institutions of Man. If it is a major or minor part of it, there is no reason for building
anything unless it satisfies an institution of Man of some kind, whether it's the institution of Government,
institution of Learning, or institution of Home. They are all institutions.

There is nothing that one builds that is not part of some institution of Man;

... something that he institutes and wants to see continued. It is true of business; it's true of shipping; it's true of all things that are done, that you are involved in. And there are people who love even those things that you don't care for. They are inspired, you see, by just the same kind of ... feelings ... about existence.

I think the greatest of these feelings is the feeling 'to express,' which, of course – this is the real reason, I think, for living: to express the inexpressible; to express that which words can never find suffi-cient to express. It's a true sense of religion of 'in-touchness' with commonness with *a* commonness.

I am going back to the example of the school. Your concern should be how – how we – what is my opportunity, when I get this building, to express this institution of Man in a way which has *lost* its sense, of expressing it with spirit?

That doesn't mean that it [school] works; it means it has a spirit. It has *in it* the character of 'a place you want to learn.' It must have that character, and therefore it must have this feeling that ... the small space, the larger space, the lecture hall, the hallway, the entrance – all particularly belong to 'School,' ... and not to some other building. Everything supports it. Just think what a wealth of opportunity you have if you were to think of it this way ... 'cause everything that's made is wrong. There's so many things, you see, that have to be done. *Even a man knows that he can only go so far as an architect, others can go, farther ... in other ways.*

He knows, if he builds a house, he can never make a home, because a home is what the *people* make of this house. You can have a wonderful house and a poor home, and a poor house and a wonderful home. And my concern [is] with trying to find those 'Form Elements':

Form to me means the inseparable parts of something –

... the realization of the inseparable parts – it has nothing to do with 'design' whatsoever. *Design is only a means.* It's only a *way,* to express one ... little ... spark ... of what Form actually conveys to you. It's a real-ization of something that has an 'Existence Will,' and has a sense of its parts. I believe the temple I spoke to you of before, you see, *had* this kind of power.

And many buildings, in the wind, yet not dreamed, just wait for the *man* – not the committee, not the machine, not anything else, not a system, not a school, nothing – just for the *man* who ... somehow sees ... the emergence of something ... which was not there before. I believe the most dedicat-ed position that a school could take is to look for those manifestations. And they're all around you.

I can think of twenty-five schools that could be built that would be nothing like the schools you have now. Schools which are based on beliefs of some kind – not just physical plants – beliefs from which a new 'Form Realization' can ... come out, and this is your beginning of 'Design.'

And this is really the same kind of realization that a forester had, let's say, who made the first axe. Could the information have been put into a machine to make this axe? No. It had first to be *made*. *Then* you can put it into a machine as to how, you see, it reacts to other things: as to whether sharp axes, for instance, can be better than ... dull axes. You can put *that* in a machine. It'll give the right answer, too ...   but that's all.

[Professor Kahn, now addressing the slides on screen:]

10

Now we'll go back to how it all started.

[Referring to the slides]
They're way up, aren't they? I'll never see *that*.
Well, it's so far away, maybe *you* tell me about it.

[audience laughter]

20

You know, of course, this is the Salk Institute, and this is the laboratory wing. I'm just about to start this wing, here, and this will start eventually, I hope – I have no great assurances, yet. But I just want to tell you a little story about – it had to do with the realization of what I *thought* was the becoming of a new institution, in that [Dr. Jonas] Salk, when we saw each other – he said he needed so much space, and that was about the *program* – the *extent* of the program. It had no other thing in it. I said, but I know: a laboratory is a laboratory. But he mentioned that he wanted to invite Picasso to the laboratory. His idea was not to limit it to just be the place where what he would call the biological engineers [would come], you see, but he [Salk] has an equal regard for all scientists. And this caused this: 30 The actual requirement is this, these two boxes – this one and that one – but realizing 'the institution of man' emerging – something which is not the same as what existed before – and just because you wanted to make it a place where the regard for 'the being biological,' regard for such – for the psyche – was there. It wasn't all a matter of scientific usage. And when you deal with the psyche, you aren't dealing with science at all. You're dealing with something which science will never know anything about.

Therefore these studies, you see, are outside. They're also there for other reasons, because – after all – these laboratories, they're all souped up with all kinds of machines and pipes and stuff, you see, and they [the scientists] don't *need* that. All they need is a pen and a rug and a pipe, you see. So that's all they need; so why have them inside?, stuffed (usually) in very small spaces, because who can afford, you see, anything with decent living with all these expensive things around? So, I just put them   40 outside, you see, in the garden. And then this was only, however, an arm of this building, which is actually the 'Unmeasurable Center' – the center of the unmeasurable – where *nothing* is measured, except maybe one jigger after another.

[audience laughter]

And these are, of course, houses for people who like to be near their experiments, for some ungodly reason, you see. It's true. (I know.) But the separation, you see, was important. If you put them together, the one worked more or less *behind* the other. So, I purposely put them one quarter of a mile away from each other.

That's only a humorous story. I'll just go through – well,

Next slide.

Salk was so taken with the distinctions between one and another that he helped *me* – the leader he is – and believed in what I had to say. He even believed it more than *I* did. Because, see, the labora- 10 tory is here – there and there – but that which serves the laboratory are these spaces between. This came as a result of many studies. And I had three studies [offices] over each other, you see, but he said, 'No.' He said you must have the study here, but you must not *think* of having the feet of the other scientists on the head of another scientist. And what he said to me was this porch, you see, also came out of the laboratory, as though it had to have its own garden, facing out from the laboratory. This has one, and this one below has one too: that bridging across – separating them. Also, by separating I was able to make a sun-shield [as] a *glare*-shield for the laboratories, so that they don't need curtains, you see. But I noticed a few curtains coming in. Because habit, you know, is a funny thing. This is the one thing where the machine could help. You see, the machine would say, 'No curtains necessary,' and then the scientists would [unclear: say, 'I ?] understand.'

20

[audience laughter, applause]

Next, please.

The first time I did this thing, I had this idea of having two levels of laboratories and a con-struction which would take pipes. And I thought this was really terrific. Then I found that other people had better thoughts on this matter, because knowing, you see, that the machines that serve the laboratory are 30 multiple, and also that to crawl in the pipe space is really pretty cruel – not to the pipes, but to the people. And so the idea, then, became one of making a regular *floor* for the pipes, which I did in the other thing I showed you. That floor is nine feet high, and even there it's crowded, you know. The laboratory's eleven feet, the pipes are nine feet, the pipes want to spread out more and more. It's sort of a laboratory of pipes, you know; two lab-oratories, I mean – one for the pipes, one for the people. So this, maybe, was not a good solution, although it looked terribly pretty. We were paid for making this terrible solution and, and then we went into the other one, of course, and all the time I'm thinking that the thing is not as exciting, but, sure, that's very important. How did we even get that? It's a combination of studies – knowledge, too. But a part of it is your willingness to see the truth, and that's very important: to face up to the truth. My engineers, everybody, said, 'You're a fool for going into the other, because it's nothing but a box, just a box.' No. I felt that I had to get something out of this 40 box, and I think I really did. And, as the subsequent slides will show, I'm very proud of this.

Next, please.

This shows the various levels, you see. The darker bands are the laboratory – pipe laboratories, you might say, and the laboratories in between. Now that building will last for a very long time, because you can make any number of changes without making any drastic changes of appearance.

Next, please.

Now you see the separation: there are your studies, and there are the connections, the stair connections to the studies. This is that walkway that feeds the laboratory. Now, I think this kind of thing could be interpreted many, many ways. But the separation, the *realization* of the separation, [is] for many reasons, reasons of pure economy (I don't mean budget; I mean economy – it's a different thing, economy). The budget's a deadly thing. Economy can be important.   10

Next, please.

I'll show you the various aspects of the separation. The separation is exciting, here. It really feels like getting away for miles from what you're doing, and still you're very close.

Next, please.

The service towers [are] in back, which take all the toilets and all the necessary things you need, you see. The laboratories are completely clear; they don't have any obstructions, whatsoever. All the services of the laboratories are in *these* buildings and, you call it the rear – actually, it isn't – I mean it's just a bunch of laboratories on this side, as the other – and you go downstairs to the lower gardens, here. And the next slide shows what – you continue the stairway down. And the next slide is – you go through this, finally, to get to the lower gardens. This wood has turned very much grayer. And I was disturbed about the   20
color at first, but I knew, of course, that time would erase it, and now it's a very nice, brown, nutty color.
'Highly *nummy!*'

[audience laughter]

Next, please.

This shows what you go through, you see, to get to the lower gardens, which now I'm trying to finish. They were still left undone. But these are all pools. This is actually a trough for plants, and up above is a place for water. So, these are the studies that you see. Then, these, also the studies are up around the west side towards the Pacific.   30

Next, please.

This probably gives you a better view of the unfilled pools, here, which will cascade down to this one. And you'll sit there, and this will all be paved, and, here, these will be flower pots.

Next, please.

This is another detail of the lower section.

Next.

These are some others [pools], just running.

Next.

These are the porches, by the way, the intermediate porches. This is all poured-in-place concrete. There's no prefabrication; no precast work. The forms were all done by the architects, and they   40
were very expensive, but they actually saved. I've gone up three hundred thousand dollars in concrete, in the end. They were done very well, and actually they worked very well. We had a very, very small amount of honeycombing – in fact, a negligible amount.

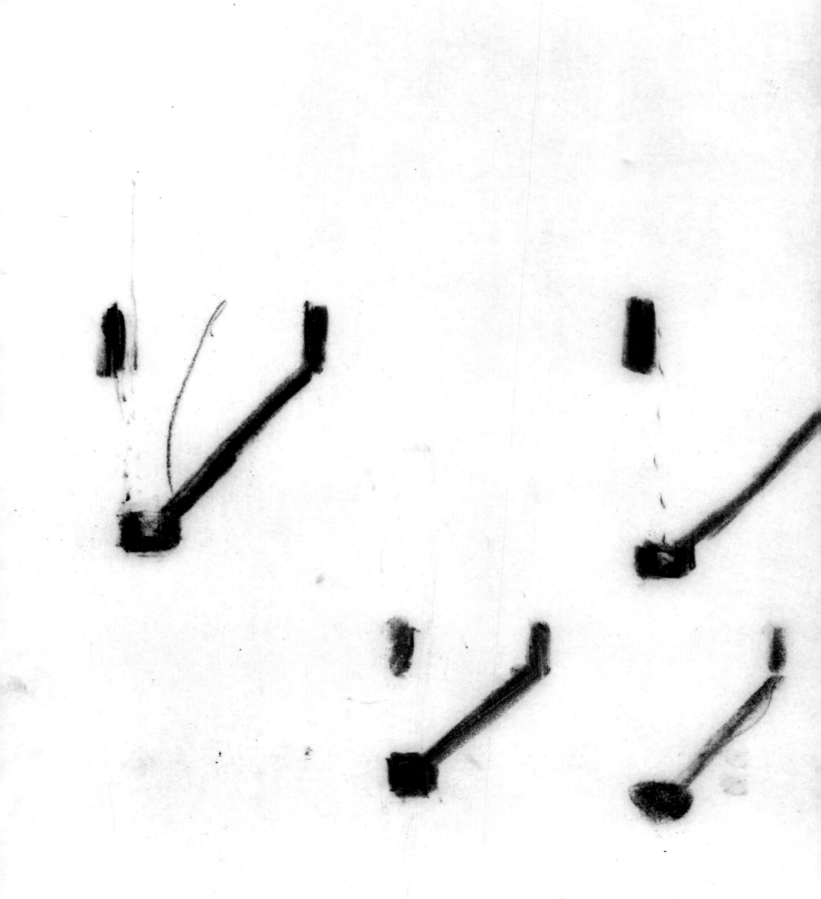

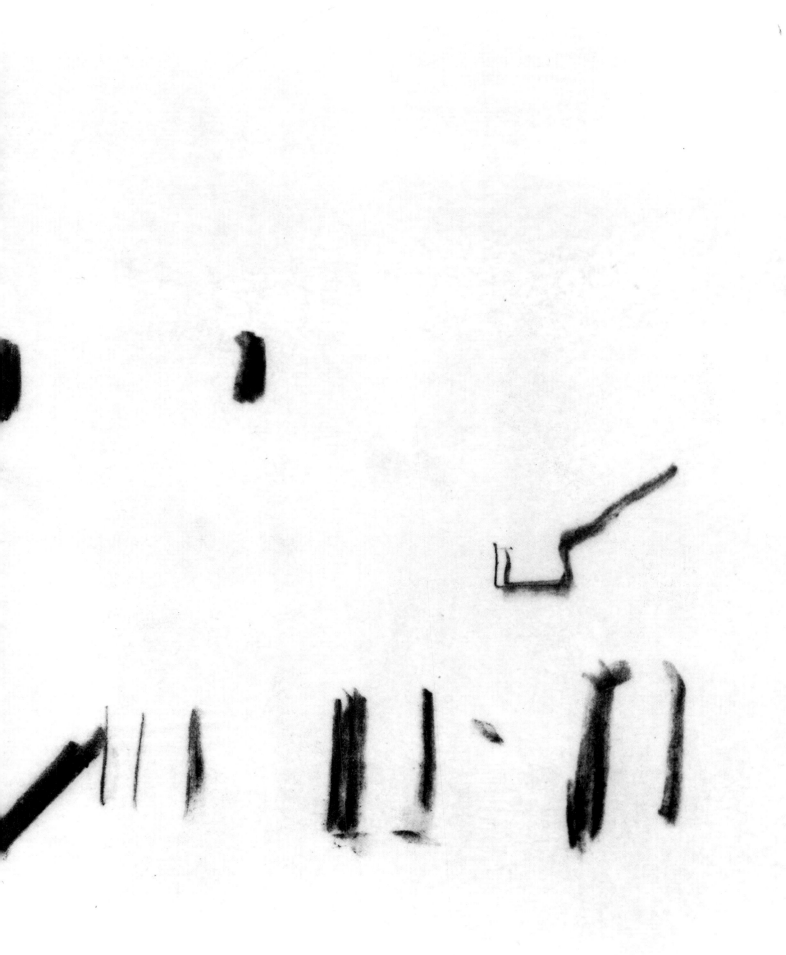

LIK
20 AUG 1962

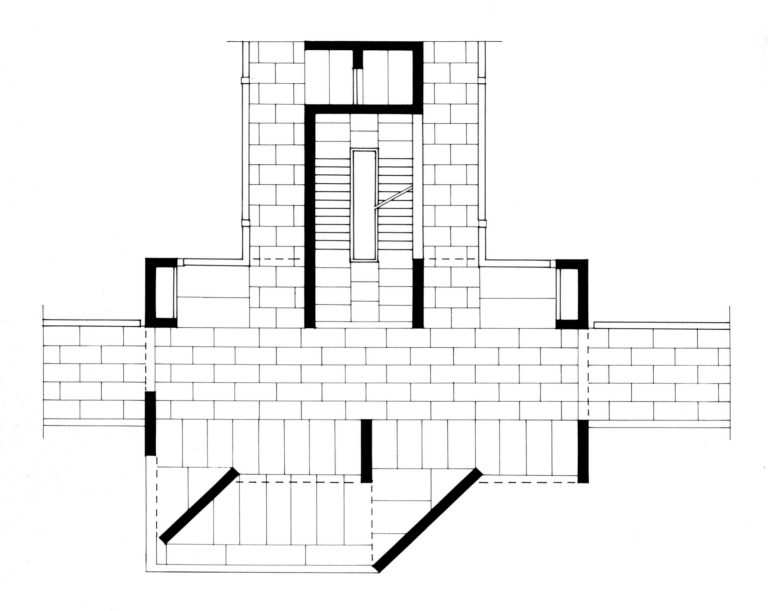

Preceding drawings by Louis I. Kahn in sequence:
Salk Institute for Biological Studies
La Jolla, California, 1959–65

12–13. Laboratories: Plan study. Various wall details
vine charcoal on tracing paper

14–15. Laboratories: Plan study
vine charcoal on tracing paper

16–17. Laboratories: Study. Window detail
20 August 1962
vine charcoal on tracing paper

Laboratories: Illustrative plan
ink on mylar

Next, please.

These are construction photographs, really, but I had them in the pile [of slides].

Next.

This is the same photograph you saw, but I thought it was rather a better photograph of the studies. You can use your imagination for the rest.

Next, please.

These are some of the details. Now these walls are made of plywood, twelve feet long and four feet wide; no [special] 'effects.' It was done with the idea, technologically capable, not recognizing from the start that concrete's no good, and that you do everything possible to make it look *not* like concrete. You know what I mean. 10

Audience member: What are the holes for?

The holes are there to hold the forms in position. You see, there are screw ties that go through the forms, which tighten them, and also space the forms so it's accurate, the wall is accurate, you see? And *that* appears, you see. And if you make it positive, and take care, they actually *are* very decorative. And then I covered them with lead, because there's some rust that can come out of it; I covered them all with lead. Lead and concrete work beautifully together.

Next, please. 20

These are some of the details, you see. The surfaces are very hard. Notice these little, little edges. That's where the boards came together. And the technique used there was to allow the concrete to bleed out slightly, 'cause you can't make a tight joint. If you try to make it tight, you'll have honeycombing there. But if you permit the joints to actually show, then the concrete is released, and it has a place to come out, and it fills it tightly, you see, and the only charm ...

[There is a short gap in tape resulting from reel transfer. The tape resumes with a discussion 30 of the Salk 'meeting-house' complex in progress:]

... the buildings within buildings. There's actually an architecture to sun. This is what we call a 'sun architecture.' Inside is the building that you use, but outside is the building to the sun. And, because it has no roof, the light that pours on the interior of this construction, which, by the way, is made paper-thin, if you notice, it's made not to be, really, a supporting structure. And [in] the interior, then, as the next slide shows, you see, you feel no glare, although there is light there, because the walls, against the stark sky and the sea, will be modified by no contrast; an opening, you see, contrasted against the sun by the 40 glare – that makes glare; this [interior] would *not* be in glare. And you could open all your windows, and look out, and you'd feel no glare. You'd feel as though you are outside, where you don't feel glare, either – very little.

Next, please.

So the meeting house I visualize as being a place where the windows would not show. They are simply openings in – this is a crude model, I mean, because you don't see the articulation of the making of it, which makes it very much better-looking.

Now here is a building – also a realization of an emerging kind of [unclear: practice?] or belief or institution; you see it there: [unclear word] Institute. Here the dormitories of this school of business management in India [are] grouped around the school. The school is this building up at the top, there, and these are the dormitories right next to it, and then a body of water separates that building from the other houses, and the houses are separate. This is near the University of Gujarat, and all the dormitories are little houses in themselves. There are no corridors in the dormitories. You go up the stairway, and there are some other utilities there – the bathrooms and so forth – and you enter a tea room from which you go to your house. That's how the plan works.

Next, please.

That's an abstraction of the school itself, showing the service room, and these are the dormi-tories, houses, the triangular building there. The corridors – well, I'll show you that later.

Next, please.

This is a more detailed plan of that.

Next, please.

These are early drawings I made of the dormitories as they approached the water. And I had some idea, you see, of having a highly *brise-soleil*-looking protection for the clubhouses, which are taking these two floors; the dormitories are above. But I was confused at that time between the *architectural* making of something and the device you use *to correct* something. A *brise-soleil*, for me, is *a correction*. Actually, *the porch* is the answer, because a porch has cool air in it, and a *brise-soleil* only translates the warm air into the building. So it was not a really, strongly functioning thing, *architecturally*, and therefore poor. And, you see, there it functions, but is architecturally poor. I mean, it functions – *apparently* functions – but it doesn't function.

Next, please.

Architecture is a kind of making of a validity, you know. It isn't an answer to something; it's a validity, like *we're* not the answers to anything, like a *mountain* is no answer to anything. It's a *validity* – it's *that – stronger* than the truth.

[Referring to slide:]

That's an early one, again [sketch], of the buildings that I saw they might be, you see. I think I was thinking a bit Indian, in this strange case, which is always a mistake, you know, because you just should think of its nature and it'll be Indian, all right, because you think of the architecture of light, and the architec-ture of water. I think to build an Indian town without the water towers being the most dominant buildings there, would be a great mistake. They should be the buildings you really see, because *that*, in India, is a tremendous sense of hope and validity. Not [unclear word] because you have the [unclear words] begin-nings, which never brought it out. But that comes from the spirit, the understanding that this *is* a wonderful thing – man *feels* it, and that a man who knows how to *express* it – he becomes the leader of this expression. And then you see it, and you know what to do. *After* it's made you can put it in the machine, but only *after* you *make* it.

Next, please.

Now that [unclear words] with what we have done, because, after all, the money involved was also a question. And that fee's better. Oh, first of all because it's built. And so the next slides will show some of the beginnings of the building. All right.

Next, please.

And this is what it's looming up to be. You see, these are the houses, you see, after this, and these are the buildings rising. I like it the way it is; I hate to see it finished, don't you? I think it's much better this way.

Next, please.

This is rather – rather not the color, but I think the piling is what I showed before.   10

Next, please.

These openings, you see, are protections for the interior building which is inside, you see – the coolness of that, you see. The *brise-soleil* would be very bad, because it makes all kinds of design in your soup.

Next, please.

It shows here – those are temporary fixtures, by the way. I think they'll be there a long while, but I think [unclear words].

Next, please.   20

That's the photograph you saw in the magazine, but I think it's quite a good photograph. The next is the interior, the buttressing, you see, of the arches is apparent on the inside as well as out with it making this sort of flow, just the way ... matching the roof.

Next, please.

Now, here is the school, and that's rather an old edition (I was trying to find a new slide, but I couldn't find it). It has a completely different arrangement – much simpler than this – it's quite a complicated pile. But this is the library, and there [are] eating places in here. I made a little theater there, where you can draw a curtain. It needs to be buttressed, you see. That's why we have them. And then, on the residual spaces in the dining hall, coming in where you come in, it becomes a stage. And these are the administration buildings, up there, and over here, the classrooms. You reach the classrooms way around the   30 corner, so you get the full protection from the sun falling on the porches.

Next, please.

This shows the section of that little theater. You see the buttressing of the arches, going this way.

Next, please.

This is a purely arched construction, and it's a straight brick work, but it is actually a composite order of brick and concrete. I can explain it to you in little places, more readily. This is your thrust, you see, that this arch would make, [and it] is restrained by a concrete member, across there. Even *these* also have concrete members. Now these little ones are there because you want [a] breeze in the balcony. You've gotta have a breeze below you, where your feet are, as well as above. Ventilation is absolutely   40 essential. And that's what caused me to think of a composite order of concrete and brick, and I'll show you some other slides which bring that out.

Next, please.

There is an indication of the composite order. You see how these concrete members, here –

you see them, there, going across – they are concrete that restrains very low arches. I could never have made it ordinarily, if I didn't have concrete. So the entrance of concrete, with its power, and brick, with its nature, come together and form shapes which are *natural* to both the orders – a composite order. You see it, there. Even this shape – it also comes out of the concentrated load that comes at this point and must find its way; and this just fell in someplace; it has very little to carry – about there. So that is really an indented thing; a wall over a wall, you might say. This is really a column, but it's trying to be a wall.

Next, please.

I think this shows the concentrated load that the ceiling has, at those points, which must be brought down.   10

I'm very influenced by Choisy's drawings, because they are very economical and to the point. I wish you'd all learn to make them, [to draw] like them, to show the integrity of your work. Even a little portion, because if you think of a little portion you can also think of an element, an element which, when repeated (like in music) – when repeated, you see – it becomes something which almost composes itself, in a way: The 'Order of Realization.' Not the freewheeling, all-over-the-place, you see, and if you ever had to make a drawing of it, you'd have to be on the job – sleep there, eat there, everything else.

Let me explain, because architecture is not that kind of thing. A sculptor's work is that kind of thing. Every imprint of the thumb, you see, must be there. I don't believe in assembled junk piles, glued together. I believe that everything should have the imprint of the artist, in the structure. In architecture, it must be the instruction. It must be the instruction because it's beyond his [the architect's] ability; he doesn't handle a   20 brick. See, 'in the instruction' means it's a tremendous 'order-sentencing' – not just a thing, really, as though you were doing some piece of sculpture with your thumb, or something.

Next, please. – I'm *mad*, don't you see!

So, now, I'll just show you other aspects of this model of the school. It's a wooden model, but very nice-looking, anyway.

Next, please.

Now this is the old plan of Dacca, and, again, the sense of 'institution' there. Good, the whole plan reveals itself to *me* just the way it is, there. Actually it's the graphic presentation of the first thought that this was a citadel of the Assembly; this was a citadel of the Institutions. Because the Assembly was a maker of   30 the institutions – the *establishment* of them – and these institutions which are basic ones of science and art and just 'well-being': a place of well-being which is – gravitates around – a stadium that has many rooms and gardens in it, to just respect the body itself: an institution which [as] yet has not been created anywhere in the world. (And the village [is] behind.)

The next slide indicates a progression of this. I turned the thing around, by the way, and I made the hostels and the assembly room in a lake. It's necessary to make lakes in Dacca because the land is so flat and the floods are high. One must have a raised area, so these all are raised buildings, and the way to make ground for, even for grading, is to make lakes there. Everybody does it, so I did it, too. But at first I saw the Assembly as a transcendent place. It don't [sic] matter what kind of a rogue you are: In the Assembly you are still – when you're having an assembly, your vote is a considered one. And I thought, also, that the mosque   40 was an important aspect of 'assembly,' being a transcendent place. And also because they are very loyal to the tenets of their religion.

And: In the program was a space, three thousand square feet, with a closet for rugs. I translated that into a mosque which is thirty thousand square feet, and nobody cried. It's because you were discovering the 'ingredients' that are good for *this* place. That's what that is; it's little, down before. In the other one, you see, you notice – but it was as big as Hagia Sophia, and that was a little bit too much, I think. So we brought it down to something more reasonable.

But, you know, a funny story about this thing: When I took the plans to the Chief Justice, he didn't want to be anywhere near the walls of the Assembly, as he put it, you see. He didn't want to be near this place. And, obviously, part of my duty was to build the Assembly building – project the building. And so, before I [had] made any sketches (I made the first sketches in front of him, because it was the first time I came here), I showed him this concept I had of a mosque. And he put the Supreme Court where I would have put it, you see. He said the mosque was sufficient insulation for him. (*Precisely.*)

10

Next, please.

Here is the way it's shaping up – always worse than your first sketch, I think. But, however, these took care of many, many problems that I had which I completely couldn't have taken in, in the first sketches which I showed. But these are some – these things have changed. But, you see, the *essential* thing is quite the same.

Next.

This is an old drawing – no, old model – which showed the Assembly in this shape. I rather still like it better than the one I have now, but the problems I have in the Assembly could not take this. It just had to grow bigger. And this is water, these are some avenues going across, these are the hostels. I changed [the program]. In the program there's a *hotel* for the visiting members of the Assembly, the judges, the ministers, the secretaries. I changed this to '*studies in their own gardens*,' on the lake, and that was accepted. Transformation, completely – the *program* asked for a hotel.

20

Next, please.

This is the way it's beginning to look now. This is the waterway that you see, the gardens beyond, the Presidential Square here, more water, and this leads to the Assembly – to the institutions back there. These are the hostels, now, as they're shaping up.

Next, please.

That's a very old one, too. I bring you this because, again, what I told you about, and it is an elemental realization, which, when once in your mind, you never want to 'think' but repeating it, because in its repetition lies its beauty. Not [unclear:forced?] circumstances – you don't know what they are. You get something which doesn't have so circumstantial a consideration. You don't know what the circumstances are. In fact, circumstance, you might say, is continuous and unpredictable. So, what do you know about it? What do you know about, say, the next moment? You can't. You can't anticipate circumstance. That's the success of Cartier-Bresson's photography. He says he looks for the crucial moment. That means he selects, out of a continuum of circumstance, *one* particular thing which, at that moment, only the camera can take. No other artist has this instrument, you see, of expression. Now, at that moment [when] I realized that, then "Whistler's Mother," and photography, and Japanese effects, meant absolutely nothing. But previously it did. I realized, you see, they were only just little – they were just 'surface.' They were, rather, *fringe* things, you see; things also you can do, but in nature, photography – No.

30

I bring this out because, in the next slide shows [sic] the construction, the light construction of the Assembly, where the finding, you see, of these courts, and for light, were equally elemental. These courts were elemental. And the white areas, you see, were light-giving areas. It's rather a move away, far, from what you may call a column. But in a way it is not. When you think of a column, you think of a construction that wants, really, to break out of the seams. It feels its strength only around the periphery. Only

40

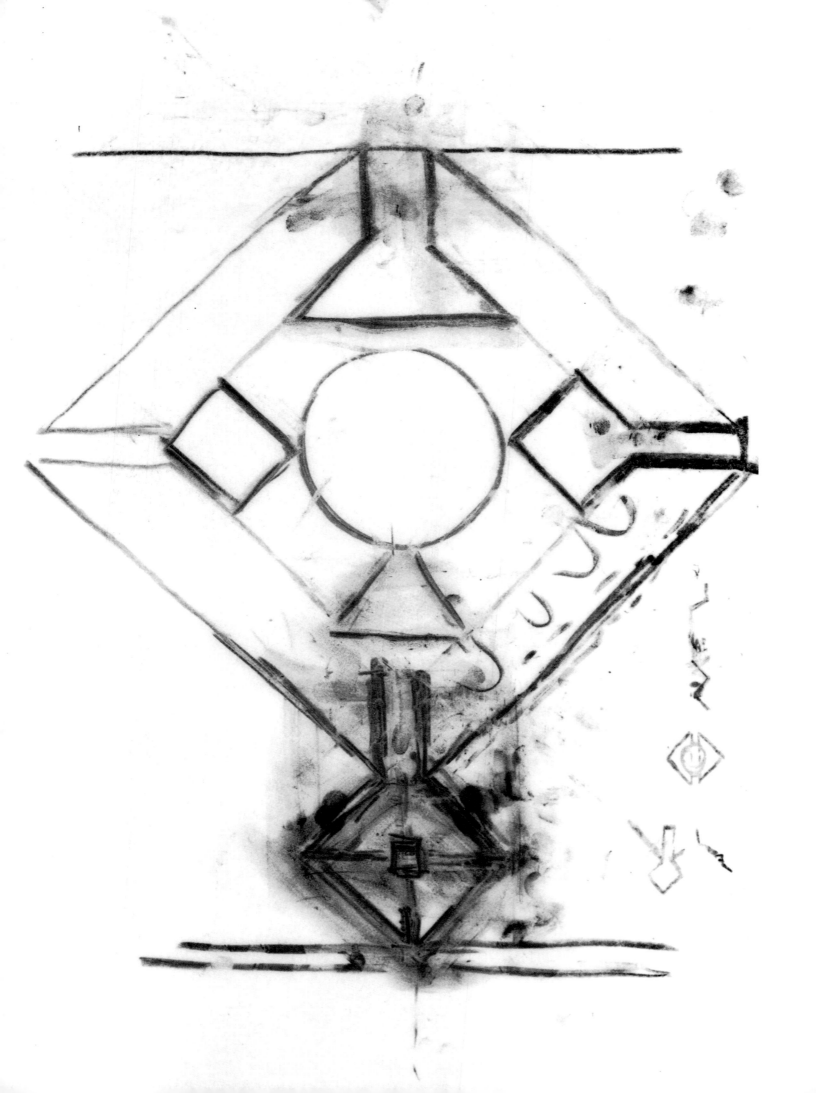

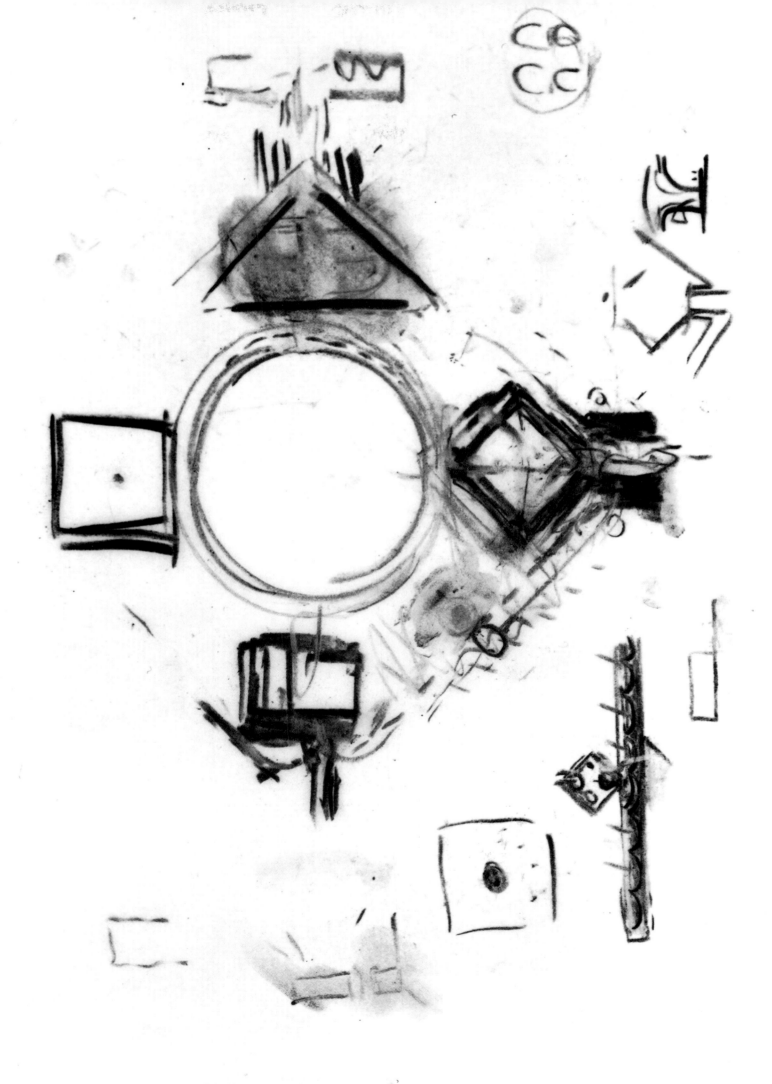

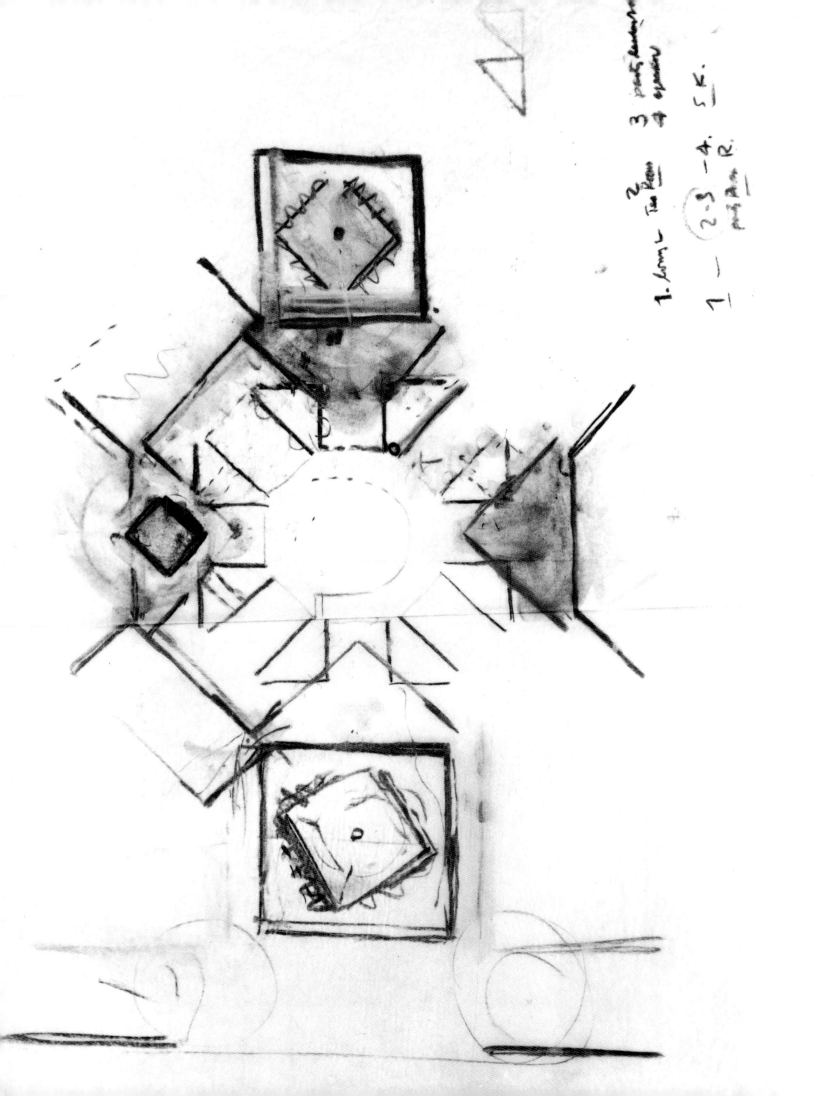

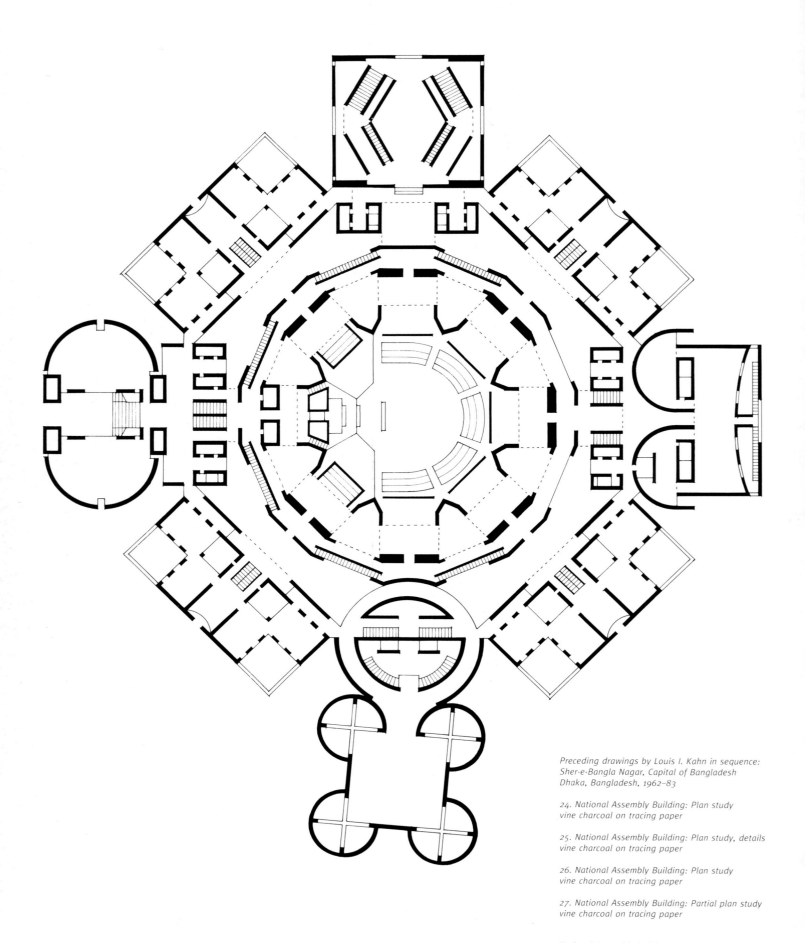

Preceding drawings by Louis I. Kahn in sequence:
Sher-e-Bangla Nagar, Capital of Bangladesh
Dhaka, Bangladesh, 1962–83

24. National Assembly Building: Plan study
vine charcoal on tracing paper

25. National Assembly Building: Plan study, details
vine charcoal on tracing paper

26. National Assembly Building: Plan study
vine charcoal on tracing paper

27. National Assembly Building: Partial plan study
vine charcoal on tracing paper

National Assembly Building: Illustrative plan
ink on mylar

inside it wants to be hollow, because its strength really rides inside. It wants to put something inside, and yet you think of it growing bigger and bigger and bigger and bigger. You see, you think of the interior having a kind of *hope* about it, or *anticipation* about it. And the word 'hope-anticipation' you can really put as a meaning of the inside of a column – all its strength is outside. And I thought of it, really, that way. This was really a column, you see, which became a court. And I can explain this some other time when I come to visit and come into, maybe, actually go with you on a column-court, maybe a week's time, which I'd love to do (when I find the time), see, to explain this to you, because it's very exciting to discover these so-called 'all-out' ideas, you see. I mean 'way out' – you call them 'way out.' Okay. You see, these are the offices – here – and then the special rooms are placed. Essentially it's a square, with just this little bit [unclear: aggravated piece ?]. 10

Next, please.

See, the mosque turns slightly towards true West. There; it's West – the building. I purposely did that. I *purposely* made that building sit there like that so I could turn the mosque the other way. In other words, how would you know that it's *particular*?

Next, please.

Incidentally, these circular openings are for light and for ventilation. It's essentially light, 20 for the light, you see, which is actually a silver light that you get inside. You get no actual edges of the shape or anything. This is the mosque.

Next, please.

This is construction of the mosque, and it's made of, actually, light-giving elements, you see, through here, which have openings in them. But they're all so made [so] that you need no windows on the inside. It can pour – and it does pour – in Dacca, 'cause they have three hundred inches of rain a year. But it can pour, and you can see sheets of water through here, but you get no water inside. And that'd be the environment of the mosque.

Now these stripes that you see there are the way I made the construction. I poured every five feet, and rested, so that all the screw ties I talked to you about just a little while ago – these little holes 30 – would all be in this little area where I placed marble. So, you would have marble inserts every five feet, and that's how it's made. Because they technically are unable to make it – the concrete – as 'Salk concrete,' you see, so I made the 'trauma' part – the part that always is bad, when you start another pour – be a, well, be a sort of cruddy event, you see. But the bar that was in there, to supplant, you see – it's like thickening – it actually becomes a wash, maybe. Because it rains so much: so the wall is not made so damp coming down. If you had the wall, with the rain coming from the top down to the bottom, it would be soaked, you see. This way, every five feet it's drained. It's a combination. It's an 'Order'; a realization of concrete, of construction, and [of] need.

Next. 40

Now this – it's the Presidential Square view, where I showed you near the garden. And it's taking away the wall of this to see the stairways and the construction of the stairways and then to the higher part that is the gardens above.

Next picture.

Again, I try to show you the construction, you see, of this particular entrance. It happens to be that *this is* the base. But what's the difference? You know? This is the base, here; it should be around like that, you see. Well, I think it looks better this way.

Next slide, please.

Now this is the construction of the Presidential Square, which is entirely in brick: brick is their material – concrete is not. I used as much brick as I could. And these are all arched constructions below the Presidential Square, and the next slide shows you some of them; there they are. These are thirty-foot arches, in brick. Brick is very cheap – these are not expensive constructions. Here it would be fabulously expensive. Now, I have made the lower part of this, which are the catacombs of the, you might say, the 10 Presidential Square – a mosque. It turns in the right direction, anyway.

Next, please. (I changed it somewhat, too.)

You see how it goes on, this construction? These are the lower arches, and they're very large, high arches. And then, you see, because the Square itself has a place where you sit, you see, and so these arches are receding, actually, in size: big ones, and the smaller ones, and finally very small ones. (Well, not very small – the small ones are ten feet, and these large ones are about thirty.)

Next, please. 20

This will all be paved. It is now temporarily paved with brick. It means nothing to temporarily pave something – take it off and put it on again. Labor is zero, as far as cost is concerned. This is *different*, too.

Next, please.

This general aspect of Dacca: [is] 'protected walls.' Inside, [unclear words] of light. In fact, light is really unwanted. But it's not so much light, as it is sun that's unwanted. You feel most comfortable when you're in a room which is flanked by other rooms which get the light.

Next, please.

Now I show you this as one of the buildings. You know – the hostels – have central buildings, and they are dining rooms and so forth. I show you this because some of the arch work I will show you now will indicate – well, one of these will show what I mean about the openings, these round openings. 30

Next, please.

That, you see, for instance, *these* arches, naturally, will be built with the brick all the way through (you see, they're actually brick all the way through), but these are openings in round openings, and they use the stairway coming up from one level to another as a brace for these openings. That is on the water.

Next, please.

Now these openings show you how the composite order works. There is an opening, here. You see this arch? – this low one? That would really break through here, but it's restrained by this concrete member, across there. Here's a floor, you see, and that supports that floor – that's what it's there for – but it involves also an opening, there. And these round constructions which I have here (not so well completed) – but they were meant to counteract a force upwards because it's earthquake country. So that round shape, well, I 40 got so fascinated with that round shape that I could use it anywhere. Because I find them – they're a very satisfying way of making an opening in a wall. It's continuous. I find that it's *satisfying*, somehow, and, well, it's *easy*, too.

Next, please.

These are all just 'mad,' you know, kinds of things to make. These composite orders going this way, you see, these great sweeps you can make because there is no reason why you can't. Now, these restraints, you see, going through there, it's making one instead of two, you see. And this could not be done in any other architecture but today, because the concrete, you see, is helping this possibility.

Next, please.

Here's where the idea really began. Because there, you see, in the porch of the houses, I needed to have ventilation at the peak. You see there? Low, otherwise this would not function. And that's what made this thing actually exist. So, you get very good ventilation there – it works beautifully.

Next, please.

Now, I thought it was an original idea, of course, until I read pages of Leonardo, where he writes: "On the remedy for earthquakes," and [in Leonardo] *there* is that reverse arch. You see it there? So, you can't win; you can't win!

Next, please.

Now, this is the synagogue building where I saw a game of light. And these are 'chambers' of light: they are twenty-foot chambers, where the windows outside are glazed, and, inside, the openings lead into the chamber itself. Now, these are useful areas because, in the High Holidays of the Hebrew religion, the women are always upstairs, you see, and they look down on what's happening, and that affords a place for them, you see, to be. There's also a place for them in the actual sanctuary itself. That's part of the ritual that you see, there. And this is a chapel built the same way. And, also, the community building has a court, made the same way. And that column I spoke to you about – that column, which has windows in it and now becomes a court – is shown, here, see. It's really a *way of thinking*. It has nothing to do with what – it's a familiar thing, but a *different way of thinking*.

Next, please.

There are the doors to enter the community building, here. And there's a *sukkah*, which is a place during the festival days – the harvest, I mean to say. And here is the chapel; here is the synagogue.

Next, please.

This shows you some photographs of a model we made. It shows the interior openings, you see. And the exterior openings you see there – they're the glazed ones. This is the building, with very little glass.

Next, please.

This is an early drawing I made, and, here, you see, I tried (I didn't have much thought, here), and I tried to imitate what I did here, until I realized that the interior light, there, is a *different* one. And that's how I got to the window, which is *much* more in keeping with the window across the way.

Next, please.

That shows some cross influences, where in the work I was doing in India I realized that some of the ways in which I tried to express these openings was not as good as to have these arches, you see, just *brace* the building as it turns around, where the glass is set into them. And that's what *this* – even *that*, you see, is really a pivoted door – triangular door – which opens in this direction, so you can walk in freely, and, when it's closed entirely in this direction, it has a door *in it*, through which you can go to get to the actual main chamber. It's sort of a 'door'; and it calls for another door, you see. Because the *spirit* says there must be another door – not any book, not any document, not any machine, not the professor. You see, it's just *you* have this '*architectural feeling*' – at least I thought I did – and, yes, this door was worth the trouble.

Next, please.

There, again, light, light, light; that's the Unitarian Church, Rochester. All these undulations are, in a way, to modify light, and to get niches for sitting, and everything that changes your feeling when you 10 enter, and that changes your feeling when you come back to where you were. *Loyalty* to what you see – with the environment.

Next, please.

That's the light that's gotten through these four walls. It's very wonderful. It's all just block construction, but these blocks are made eight by eight – they're not made long. If cut, it causes a blotching of one block to the other to – not to appear. It homogenizes much better. In the Yale Art Gallery I also used block. I made it five by five, and they have a tendency to make a wall look even more detached rather than make it look structural or something. But I'm not sure you can call cinder block a terribly worthy material, as a *structural* material. But as a making of a wall which is not structural – this is *not*, you see – it is a very strange specimen.   20

Next.

Here are the Bryn Mawr dormitories, which I have no good slides of, but the same clerestory light comes through these places. And this is where we have, you see, this miserable furniture you see back there. And the dining hall and the entry hall is made this way. It's nice – a very poor photograph. The only thing I discovered in making these things: that there's only one source of – there are very few outlets in this building, and there's plenty of light. You groove the outlets – you don't mix so many in concrete. The concrete is a treacherous material to deal with if you have too many intrusions in it. You must divorce it of all extrane- 30 ous needs; it must just be itself. So making one or two holes in the building – coming through it – are [sic] better than making many, like for outlets and all kinds of attachments. Because you can't control it, technologically, when you're pouring concrete. There's too much concern about *pouring* it, you see, and, and that's one of the faults with it.

Next, please.

Now I show you some sketches I made in Europe as an '*envoi*,' you see – just to show you I can draw. These were made in Greece, and Rome, and in Italy, and in Egypt. I'll just go through them. You just go one after the other, just as *you* want to see them, and I'll just tell you where they are.

40

[Professor Kahn speaking to the projectionist:]

Please, just go through them. I did that before breakfast. I mean, you think I had breakfast? I did.

[The slides continue.]

You think that's what it looks like? No. No, you just drew what you wanted to see. Oop, you've got to *watch* those things – they're terrible. This final service has started; it isn't in the picture. I gotta clean up before I show 'em tonight.

Now, I show you two other slides, just to remind you of something.

The next.

This is a picture of a Cruikshank drawing. And the religion there is the same as the religion in architecture. You see, in this drawing, the *fire* is the *light*, and the *paper* is the *light*, and where the light is *not* is the *stroke*. And like consciousness all over, because you see the direction of light?, the direction of stroke? – relentlessly, relentlessly, same way. Even those stones are made, you see, and cloaks are made, and modified slightly; they're the movement, but, in general, it's so controlled. And where light is struggling to exist, there's all kinds of privileges you have, you see, with your stroke. But at this point, no. That's how *'religiously'* it's made; how 'Order' enters a drawing like this, as well, as in the light. And if you think he didn't have fun doing it that way, look at the *drawing*!

The next slide shows the same kind of discipline. This is a Flaxman drawing. And here: there is the wind, you see, which is all indicated the same way. See? Right on through. And what the wind can't touch – like the stone – it is *not* done. And the fire does have no detail, except that it is outlined as a temporary kind of shape. It really doesn't look static-y; it looks as though it just loomed up like that, and he gave it position, you see, and constantly changed. It's a beautiful drawing!

And I think that's the end of my slides, and I thank you very much.

[A lengthy round of applause from the audience.]

"The Bottle." Plate VI, detail of etching
George Cruikshank

Looking Back at Berkeley:
Kahn in Context

Ellen Morris

The lecture by Louis I. Kahn was delivered to architecture students and faculty of the College of Environmental Design at the University of California at Berkeley, on or about November 28th, 1966.[1] Since that time, the original tapes have, until this publication, been the only record of what was an important lecture, a significant portion of which had addressed a major pedagogical dilemma of the day, and stood as an important delineation of ideas about the making of architecture in general.

When Kahn came to Berkeley in November 1966, he was, prior to his lecture, apprised of what many of the graduate students perceived to be a philosophical and pedagogical crisis within Berkeley's College of Environmental Design, particularly regarding the teaching of architectural design.[2] It was our hope that Kahn, through his lecture, might address the problems we presented to him, and validate our own basic beliefs in architecture as a discipline, by addressing some of the grievances we held relative to the pedagogical outlook so entrenched at Berkeley by 1966. We hungered for renewal and inspiration, and we solicited it that day from Louis Kahn. We wanted him to challenge the new Berkeley pedagogy as much as we were eager to see the slides of his recent projects—built and proposed. What we had not expected, however, was the great extent to which Kahn chose to devote himself to our concerns during the course of his lecture, the eloquence with which he addressed some of these ideas, and the reinforcement of his views on those issues interspersed throughout the lecture.

4; 27 – 43

[At Berkeley, a philosophical rift had begun around 1964, when the Architecture Department was relocated from the old 'Ark'[3] to Wurster Hall, a new home for the newly-named "College of Environmental Design."] The pedagogical crisis seemed underscored symbolically by the difference between the old and the new homes for architectural studies: the former, a cozy and understated example of Bay Area regionalism; the latter, a neo-brutalist concrete behemoth. Most significant of all, though, was simply the change in name—a new name for a new concept of architectural education.

3; 31 – 35

Although many of our own ideas on the subject of architectural design—what architecture was and how it was to be accomplished—were scarcely formed, many graduate students shared a simple, broad concept of the nature of architecture; that, [first and foremost, architecture was a discipline of 'artistic expression,'—an 'art form' different from, though no less than, painting or sculpture.] **We believed above all else that design resulted from a conceptual, expressive activity of the intellect.** At Berkeley, by 1964–65, however, this notion of architecture had become challenged by a revisionist architectural curriculum supported by a host of new types of courses and a very different perspective on the nature of architectural design—a direct challenge to the notion of architecture as an art form.

2; 24 - 34

[The new Berkeley view was characterized by a mechanistically oriented, social-Darwinist view of architectural pedagogy. Pseudo-scientific pedagogical mechanisms proliferated, with the newly emergent computer their most conspicuous apparatus.[4]] The 'traditionalists' who adhered to architecture as an expressive activity grew to view the new pedagogy as bent on automating the practice of architectural design. A new atmosphere in the school seemed to say that 'the old architecture' was dead. By the time of Kahn's visit at the end of 1966, it was plainly evident that something different and invasive had woven itself into architectural studies at Berkeley. What was truly radical was the assumption that the architect was duty-bound to broaden the *interpretation* of architectural design as well as the *procedure* for accomplishing it. The redesigned curriculum required a host of new types of required course work and in many instances employed faculty who were architects neither by training nor degree, but who proclaimed at least a marginal interest in 'Building Science.'[5]

A spate of new courses was intended to 'feed into' the design-studio sequence. The dominant canon was that the architect must face the task of designing 'without pre-conceptions.' It was precisely such *preconception*—the intuitive, associational, culti-vated perspicacity of the *traditional* architect—that was deemed as restraining and inhibiting, rather than facilitating, the 'doing' of architectural design. An inversion of the conventional notion of architecture as rooted in individual artistic inspiration, the new curriculum at Berkeley viewed *newness* as inherently good, *distinctiveness* as inherently bad. Conformity or 'sameness' in design was seen as positive, especially when it reflected some vague notion of social consensus, well-being, and political purpose. [Above all, architectural design was seen as something to be derived from linear, formulaic *procedures*—in short, what was called the *Program*.]

3; 1 – 22

This new curriculum, eschewing extra-programmatic invention, strove to quell the quest for architectural individuality by emphasizing adherence to socio-technic deter-minants, presumed to be immanent in the architectural program. Backed by a utopian vision, proposed in a vaguely *scientistic* way, the 'new methods' for design would produce accordance and propriety in the resultant built product. It was believed that such a 'correctness' could be achieved only by absolute allegiance to the program. The underlying assumption was that different architects could—and indeed *should*—produce substantially similar—if not completely identical—'responses' to a given set of programmatic requirements.

Thus, for example, in the new architectural curriculum mathematicians taught classes wholly devoted to what had become termed "Design Methods."[6] These courses undertook the analytical dissection of the activity of designing in order to produce and promote a "methodology" of design. **The implicit objective was to employ scien-tific methodology in order to make architecture more scientific. The result, however, was largely methodology for its own sake. The old way of responding to the pro-gram, through the assimilation of culture—that is, expressively demonstrating an 'ideology' of design—had now been shunted aside.** Better and more *programmatical-ly responsible* buildings would result, it was proposed, from a clearer understanding of 'method.' Various mathematic formulae and geometric constructs of 'procedures for thinking' were put forth—some of these superficially resembling symbolic logic, all of them purportedly *logical,* and all emanating from the dubious assumption that the study of Methodology, in and of itself, could and must lead to 'products' of archi-tectural design.

The philosophical underpinnings of this new pedagogical orientation were, if not directly the result of, certainly abetted by, the appointment of Christopher Alexander to the Berkeley faculty, fresh from Harvard, and following the publication of *Notes on the Synthesis of Form*. Alexander was seen as the standard-bearer of the new peda-gogy, and Berkeley wanted to be at the 'cutting edge' of a new vision of architectural education. With Alexander's arrival the atmosphere of the school, especially in the design studio, had changed dramatically. The phrase 'design concept'—used tradi-tionally to refer to the expressive *raison d'être* or *parti* of a building—was eschewed in favor of a new notion of design which was to be programmatically determined. **Process subsumed Concept.** [A 'concept,' being an unprovable 'idea' rather than a demonstrable 'fact,' had little place in a 'rationalized' Design Process, whose explicit objective was to make design-*ing* 'objective,' 'straightforward,' and 'predictable.']

2; 40 – 43

Christopher Alexander himself ran independent, methodologically oriented design stu-dios and gathered his own coterie of graduate students—many, if not most, of whom had first degrees in disciplines never before linked to undergraduate preparation for architecture.[7] To the majority of the graduate student body, these methodological studios were exclusivist, but more so, they were antithetical to essential aspirations in architectural design. By the time of Kahn's 1966 visit, not having seen any physical, 'designed products' coming from Alexander's studios, there had emerged the sense that nothing—at least in conventional architectural terms—might ever emanate from those studios in the form of real design projects such as the rest of the students would produce at the end of each academic term.

The essential, more general, feature of the new curriculum was a series of required courses in which 'human-needs,' in and of themselves, formed the focus of study. The roots of this lay in a concentration upon *program* as an end in itself, and the operative goal was architectural *programming,* in which an architect's individual desires were to be subjugated to the perceived sociocratic demands of the day. Such courses were taught by sociologists and/or psychologists, who were to help instill in architectural design a more accurate reflection of the 'socio-political concerns' latent in the typical architectural program, above and beyond simple space requirements. "Social and Cultural Factors in Design" was the subsuming banner for these courses, with the assumption that society could benefit only from an architecture that was the literal translation of behavioral, psychological, and cultural needs into physical form. 'Building' was to be *determined by* 'Program.' Accordingly it became necessary to ensure that the program was a sufficiently accurate document of social needs and aspirations. It thus became the task of design students to assemble for themselves the raw data for the program, to interpret this data mathematically, and, finally, to generate the product of this work as 'The Program.' Often this became the sole objective of a given term's work.

Additional imperatives paralleled the sociocratic and deterministic ideology of the day, and found vehicles in other aspects of the curriculum. Urban planning was to be made manifest in the form of sociologically grounded 'policy planning' rather than 'physical planning.' When the so-called "Urban Master Plan" became the focus of study, the individual building as 'object' was eschewed in favor of 'superblocks' and 'megasystems.' Even in the late Sixties, when *urban design*—as a subdiscipline of urban planning—was newly elevated to a subject for design studios, the results were largely diagrammatic and very rarely truly architectural.

Newly discovered 'vernacular' traditions became the rage: 'architecture without architects' was the buzz-phrase. The closest a student got to the great marvels of architectural history were slides of one or another instructor's summer trip to Italian hill-towns or the Greek islands. Emphasis upon the impact of climate on building design (housing, usually) grew out of an obsessive concern with vernacular architecture, fueled by a backlash against conventional notions of monumentality, and energized by a sincere yet naive vision of a more 'humanistic' architecture to come. In general, the use of history and precedent in the design studios was severely restricted or altogether ignored. [Examples of historical 'high-architecture' were unseen and unused: built form was to be determined by factors external to the architect's individual imagination and independent from historical association.]

6;   *14 – 28*

A corollary of the diminished role of the past was an emphasis upon a so-called 'new architecture for the future.' Mass-produced, 'pre-fab building systems' proliferated— mostly intended for repetitive building types such as elementary schools or suburban houses. Paradoxically, despite the emphasis on vernacular associations, the mood of the day swung away from 'the hand-made' and 'the site-specific.' Moshe Safdie's "Habitat" at Expo '67, for example, embodied such contradictory imperatives, and was celebrated as the epitome of a 'new environment.' Safdie, Archigram, and the Japanese 'metabolists' were *in*; Frank Lloyd Wright was very definitely *out*.

The architectural pedagogy of Berkeley in the heyday of the 1960s was thus heavily characterized by a numbing, deterministic attitude, whose most proximate antecedent in architectural theory was likely of early-modernist, German derivation—*die Neue*

Sachlichkeit—taken to its most utilitarian extreme. The message was loud, clear, and insidious: ['Architecture' and the 'Architect' as we knew them were *passé,* and would be supplanted by the newly emerging autocracies of sociology, statistics, mathematics, and, more generally, 'Rational Methodology' in design.] **Design was merely the by-product of program.** Naturally, by focusing so insistently (first) on the *nature* of the program and (second) on the *procedural implementation* of this program, this attitude sought primarily to extract a three-dimensional correlative of the program itself—architectural design viewed merely as the cool reflection, logically deduced, of programmatic directives. Architecture was treated as the natural, inevitable outgrowth of socio-techno-determinism—Architecture reduced and degraded to the phrase, "Built Form." It was perhaps the utmost instrumentalist attitude toward design—a view of architecture, actually, much more *mechanistic* than scientific, in which the guise of social obligation was used to denude architecture of its fundamental cultural aspects. The ultimate hope—the methodological *grail*—was that the computer, then in its infancy in architectural applications, would prove capable of *logically* and *infallibly* sifting through programmatic elements and relationship, in order to produce the 'optimum' design for any given circumstance, without the inherent prejudices of the conventional architect.

3; 1 – 22

It was into this atmosphere that Louis Kahn came to Berkeley to speak in November 1966, and it is in precisely this context that much of his lecture should be understood and appreciated. Kahn's lecture that day was delivered in a vast chemistry amphitheater, filled to capacity. His audience was the assembled Berkeley architectural community, and the applause noted at the beginning of the transcript occurred at the moment Kahn entered the room. As it turned out, Kahn would be preaching to the converted. The resounding applause that greeted him, as well as during and after the lecture (noted in the transcript), serves to demonstrate that this was an audience who already knew well Kahn's position on the issues at hand.

An appreciation of the context of this lecture also helps to explain the methodologists' 'boycott' of Kahn's lecture,[8] and their general antipathy toward Kahn's quest for 'what a building wants to be.' That aphorism, of course, stood for the fundamental, theoretical proposition that 'concept' was essential to the creation of any architectural design. From the scientist, methodological standpoint, Kahn's idea of 'what a building wants to be' was erroneously viewed as a *romantic* notion, when in fact it was, for Kahn, a *rational* one expressed in a romantic construct. It was clear that day that Kahn and the new Berkeley revisionists resided in altogether different architectural worlds. [Kahn, however, viewed his mission in terms of the *students,* not just a coterie of ideologues, and made this eminently clear when he stated at one point, "school is my chapel."] In addressing the pedagogical situation at Berkeley, Louis Kahn provides us with as telling a sign of his dedication to architecture as a discourse of ideas, as much as his slides demonstrate a devotion to architecture as a matter of practical consequence.

6; 37 – 39

Had the methodologists listened to Kahn's lecture that day, they need have heard no more than one morsel of the lecture in order to fully comprehend **Kahn's position on the issue of making architecture an expressive endeavor.** Kahn, in speaking of Dacca—of the change in axial relationships between the huge Assembly building and its small ceremonial adjunct, the mosque—showed a plan of these two components. Pointing to a subtle shift in principal axis from the Assembly building to the mosque at the very point where the two buildings intersected, Kahn said:

29; 16 – 18

See, the mosque turns [relative to the Assembly] slightly towards true West [to Mecca]. There; it's West—the building. I purposely did that. I *purposely* made that building sit there like that so I could turn the mosque the other way. In other words, how would you know that it's *particular*?

This has always stood for me as a defining moment in which architecture *as idea*, architecture as *concept*, had been made evident with but a simple formal gesture. It was a moment of vintage Kahn, but it also represented an emblem of the intellect, a model of thinking about design as many of us wished it had been propagated at Berkeley during those years, instead of as it actually was.

Endnotes

1 *The exact date of this lecture cannot be precisely verified at this time. Kahn visited Berkeley at least three times during the 1960s, including June 1968, at which time he lectured to the university community as a whole on the occasion of the centennial celebration of the University of California. The present lecture, however, was the most significant — especially so because of its strong theoretical content. It is virtually certain that this lecture was given toward the end of 1966. A two-day visit at the end of November is documented in the Kahn Archives at the University of Pennsylvania. Additional clues are audible at the end of the lecture tape (not transcribed here), in which Kahn was engaged in a brief conversation with Patrick Quinn (a former student, by then a member of the architecture faculty at Berkeley) discussing the progress of the project for St. John's Priory in Valyermo, California, begun in 1966 and abandoned in 1967. As Kahn visited Berkeley only once in 1966 and did not visit the campus in 1967, the date of the present lecture is therefore reasonably certain.*

2 *As I had studied architecture at the University of Pennsylvania as part of my liberal arts studies, I was asked to escort Professor Kahn around the campus during the afternoon preceding the lecture. I used this opportunity to inform Kahn of our concerns.*

3 *The building, officially called North Gate Hall, was designed in 1906 by John Galen Howard, and served as the original home of the School of Architecture. It was affectionately referred to as 'The Ark' by its denizens.*

4 *It bears mentioning, of course, that this position was oddly out-of-synch with the humanistic, 'let-it-be' spirit so pervasive at Berkeley as a whole during those years.*

5 *'Building Science,' as distinguished from 'architecture'—a distinction which Kahn was to stress in his lecture. By the time of Kahn's visit, the core curriculum in architecture had been re-structured into a new four-year undergraduate program leading to the degree 'Bachelor of Environmental Design,' supplemented by a two-year graduate program leading*

directly to a Master of Architecture degree: the traditional five-year Bachelor of Architecture program was abandoned altogether. Key faculty members who, together with Christopher Alexander, exerted considerable influence to change the curriculum and, in particular, to advocate the new interpretations of architectural design were Joseph Esherick, Horst Rittel (a mathematician), Gerald McCue, and Roslyn Lindheim. Sim Van der Ryn and Jesse Reichek were also participants in some of these changes.*

6 *After Christopher Alexander's "DMG" (Design Methods Group).*

7 *I recall one such student arrived in Alexander's studio from Harvard with the distinction of having single-handedly created a concrete dinghy.*

8 *Christopher Alexander was conspicuously absent from the lecture. Although there was no formal boycott as such, many of his students likewise chose not to attend, as an ideological statement.*

The Berkeley Lecture - A Postscript

Ed Levin

It is only possible to create interwoven spatial systems by getting rid of circumstantial pressure. In order to get complexity in architecture you have to get rid of several things: first, you have to get rid of architectural, historical laws; second, you have to stop thinking about clients; third, you have [to] stop thinking too much about the money you're making; and, finally, you have to stop thinking about cost.[1]

Wolf Prix, Coop Himmelblau

The subjective theory of knowledge – which tells me to construct the physical world out of my own 'egocentric' perceptual experience – has set itself a task which is both unnecessary and impossibly difficult. This is why it always relapses into some kind of idealism. And what makes idealism so unattractive is, precisely, the fatal ease with which it explains everything. For idealism does solve all problems – by emptying them.[2]

Karl Popper

If the first quotation succinctly summarizes a currently fashionable posture, regarded by many as a viable extension of 'the modern program,' then it is no small irony that a 25-year-old lecture by a lately unfashionable architect – who also cared more about architecture than about the money he was making – may provide a useful critique of that fashionable position. In this context, this hitherto untranscribed lecture may be as timely now – as a *rappel à l'ordre* – as it was when originally delivered.[3]

Louis I. Kahn, reduced in recent years to something of a cult figure, seems, in fact, to be coming back into 'fashion,' if a current, major retrospective exhibition and a spate of recent publications serve as any evidence.[4] Unfortunately, the retrospective and publications seem likely to contribute more to the simple rehabilitation of Kahn's historical stature than to a genuine critical re-examination of his work. It could hardly be otherwise, given contemporary critical prejudices. Despite a well-researched and generally insightful catalogue to the retrospective, the conventional perception of Kahn's work will almost assuredly remain colored by the tendency of historians and scholars to treat Kahn's writings and buildings as indistinguishable, one from the other.

In this, of course, Kahn is not alone. **One of the general presumptions historians and critics hold about architects – especially about great architects – is that their deeds mirror their words: that their buildings may be best and most cogently explicated by literal recourse to their rhetoric, their polemics, and their theoretical musings.** This axiomatic view of intentionality tends to hobble critical thought, even in cases in which it appears, *prima facie,* to be blatantly gratuitous. To read Frank Lloyd Wright, for example, on the subject of his own work is to recognize dissemblance and puffery at every turn. Nonetheless, Wright's avowal that he 'invented' architecture in his nursery by playing with Froebel blocks is largely accepted at face value,[5] while the influence of either historical architecture or his contemporaries is little studied. Compounding the critical problem in his instance, Louis Kahn's writings are, in their own way, far more seductive than Wright's. [To read Kahn on the subject of his own work, or on the subject of architecture in general, is to hear a very genuine voice. It is, accordingly, to believe – deeply in the case of many of his admirers – that Kahn can be taken exactly at his word, and that, by his words, the buildings can be exactly and completely comprehended, without need of further, critical mediation.][6]

Architects, however, are notorious for camouflaging their true intentions either unconsciously – through neglect or lack of introspection – or consciously, generally in the hope of suppressing any apparent influence of their contemporaries. This latter desire reflects a typically modernist interpretation of 'originality,' which places great value on novelty of image and views novelty of interpretation as merely 'derivative.' Subterfuge in the name of appearing original may extend beyond suppression or

1; 19 – 38

camouflage to dis-information, with architects purporting spurious, non-architectural influences rather than acknowledging the pull of contemporary architectural fashion.[7] [Consequently, the naive belief in intentionality – that architects mean what they say and say what they mean – is perilous ground upon which to re-construct the 'meaning' of works of architecture.]

Admittedly, Kahn's speaking style does not encourage a detached criticism of his work. Kahn's 'writings' are, for the most part, transcribed lectures, and the process of polishing his prose for publication – massaging his fractured syntax into more or less grammatically correct form – has often resulted in the loss of a sense of Kahn's staccato delivery that, paradoxically, more readily conveys his intent to the listener.[8] **Instead of a cogent, albeit disjointed, discourse, what emerges from the printed page is generally too neat, too tidy, and, too often, something of a poetic babble. In this regard, if the Berkeley lecture seems somewhat more 'raw,' and in that way somewhat uncharacteristic of Kahn's other lectures and writings, it is probably for the better.**

Indeed, perhaps *because* it has been neither over-polished nor 'laundered' by well-intentioned editors, what emerges from the Berkeley lecture are fascinating insights into the nature and the complexity of Kahn's thought, for to say that buildings are other than constructed words is not to say that Kahn's words are of no use in attempting to understand his work. [If buildings are not the mirror of words, it is at least fair to say that an architect's words – what is only *implicitly* stated as much as what is *explicitly* stated – provide useful clues to the assumptions, prejudices, and influences that underlie those buildings.] In fact, it is in this sense that the Berkeley lecture may be among the most valuable of Kahn's lectures and writings.

Further complicating any genuine analysis of Kahn's work, most historians and critics also continue to believe in the progressivist notion that the whole of an architect's production – words and buildings – can be, and therefore ought to be, reduced to a seamless, coherent continuum. Indeed, modern historiography typically holds a superficial consistency to be one of the principal attributes of the 'mature' architect. This attribute is considered so pivotal, in fact, that architects who do not exhibit a 'signature' style tend to be relegated to the ash heap of history, at least in the short term. Consequently, many architects have made a practice – literally, as well as figuratively – of exploiting this critical prejudice.

Such would certainly explain why some of the greatest architects of this century have felt compelled to manicure their reputations as carefully as they crafted their buildings. Le Corbusier, for one, took elaborate pains with the publication of his writings and buildings. He augmented, edited, and adjusted nearly every edition of each volume of his *Oeuvre Complete,* omitting all of his earliest work, and occasionally even excising from later editions such originally published projects as he subsequently found embarrassing.[9] Corbusier almost assuredly participated in the composition of the published photographs of his early buildings. These images are replete with the iconic objects of Purist still lifes, his own furniture,[10] and a Voisin automobile – all intended to concatenate the *"Esprit Nouveau"* polemics of *Vers une Architecture* and *L'Art Décoratif d'Aujourd'hui.*[11] Frank Lloyd Wright, too, wrote, published, re-wrote, and re-published his own writings and buildings – even revising and augmenting *An Autobiography* 11 years after its original publication – seeking at every opportunity to present himself as a 'genius,' and his work as the very embodiment of originality.[12]

Kahn himself did not engage in such overt self-promotion, nor was he particularly adept at professional propagandizing,[13] which, parenthetically, may explain why more than fifteen years elapsed after Kahn's death before a major retrospective and critical compendia of his work emerged.[14] Rather, in Kahn's case a corollary phenomenon has been at work: that the work of an architect who is considered 'great' must be construed as being consistent. As such, architects who are adjudged to be 'great' on the basis of their ideas find that their work is viewed through a predetermined ideological filter that sees only the continuities and consistencies in that body of work. By thus removing from critical discourse the consideration of any disparate or apparently contradictory aspects of the work, this 'shorthand' method ultimately reduces complex historical meaning to simple allegory.

Kahn's particular circumstances also conspired to shape the perception of his *oeuvre*. Kahn's early work remained largely buried in obscurity, at least in part because of the unheralded treatment of Depression-era and wartime projects. It may also be argued that Kahn's reputation was aided by the fact that his large-scale urban projects for Penn Center, the Philadelphia College of Art, and the Baltimore Inner Harbor were never realized, as their imminent quality as drawings and models far exceeds what would have been the banality of their urban vision as constructed works. Finally, of course, Kahn's untimely death cut short any further development of his work. It is thus on the basis of comparatively few buildings – almost exclusively institutional – that most of the critical judgments of Kahn's work have been made. Consequently, Kahn's work has remained an easy victim of simplistic critical analysis.

It hardly matters whether such reductivist pigeon-holing is promulgated by historians, by the professional press, or by architects themselves. In any case, buildings are stripped of a significant portion of their substance – especially when elevated to the status of architectural icons.[15] For architects, the equivalent condition is their 'labeling' according to their supposedly singular ideological predilection. An architect is adjudged to be, more or less exclusively, a 'Classicist,' a 'Modernist,' a 'Postmodernist,' a 'Deconstructivist,' or whatever. It would be over-simplifying matters, though, to attribute this condition solely to mediocre historiography or journalistic trends, however much the impetus for such 'niche positioning' would seem to stem principally from an implicit recognition that simple-minded labeling requires less effort than complex thinking. It must be added that, while such shorthand thinking may not be particularly useful from a critical historical perspective, from the standpoint of architects in the commercial marketplace, not all of its consequences are negative. To 'define' an architect is, in a cynically pragmatic sense, also to position that architect as a clearly recognizable, consumable commodity.

Conversely, [to be an ideologically complex architect is to risk being perceived as 'difficult' by the marketplace as well as by historians, and indeed, Louis Kahn has generally been perceived by both parties – probably correctly so[16] – as 'difficult.'] Too 'Beaux-Arts' for doctrinaire modernists, but no less obviously 'modern' in the abstraction of his forms, Kahn fits traditional historical straitjackets badly, and fits the commercial marketplace even worse. In the context of these reductivist critical prejudices, the breadth, richness, and complexity of the Berkeley lecture makes it altogether apparent why Louis Kahn has remained a problematic figure.

20;   19 – 26

This lecture also throws Kahn's formalist predilections into sharp relief. Perhaps because he is addressing students of architecture, [Kahn speaks quite openly about false starts and bad initial design assumptions, most of which involve formal preconceptions. Kahn acknowledges that his initial design for the Indian Institute of Management dormitories featured *brises-soleil,* without regard for their functional inappropriateness; in other words, purely as a preconceived formal gesture.] More than just a genuine (and genuinely refreshing) admission of a fallibility that all architects share, in alluding to this formalist bias of his design method, this particular example also underscores the underlying influence of Le Corbusier's postwar work.[17] Kahn's radical divergence from Le Corbusier's planimetry has generally led Kahn's admirers to ignore or to downplay his broader dependency upon Corbusier's imagery and use of materials, as though the acknowledgment of such would diminish the freshness and originality of Kahn's subsequent manipulation of that material.

The formal influence of Kahn's Beaux-Arts education on his work has, too, been extensively discussed, either to stress or to attempt to downplay Kahn's formal alliance with its tenets.[18] While the formal influences must, by now, be thoroughly acknowledged, the Berkeley lecture provides some telling insights into another, equally crucial aspect of Kahn's connection to Beaux-Arts theory. Kahn speaks to the very origins of the Beaux-Arts methodology when he states:

7; 41 – 43
8; 1 – 33

[T]here is no reason for building anything unless it satisfies an institution of Man of some kind, whether it's the institution of Government, institution of Learning, or institution of Home. They are all institutions. *There is nothing that one builds that is not part of some institution of Man*; something that he institutes and wants to see continued. ... It's a true sense of religion, of 'in-touchness' with commonness with *a* commonness. ... Your concern should be how – how we – what is my opportunity, when I get this building, to express this institution of Man in a way which has *lost* its sense, of expressing it with spirit? That doesn't mean that it works; it means it has a spirit. It has *in it* the character of 'a place you want to learn.' It must have that character, and therefore it must have this feeling that the small space, the larger space, the lecture hall, the hallway, the entrance – all particularly belong to 'School,' and not to some other building. ... And my concern with trying to find those 'Form Elements': *Form to me means the inseparable parts of something* – the realization of the inseparable parts – it has nothing to do with 'design' whatsoever. *Design is only a means.* It's only a *way,* to express one little spark of what Form actually conveys to you. It's a realization of something that has an 'Existence Will,' and has a sense of its parts.

Such a statement directly connects Kahn with those aspects of architectural theory that might rightly be termed 'proto-Beaux-Arts.' In this quotation we can easily recognize that Enlightenment dialectic between *type* – what Kahn terms *'form'* – and *associational character* – the *idea* or spirit of the building program – that, once codified, formed the kernel of Beaux-Arts theory. Indeed, such thinking aligns Kahn less with the instrumental rationalism of Durand's *Précis des leçons*[19] than with the associative expressionism of Boullée's *Architecture*.[20] It is Boullée's view of the roots of architecture in naturalistically expressive typologies, rather than Laugier's ontological primitivism, to which Kahn alludes when he speaks, as he does elsewhere, of wanting to read Volume Zero of the history of architecture. **Kahn is captivated by this desire to work directly from an original idea – that is to say, literally, an idea of the origins – of the dialectic of type and character.** As such, if the Beaux-Arts did not already exist, Kahn would have been compelled to invent it. As it is, Kahn may be said to have reinvented – or at least reinterpreted – the Beaux-Arts by superimposing upon its attitude toward typology an abstract character that was simultaneously modern and premodern.

The character of a building – the *idea* of its intended use and the way it expresses that use – is more important to Kahn than the mere fact that it accommodates that intended use. Consequently, although Kahn strongly believes that functional requirements must be accommodated – that a building cannot be considered successful if it does not 'work' – the building program itself, as a list of functional requirements, is to be accepted as *fact* and rejected as *truth* – to be considered *a posteriori* rather than *a priori*. It is the human institution in question that is primary, and the program must be adjusted if it is not adequate for the typological expression – an expression of a 'commonness' – of that institution:

2; 40 – 43

I think it must be *assumed* that a building, when made, is a 'solution of the problem': and not to think that you are doing so marvelous a job in doing *that*. Because it's probably the most easy thing to do – if you have the predilection for it. The reason why some deviate from this is because the program *itself,* is not worthy to be extended in the form of a building.

This attitude toward the program distinctly separates Kahn from doctrinaire, 'scientific' functionalism. Function plays a central role in Kahn's architecture, but primarily as the implicit, 'shadow' expression of a human need. Thus, [function is not a matter of problem-*solving* but rather one of problem-*defining;*] the former capable of being addressed by a *brain* – by a machine – but the latter only capable of being resolved by a *mind*. This distinction is wholly familiar to the Beaux-Arts sensibility, but is so completely alien to the modernist, *sachlichkeit* sensibility that the role of function in Kahn's work has remained ambiguously considered by both critics and admirers.[21]

[In that sense of problem defining, when Kahn 'violates' the program, he is not, in his mind, violating function. The program is manipulated not principally to ignore genuine functional requirements but rather to add some transcendent, typological element which is missing from that program yet essential to the function of the human institution *qua* institution:]

3; 6 – 18

A school is an environment of spaces where it is good to learn, where even the corridor must be changed into galleries, because galleries then become the only classroom the student has. ... A man has to realize that suddenly one element of architecture, 'the gallery,' is an important part of 'School' – something which is not in the program at all. Do you find a gallery in a program? No. You will find a *lobby*, but you'll never find a 'Place of Entrance.'

22; 43 – 44
23; 1 – 9

[This attitude clearly explains why Kahn has absolutely no compunction about eliminating or 'transforming' major programmatic elements – as in the transformation of a rug closet into a mosque at Dacca – when such transformation serves a larger purpose, and it also explains why Kahn never discusses his larger purpose purely in terms of formal intentions.] Instead, for Kahn, the larger purpose concerns "discovering the 'ingredients' that are good for *this* place." This is not merely a formal investigation into the aesthetics of the plan. It is, instead, an investigation into typological 'correctness,' in which the *collective* aspect of a human need must be explicitly expressed. In that sense, the type and its expressive or associational character are regarded as an inseparable dialectic, the accommodation of which is more highly valued than the simple satisfaction of programmatic function.

That same sensibility carries over into the detailing of Kahn's buildings, as the Berkeley lecture also demonstrates. Kahn intersperses his theoretical discourse with practical instruction on the making of buildings, patiently explaining, for example, the purpose and nature of form ties in concrete construction. Yet, whether describing the concrete work at Salk, the 'composite order' of brick and concrete at Ahmedabad, or the concrete and marble at Dacca, Kahn emphasizes not simply the facts of construction but also the ordering effect of construction methods; that is, the expressive potential of the materials and their combinations:

29; 29 - 38

Now these stripes that you see there are the way I made the construction. I poured every five feet, and rested, so that all the screw ties I talked to you about just a little while ago – these little holes – would all be in this area where I placed marble. ... This way, every five feet it's drained. It's a combination. It's an 'Order'; a realization of concrete, of construction, and [of] need.

As with the dialectic of type and character, Kahn presumes an inseparable relationship between construction method and material expression, which supersedes pure practicality. Always, the *idea* of the detail is paramount, but, unlike Mies van der Rohe, for Kahn, God is not so much in the details as much as in Man, and Man's imprint in the act of constructing. Kahn's details are the perfect manifestations of their making, whether or not this making is perfect. This attitude, though, is not without its price. Kahn's buildings were generally quite expensive, due in large part to his preference for expressive, but atypical, detailing and construction methods. Many projects were either substantially re-designed or abandoned due to serious budget overruns. Furthermore, Kahn's buildings, when constructed, sometimes suffer from details that, while they are eloquently resolved from a conceptual standpoint, do not function as intended.[22]

2; 16 – 19

[In the end, however, Kahn's buildings are ennobled by the evident struggle toward their 'realization,' in which what is realized is not *architecture* but rather *a work of architecture*.] **A great work is not an abstract entity but a human thing – for Kahn, the most human thing:**

5; 16 – 19

It's true of a painting: it gives you a different sense of point of view about things. You certainly realize that a painter can really paint a red dress when he sees a blue one. You wonder why he does it, but still, you see: well, he really can – you see, he *does* it. Is he inhuman? Of course not. *Terribly human* – in fact, more so than those who are amazed by it.

Kahn's often-expressed preference for the temples at Paestum over the Parthenon may be understood in exactly these terms, as the former embodies the struggle by which the latter was made comparatively easy. However great the Parthenon may be as a work of architecture, the temples at Paestum are more human for being less perfect: less literally an ideal type and therefore more pregnant with human possibilities.

8; 19 –23

2; 24 – 26

[Anthropocentrism and egocentrism are not, however, one and the same, and it is Kahn's core of humanism – his sense of the collective commonness – that prevents him from lapsing into Popper's egocentric idealism.] Indeed, [it is not difficult to imagine that the battle Kahn wages in this lecture against the architectural Left, in the form of "machines taking the place of men" he would equally wage against the architectural Right, in the form of the present regressive tendency toward egocentric expressionism.]

All of this does not make Kahn an easier or less complex figure to deal with, and perhaps this in itself is the reason that the Berkeley lecture seems to have such resonance today. Ultimately, what appears most inspiring and most timely is Kahn's consistent unwillingness to 'empty' the problem of architecture by what Wolf Prix terms "getting rid of circumstantial pressure." Kahn's personal field of battle was precisely those circumstantial pressures, both intrinsic and extrinsic, that impinge upon a project from all directions. **For Kahn, the personal must always remain suspended in a dialectic balance with the collective.** In this insistence upon both type *and* character, 'Form' *and* 'Design,' the rational *and* the expressive, we might find in the Berkeley lecture a lesson at least as important today as it was more than a quarter century ago.

Endnotes

1 *Wolf Prix, "On the Edge," Deconstruction III, Architectural Design Profile No. 87 (London: Academy Group Ltd., 1990): 65.*

2 *Sir Karl R. Popper, Realism and the Aim of Science (Totowa, New Jersey: Rowman and Littlefield, 1983): 103.*

3 *See Ellen K. Morris' introduction for an extended discussion of the contemporary context of this lecture.*

4 *The first major retrospective exhibition of Louis Kahn's work, organized by The Museum of Contemporary Art in Los Angeles, opened in October 1991. The massive exhibition catalogue, Louis I. Kahn: In the Realm of Architecture, David B. Brownlee and David De Long, eds. (New York: Rizzoli International Publications, Inc. and The Museum of Contemporary Art, 1991) [hereafter, In the Realm of Architecture]: 423, lists 28 substantial, English-language publications on Kahn, beginning as early as 1962. Of these, 6 were published between 1989 and 1991.*

5 *For an example of the exclusive examination of prima facie influences on Wright, see Jeanne S. Rubin, "The Froebel Wright Kindergarten Connection: A New Perspective," The Journal of the Society of Architectural Historians, Vol. XLVIII, No. 1 (March 1989): 24–37.*

6 *This belief is epitomized by Light Is the Theme: Louis I. Kahn and the Kimbell Art Museum, Nell E. Johnson, ed. (Fort Worth, Texas: Kimbell Art Foundation, 1975), which consists solely of Kahn quotations juxtaposed with black and white photographs of the Kimbell Art Museum. An interesting, if ultimately unsatisfying, variation is Romaldo Giurgola and Jaimini Mehta, Louis I. Kahn (Boulder, Colorado: Westview Press, 1975) [hereafter, Giurgola and Mehta]. The authors initially state their belief that there is "no obvious methodological connection between [Kahn's] thought and the architecture" (p. 11), but then proceed to base most of their analysis of Kahn's work upon just such a connection.*

7 *Although architects such as Peter Eisenman and Bernard Tschumi have produced work that depends upon Deconstruction for its critical base, much of the current architectural work which is self-described as 'Deconstructivist' employs that term to mask the latest iteration of a retardaire Expressionism, as it is more intellectually 'chic' to be perceived as relying upon the theories of Jacques Derrida than to be perceived as merely engaging in the latest formalist trend.*

8 *The most significant exception to this generalization is the article entitled "Form and Design," written in 1959, and re-written at least twice in 1960 [see In the Realm of Architecture, p. 71, and note 116]. In this instance, the 'polishing' is Kahn's own, and the extensive use of capitalization and italics serves to maintain the emphasis of Kahn's original, spoken words.*

9 *With the publication of the first edition of Volume One of the Oeuvre Complete, [O[scar] Stonorov and W[illy] Boesiger, Le Corbusier und Pierre Jeanneret, Ihr Gesamtes Werk von 1910–1929 (Zurich: Verlag Dr. H. Girsberger, 1930)], Le Corbusier omitted all of his youthful, Jugendstijl-influenced work at La Chaux-de-Fond. With the subsequent publication of the second edition of Volume One [W[illy] Boesiger and O[scar] Stonorov, Le Corbusier et Pierre Jeanneret, Oeuvre Complete de 1910–1929, Nouvelle Édition (Zurich: Editions Dr. H. Girsberger, 1937)], Corbusier removed a handful of 'modern' projects built as well as unbuilt – including several industrial projects and an executed town house in Bordeaux.*

10 *Le Corbusier's 'own' furniture was, of course, designed in conjunction with Charlotte Perriand.*

11 *Le Corbusier, Vers une Architecture (Paris: Les Éditions G. Cres et Cie., Collection de "L'Esprit Nouveau," 1923). Le Corbusier, L'Art Décoratif d'Aujourd'hui (Paris: Les Éditions G. Cres et Cie., Collection de "L'Esprit Nouveau," 1925).*

12 *Frank Lloyd Wright, An Autobiography (London, New York, and Toronto: Longmans, Green and Company, 1932; revised edition, New York: Duell, Sloan and Pierce, 1943; revised (posthumously, from manuscript) edition, New York: Horizon Press, 1977).*

13 *Despite its relative geographic proximity to New*

York, Philadelphia – at least during Kahn's lifetime – was a comparatively parochial place, and remained aloof to, if not ignorant of, the professional architectural press. This attitude is alluded to by Mimi Lobell in her article "Kahn, Penn, and the Philadelphia School," Oppositions 4 (New York: Wittenborn Art Books, Inc., October 1974): 63–64.

14 The emphasis here is on critical compendia; several significant, albeit non-analytical, compendia were published prior to 1989. Alexander Tzonis, ed., The Louis I. Kahn Archive: Personal Drawings: The Completely Illustrated Catalogue of the Drawings in the Louis I. Kahn Collection, University of Pennsylvania and Pennsylvania Historical and Museum Commission (Hamden, Connecticut: Garland Architectural Archive, 1987) is, despite its introductions, a non-critical catalogue. Heinz Ronner and Sharad Jhaveri, eds., Louis I. Kahn: Complete Works 1935–1974 (Basel and Boston: Birkhäuser Verlag, 1977; revised edition, 1987) is avowedly non-interpretive in its approach. A third earlier compendium, Giurgola and Mehta, is interesting, if quirkily organized, from a critical standpoint (see note 6).

15 One example of this would be Kahn's Richards Medical Research Building. Virtually all of the contemporary discussion of the project centered on the purely iconic aspects of the separation of 'served' and 'servant' spaces. Even those critical of the building tended to remain focused less on its mediocre technical performance than on the iconic aspects of function, as in Reyner Banham's otherwise seminal essay, "On trial / 2: Louis Kahn / the buttery-hatch aesthetic," The Architectural Review, Vol. CXXXI, No. 781 (March 1962): 203–206.

16 Undoubtedly, Kahn's painstaking and time-consuming working method largely contributed to his perception as a 'difficult' architect from a commercial standpoint. Kahn received a relatively small number of commercial commissions, of which even fewer were built.

17 This influence is apparent upon examining the material vocabulary of Le Corbusier's Maisons Jaoul at Neuilly, the Maison 'Weekend,' and Villa Errázuriz, among others. Beyond any architect's general awareness of Le Corbusier's work, Kahn worked with Oscar Stonorov, a former employee of Le Corbusier and co-editor of the first volume of Corbusier's Oeuvre Complete [c.f., In the Realm of Architecture, pp. 24–25, 29, 30].

18 These discussions tend to be split into those who see Kahn as influenced by the Beaux-Arts on a fundamental level, and those who see the Beaux-Arts influence as incidental. For the former, see especially, Kenneth Frampton, "Louis Kahn and the French Connection," Oppositions 22 (Cambridge, Massachusetts: for The Institute for Architecture and Urban Studies by the M.I.T. Press, 1980): 20–53; and In the Realm of Architecture, pp. 21–22. The latter viewpoint may be represented by Giurgola and Mehta, "[T]he association which Kahn is supposed

to have with the Beaux-Arts academic tradition." [italics mine], p. 184; and Maria Bottero, "Organic and Rational Morphology in the Work of Louis Kahn," Zodiac 17, 1967, quoted in Kenneth Frampton (above), p. 48, "The Beaux-Arts aspect which has so long been discussed and accepted as a main element characterizing and determining [Kahn's] work seems to me only secondary and incidental, in any event, in no way central to the real historical meaning that his work has taken on for us."

19 J[ean] N[icholas] L[ouis] Durand, Précis des leçons d'architecture données à l'École polytechnique, 2 vols. (Paris: Chez l'Auteur, 1802/1805).

20 Etienne-Louis Boullée, Architecture, Essay on Art in Helen Rosenau, Boullée & Visionary Architecture (London: Academy Editions; New York: Harmony Books, 1976): 81–116. Portions of Boullée's Essay were condensed and paraphrased in Emil Kaufmann, "Three Revolutionary Architects, Boullée, Ledoux, and Lequeu," Transactions of the American Philosophical Society, New Series - Vol. 42, Part 3 (Philadelphia: The American Philosophical Society, 1952): 469–473. Kaufmann notes Boullée's emphasis on an architecture of dramatic light and shadows.

21 An example of the ambiguous critical consideration of Kahn's relationship to functionalism may be seen in Wilder Green's 1961 essay on Richards Medical Research Building in "Louis I. Kahn, Architect / Alfred Newton Richards Medical Research Building," Museum of Modern Art Bulletin, Vol. 28, No. 1 (New York: Museum of Modern Art, 1961): 5: "Kahn's work also continues in the mainstream of the functionalist movement of early modern architecture. Many contemporary architects have now found this to be an inadequate, or even irrelevant basis for their own work, but Kahn, by his redefinition and expansion of the limits of the functionalist theory, has disclosed its continuing usefulness as a generator of meaningful form."

This ambiguous attitude continues to the present. Richard Ingersoll, in his essay "Louis I. Kahn: The Last Master," Design Book Review Issue 21 - Summer 1991 (Cambridge, Massachusetts: The MIT Press, 1991), also oversimplifies Kahn's dialectic between function and expressive character as a shift from functionalism to formalism, when he posits that "Kahn abandoned an architecture of program for one of form."

22 Kahn's penchant for flush detailing, for example, has led to problems with a number of buildings. A recent example would be the Yale Center for British Art, whose exterior walls and windows are streaking due to the combination of a flush-detailed metal facade and a system of reveals and drips which, while elegant, do not actually channel water off the wall.

KAHN, Louis Isadore. American. Born on the Island of Saarama, Estonia, now Russia, 20 February **1901**; immigrated to the United States, to Philadelphia, **1905**; naturalized, **1915**. Educated at the Central High School and Pennsylvania Academy of Fine Arts, Philadelphia, **1912-20**; Graphic Sketch Club, Fleisher Memorial Art School, and the Public Industrial Art School, Philadelphia, **1916-20** (Pennsylvania Academy of Fine Arts Prize, **1920**); University of Pennsylvania, Philadelphia, **1920-24**, B. Arch., **1924**. Married Esther Virginia Israeli in **1930**; daughter: Sue Ann. Draftsman with the architects Hofman and Henan, Philadelphia, **1921**, and with Hewitt and Ash, Philadelphia, **1922**; Teaching Assistant, University of Pennsylvania, **1923-24**; Senior Draftsman, **1924-27**, and Chief of Design for the Sesqui-Centennial Exhibition, **1925-26**. City Architect's Department, Philadelphia; studied and travelled in Europe, **1928-29**; Designer, Office of Paul Cret, Philadelphia, **1929-30**, and Zantziger, Borie and Medary, Philadelphia, **1930-32**; Organizer and Director, Architectural Research Group, Philadelphia, **1932-33**; Squad Head in charge of Housing Studies, City Planning Commission, for the W.P.A. (Works Progress Administration), Philadelphia, **1933-35**; Assistant Principal Architect, office of Alfred Kastner and Partner, Philadelphia, **1935-37**; in private practice, Philadelphia, **1937** until his death, **1974**; in association with George Howe, **1941-42**, with Howe and Oscar Stonorov, **1942-43**, and with Stonorov, **1943-48**. Consultant Architect, Philadelphia Housing Authority, **1937**, and United States Housing Authority, **1939**; Consultant Architect to the Philadelphia City Planning Commission, **1946-52**, **1961-62**; Consultant Architect, Philadelphia Redevelopment Authority, **1951-54**. Chief Critic in Architectural Design and Professor of Architecture, Yale University, New Haven, Connecticut, **1948-57**; Resident Architect, American Academy, Rome, **1950-51**; Albert Farwell Bemis Professor, School of Architecture and Planning, Massachusetts Institute of Technology, Cambridge, **1956**; Professor of Architecture, **1957-66**, Paul Cret Professor, **1966-71**, and Emeritus Professor, **1971-74**, University of Pennsylvania. Member, Team 10. Died (in New York City) 17 March **1974**.

inspiration and making

"I LOVE   to be critical, instigative, accusatory." [60]

"I REACT   to conditions outside myself." [64]

"I IMAGINE   moving through things; I imagine journeys." [87]

"I TAKE   the good wherever I find it." [111]

"I RESPECT   things that have sprung from this land; forms subjected to our
          early sense of economy, inventiveness and questioning." [114]

"I THINK   the recent past is the hardest thing to understand." [127]

"I EXPLORE   social insight in an architectural way." [133]

We are all excitable, sensitive, fragile creatures, inspired and encouraged, or frightened, by the myriad forces of the world around us. What do we fancy? How do we respond— what do we "make" of this world? The following seven essays of selected architects present a wide, if not intentionally wild, array of very personal perceptions, sources of inspiration and ways of making, or constructing, a world beyond oneself.

The presentation of each essay brings together the voice of an architect, in one or more texts, and their images of inspiration in a highly integrated, if not investigative, fashion. If buildings are the final form of an architect's ideas, then the images selected to accompany each text are clips of the ever-evolving scaffolding which surrounds an architect's work. The particular context or adjacency of text and image in each essay is established to alternately isolate, integrate, or reveal significant verbal and visual moments of each contributor's inspiration.

Contributing Architects:

Jean Nouvel, Günter Behnisch, Adéle Naude Santos, Aldo Rossi, W.G. Clark, Denise Scott Brown and Robert Venturi

"The eye sees not things but forms of

Italo Calvino, 1980.

L'Avenir de l'architecture n'est pas architectural

Doctrines and Uncertainties

"The eye sees not things but forms of

Doctrines and Uncertainties

things which signify other things."

Architecture today is still the art of choosing the formal vocabulary of

With few exceptions, Architecture is sad, monotonous, and unsurprising.

Jean Nouvel

The Moderns never cease to hark back to their CORBU, grey and fat. The Rationalists make their final stand before surrendering. The Technocrats no longer dazzle anyone with their feats in tow. The Nostalgics are afraid of losing their memory and make us cry over the lost charms of the 17th-century city. The Formalists obsess over the triangle, the circle, or the square, depending on their genetic determinism or a bad encounter not discovered by their psychiatrists.

The skillful, correct, and wonderful game of volumes no longer amuses anyone.

The city suffocates, grows fat and flabby in the so-called peripheral zones. The circulation is poor. The bad cells are spreading. The heart is ill. The limbs are tingling.

In these circumstances, Architects have perfectly understood that Architecture was not accessible to the people and decided not to speak about architecture any longer except among themselves in order, so they say, to deepen their inner knowledge.

They speak so much of architecture that they no longer speak about anything else. The others (non-Architects), no longer hearing anything said about architecture, speak about everything else. When an Architect hears someone else (a non-Architect) speak about architecture, he treats him as an incompetent and advises him to speak of something else.

When someone else hears Architects

This has nearly turned out badly for them because other people were no longer calling on the Architect for building.

Fortunately, the Law came to the rescue of the unfortunate Architect in decreeing that henceforth only the Architect could build for other people, which the Architect totally accepted, being able to build calmly, without any surprises, and in complete legality. As a way to deliver him from every anxiety (the solitude of the Artist in the face of his empty building site is absolute), the Legislator strongly advised him to heed his prescriptions. Thus, the Architect, reassured and guided, henceforth follows the few recipes written today in the wretched menu of the government cafeteria. Mistakes are no longer his fault. As long as he follows the Civil Code, mistakes are the fault of the Administration.

Architects then discussed the matter and became divided. The greatest number of them, respectful of the Established Order, have decreed that the urban and periurban [suburban] chaos was not of their doing and that their

(break, page 55)

Toward a Number of Architectures – A Parodic Anti-Manifesto in Favor of a Pluralist Architecture:

I love architectures to be

I love them as one loves an epoch or civilization. As a revealing sign of savoir-faire and of esthetic and practical preoccupations. I love them above all as an instant of imagination turned into stone. I also love them as realistic intentions. As the result of an act of will and mastery. As the statement of a proposition which knew how, in order to exist, to have itself admitted. I love them as illustrations of the dated possible. I judge them as witnesses of economic and cultural consensus.

I am ready to love more of them. Pure and impure ones. Virtuous and whorish ones ...

Spontaneous and sophisticated ones. Nude and well-dressed ones. Proletarian and bourgeois ones. Provided that they be alive! **I am afraid**
Let us leave Frankenstein his bride. Provided that they be tolerant! Slave in search of mistresses, this does very little for me.

As for the rapport of the sadomasochistic type and those who impose their way of life and perpetually show off their strength, no thank you! As long as they are intelligent! ... one gets tired even of bimbos! If they are witty, that's all right! If they are cultured and do not show off their knowledge, I will listen to them. If they are knowledgeable, I will pay them a visit and interest myself in their discoveries. And while I'm at it, I prefer beautiful ones. It seems that this is no longer in fashion, but I can't help myself!

When I say beautiful, I do not

no more than ... what I want to say is one with the charm and minor yet engaging faults of someone like Barbra Streisand, for example. I do not like to imagine them as systems or as robots made of the same interchangeable parts and well programmed to answer some limited ques-

Nouvel

one building in a thousand. It could collapse tomorrow without making many

intelligent and unmistakable.

of mummies and things brought back to life!

speak of architecture, he does not understand a word of

L'AUBE DE 92

necessarily mean Marilyn Monroe,

ople cry. profession consisted above all in covering one's expenses and coming in on time with a technically reliable product. Certain Architects took refuge on their planet of paper, in their utopias of the future or past, taking themselves for a PIRANESI or BOULEE.

A minority (acting as is right and proper) have decided to await the Great Evening which would, miraculously, make everything possible once again.

There remain the Don Quixotes, the hot-blooded ones, those who think

I am that way for all the reasons which flow from the pernicious preceding statement.

And, against the windmills, the winds, the City Halls, the swamps, the urbanocrats, and above all those with a doctoral degree in Architecture,

The solution is not hidden in the codicils of ALBERTI, PIRANESI, LEQUEUX, or LEDOUX. The key is not in knowing in whose wake to follow, which master to worship, which architecture to impose, or which architects to excommunicate. Architecture can no longer be that which it claims to be, some kind of "art of organizing space" or some "skillful game of volumes." Architecture can no longer be one building in a thousand financed by adoring patrons or the authorities in search of style. Architecture must go beyond its borders, overturn its elitist guardians, and stop being a privilege that no social revolution will ever abolish. It is the role of architects to liberate their muse.

For this, one must express oneself by every means, principally by that which

it and advises them to speak of something else.

is built. One must echo an entire culture, and draw from an entire civilization. The example of the modern movement is significant in this regard. Is it the history of Architecture which inspired it? Or was it the industrial revolution, or FOURIER and PROUDHON, followed by KANDINSKY, MONDRIAN, KLEE…?

Architecture can no longer be the simple visual quest for beauty (for many years artists, those who work with form [plasticians], painters, sculptors, photographers, filmmakers, musicians, and poets have gone beyond aesthetic value alone to accompany, supplement, and replace it with the quest for signification).

From now on, Architecture must

Architecture should speak, tell, and question at the cost, if necessary (and it often is), of technological purity, the constructed tradition, and the conformity of references to cultural models (whether they be of classical or modern origin).

tions. I prefer to think of them as unique and bringing with them the qualities and defects inscribed in their genetic heritage. I imagine them as fragile and mortal, in need of love, care, and attention. *With, like everyone, an uncertain* I love them for themselves, for their singular personalities. I have a weakness for cool ones, sensitive to the esthetic of the times, influenced by literature, comic books, television, movies, photography, and the artistic creation of the hour. Making discerning use of all aspects of their life in order to make it easier and make themselves happy, with up-to-date electronic

I predict that the

devices and the most recent inventions. I am interested in intellectual ones, those who know how they are made and who ask themselves existential questions: Where am I? Where did I come from? Where am I going? I love those who organize themselves to exploit to the fullest their qualities and their faults, conscious of the importance of their subconscious.

I do not despair in knowing many of them. From one to another, I take upon myself the quarrels and am the champion of pluralism. To one and the other, I add still others. To black and white, I add all the colors, nuances, ornaments, and motley hues. They are only valued for being alive, tolerant, and different. Rather than taking out one or the other, or one and the other, I choose among the others in each city and port on the spot. With a number of them, it's more of a sure thing.

Jean Nouvel - Extracts from a lecture at the Centre Georges Pompidou, January 1992:

If asked to define architecture today, we would have to begin by saying what it does not do. In modern times, architecture wanted to create the world. It failed through overambition, without properly understanding that the world does not belong to the architect, but the architect to the world;

(break, page 57)

"horizon" montage, video image, text and photograph

Nouvel

destiny linked to chance and to the community to which they belong.

future of architecture is not Architectural.

Signify.

(page 55, pick up)

Architecture should address itself to the spirit more than to the eye and

In order to do this, all means are good ones: symbol, reference, metaphor, sign, decoration, humor, game, irony, plagiarism, innovation, tradition, style.... All words are permitted if they are useful in the sense given them and if they are understood.

without understanding that architecture modifies and extends the world through the defeat of chaos, an adventure into the involuntary. The architecture of each era must reinvent the tools of its evolution, together with other disciplines which

From this point of view, the future of architecture is

... who are going to live in the space that he defines. What he says, what he chooses to say, is at least as interesting as his way of saying it. The content of the architectural message is no longer something to be chosen from history, as if architecture were a literary author of the 17th century, choosing his drama from mythology or ancient history.

How is the Architect going to choose what he is going to say? Is he always going to repeat himself like an obsessed artist? Only the consciousness of

share the same characteristics. For an architect to embark on an adventure of such magnitude involves familiarity with thought.

It is never easy to plunge into philosophy or to organize thoughts. For my part I have always worked by displacement. In philosophical terms, I'm told one should talk about concept migration.

t is not by our inner knowledge that we

context, the knowledge of the milieu in which he constructs, can permit him to find a real sense. That is to say, a physical, historical knowledge of this milieu – the consciousness of the possibility of evolution during the life expectancy of the proposed building – and a human knowledge – how the milieu is felt by those who live in it, what is expected of the building to be created, whether there is a suitable balance between the program and its social vocation....

The sense of this preliminary dialogue, of this "participation" so disparaged by some and so demanded by others, lies precisely here.

Gathering information and verifying hypotheses in order to orient one's choices constitute the necessary condition for creating an architecture. But this condition is far from being sufficient. Integrating the givens does not imply finding the solution. Refusing to integrate them implies refusing to answer to them.

It is in these preliminary dialogues that the Architect has the greatest chance of finding a social sense, a common sense to what he is going to edify.

It is characteristic of the Architect-Artist to deny this. His own satisfaction is the criterion of Good. His is the only solution.

How does taking into account a request limit the quality of the architectural response? Let us be done with this bad process which would have it that an architect who integrates a precise request abdicates his knowledge and "cuts his wings." **It is often in the request that the architect finds the response**

In the work of Michel Foucault I've found a number of procedural rules and exploratory methods. In particular, I appreciated the values of the order of discourse — of discontinuity — exteriority, specificity, and inversion as effective methods of investigation; and the idea of developing rules of formulation which lead to a concept.

Today, I am attempting to take this research further. After Foucault, I found the work of Deleuze and Guattari interesting and a little disturbing — particularly their latest book, Qu'est-ce que c'est que la philosophie? *They explained things which have been familiar to me for ten years, but in a much more precise, highly involved, and intelligent way. But they speak of concept, precept, and effect, while I was talking about concept, sensation, and emotion. And on reading that the notion of concept is reserved for philosophy I realized that this was perhaps a misuse. Then I read that "there is no such thing as a simple concept. Every concept has an indeterminate number of elements ... it is a multiplicity." When I read that a concept "has an irregular form, defined by the number of its components, that each concept has a past and a future and may be considered as the point at which its composing elements coincide and are condensed," I understood that this could be applied to a purely architectural concept. That*

On this level, the future of architecture is democratic

But let us talk of the context, of the environment in which the project is sit-

there could be a link between the world of philos-

(break, page 59)

"exterior" montage, video image, text and photograph

Nouvel

translate a living civilization rather than a heritage.

more literary than architectural, more linguistic than formal

will undo the crisis of architecture.

(page 57, pick up)

uated. Does this context permit a sensible response? Does the urban and suburban [periurban] jumble still permit the architectural object to find a sense? If not, what good is it to think about architecture? Can one content himself with creating isolated art/architectural objects in making an appeal to an architectural knowledge which is less and less shared?

ophy and the world of architecture, even if an architectural concept differs in that its aim is not formulation, but fabrication, its aim is to attain reality. The question of reality brings us back once again to an exploration of the physical world.

f architecture becomes this means to convey ideas and

Today, architecture stops at the object (taken in the sense of unity and mastery of the work or the working). Should one not consider as a preliminary architectural problem the rapport to be created between several masteries of the work?

Therein lies one of the principal architectural problems — outside the domain of the competence acknowledged for architects and on the other side of the administrative barrier.

When a philosopher says that philosophy proceeds by concept, science by prospect, and art by precept and effect, he is drawing our attention to the prospect, to that which science can contribute. Heidegger's provocative statement comes to mind: "Science doesn't think." That's not what it's there for.

It is a problem of power,

Under this essential aspect, the future of architecture is urbanistic.

The field of architecture should stretch to include the spatial organization and definition of the vocabulary of the new neighborhoods, to the orientations to be given to urban modifications. There, where the rules of urbanism are in force, where the technocratic norms apply, where the censor of good taste reigns, architecture no longer carries except by mistake. Well, then, what is to be done? **Construct. In the most significant way. In 90 percent of**

One sometimes doubts when one sees the state of mathematics today, with its ingenuity, its strategies or the theories surrounding falsification, for example, presented as a kind of prototype novel, as it were, stories where points of passage can be read.... One realizes, then, that similar methods of exploration could well have a relevance to archi-

... the nature of what it should or could have been. Here are some personal examples. When you are asked to construct in a lot of the worst type (with all the same consummate houses), surround your house with an embankment two meters high and drive it into the soil so that it recreates its own landscape. When someone wants to make you make a pastiche with a seated dog, in order not to deface the landscape, make an invisible, pedestrian, chameleon-like house with rusty steel and a chestnut tree overgrown with vegetation. When you are refused a building permit and are obliged to carry out some modifications, mark them all in red on the constructed house. If you are made to work with an industrialized and repetitive model, use a single element and number from 1 to 3000 on the front.

tecture.

Seeing the images which can be produced by fractals — an iterative mathematical process leading to infinity and an infinity of forms — or the geometry of meaning suggested by Thom's catastrophe theory, one suddenly realizes that the ideography generated by science is an extraordinary foundation for image makers such as us architects. Science supplies the conditions in which ideas can change. It provides the material and the spark which kindle philosophy and art as well as art on the borders of all of these disciplines.

People will object, telling me that these attitudes are of little interest to the man in the street and are difficult to comprehend. If the story told were so simplistic, that would be true. But it is not easy to escape from the question posed by this attitude in relation to the context. It is an architectural reading at different degrees which is carried out. The author (architect) should know that his book (object) will be read, seen, and decoded [decrypted] by a very large audience.

For the architect of course, a man working with reality, it is the everyday applications of science which are useful. The evolution of technology and technical procedures and the contribution of new materials endowed with incredible properties are,

The characteristic of a strong architecture is to be

Where are these positions in architectural thought situated today? Some people call them post-modern. Under certain aspects (the different codes of possible readings, eclecticism, irony), they probably are. But does there exist

so to speak, grounds for a reappraisal. In its relationship with science and its applications, architecture aims for synergy of performance.

(break, page 61)

"interior" montage, video image, text and photograph

signify space, then the architect is a man who says (with

and architecture is weak.

the cases, we must take positions that are critical, instigative, accusatory,

read by all and to resist this reading, to be sufficiently profound to guard a little

(page 59, pick up)

a post-modern thinking? I do not think so. For me, at present, the post-modern is defined by a process of elimination. Those who are post-modern are the ones who are not pre-modern and who are not modern. The pre-modern ones are those in love with Quincy de Quatremere, those from the Versailles school who reverently make everything from the window to the

the constructed as language) and

garden in the French style, the doctrinaire ones who prophesy that the laws of estheticism and architectural knowledge are going to overturn economic phenomena, those who preach a European city with arcaded plazas and triumphant obelisks, the carvers, copiers, and masters. The modern ones are in line, the repetitive ones, the square ones, the boxes, the socio-social ones, the legitimate offspring of Corbu, the bastards of Mondrian, the involuntary supremacists, the simplifiers, those with a limited outlook, the vocabulary amnesics who have forgotten words from other centuries.

Here a new factor intervenes in the evolution of our discipline, a factor which, historically or critically speaking, is rarely considered: if architecture integrates this synergy of performance, its relationship with modernity is no longer one of uncritical

who speaks to those

wonderment. Technical prowess, once the guiding light for architects of heroic modernity, has lost its value as a symbol. The role of the engineer loses none of its power, its nobility, or its prestige. But today we no longer want to see the workings. Architecture has to be a force of its own; to be guided by something other than contingencies and the harsh realities of construction.

There remain the others, the

Those who formulate three ideas at once, who remember, who actualize, who decorate, who denounce, who keep their distances, who laugh, who multiply the signs, whose eyes fill with tears, who mix together cultures, memories, hopes, despair, and fantasies.

"Radical eclectics," manufacturers of "canards" or "decorated sheds," "symbolists," "ugly and common," spectacular, and ironic. They live in and trans-

impure ones.

foundations for the conscious development of a true work of architecture. It is important to remember that the evolution of ideas, of science and the arts, is not without consequence for architecture. With this in mind, in what direction should architecture evolve?

questioning, and ironic. Each building should provoke a question on ...

late their epoch.

mystery and also to give rise to some questions without hope of an answer.

"The Arab World Institute" montage, text and photograph
Paris, France, 1981–1987
detail view of interior

NOUVEL, Jean. French. Born 12 August, **1945**. Educated at The École

Nationale Supérieure des Beaux-Arts, **1966**; DLPG Degree, **1974**. Co-

founder of the Movement of French Architects "March 1976," **1972**; Co-

founder of the Architectural Union and one of the key organizers of the

International Consultants for the Development of the Paris Halles,

1979; Founder and Artistic Director of the Architecture Biennial, part

of the Paris Biennial, **1980**. Merger with Emmanuel Cattani of all activ-

ities and projects, **1988**. Vice-President of the French Institute of

Architecture, **1991**. Exhibitions: Paris Universal Exhibition, **1989**; "Les

Chemins de la Liberté" (The Road to Freedom) Competition, **1983**, Paris,

La Villette Biennial, **1985**; Paris, CCI Exhibition, "Chemin du Virtuel"

(The Road to the Virtual) Study, **1987**; Paris, French Institute of

Architecture, **1987**; Paris, Centre Georges Pompidou , "Les Années 50"

(The Fifties), **1988**; Paris, Hauts de Seine, "Les Lumiéres de la Ville"

(The City Lights), **1989**; Paris, Arab World Institute, "Égypte, Égypte,"

1989; Barcelona, Spain, "Jean Nouvel - College of Architecture" Nouvel-

Cattani, **1990**; Austrian Biennial, Expo 95, Nouvel-Cattani Competition,

1991; Paris Austerlitz Station, "Georges Boudialle" Nouvel-Cattani,

1991; Nara, Japan, Workshop for Architecture Nouvel-Cattani, **1992**;

Tokyo, Japan, "La Métropole selon Jean Nouvel" Nouvel-Cattani, **1992**.

Awards: Chevalier of the Order of Arts and Letters, **1983**; Silver Medal

of the Academy of Architecture, Doctor "Honoris Causa" of the

University of Buenos Aires, and Winner of the Grand Prize of

Architecture, **1987;**, Aga Khan Prize, honorable mention, **1987**; Winner of

Silver Square for the Arab World Institute, **1987**; Prize for the Best

French Building, **1987**; Creator of the Year, **1987**; Architectural Record

Prize for the Hotel St. James, **1990**. Address: Jean Nouvel, 4 Cite

Griset 75 011 Paris, France

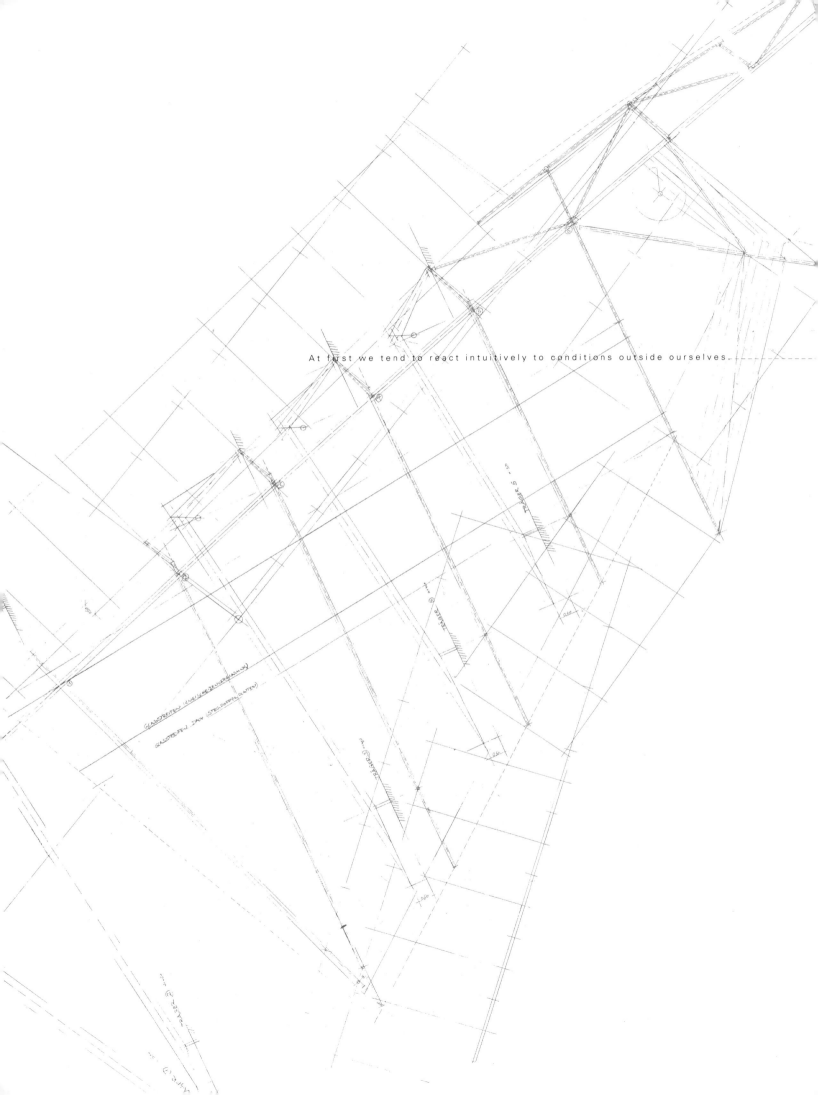

At first we tend to react intuitively to conditions outside ourselves

For an Open Architecture

Finding Form

Gunther Behnisch   **It was forty years ago, in 1952, that a friend of mine and I established our practice. In the four**

The idea that the form of buildings and open spaces should be determined at the beginning

decades that have passed since then, much has happened and much in the world has changed.

of work on a project seems absurd to us.   What a boring and unworthy way of working

this would be! One can imagine a group of several architects spending three or four years

Our architecture and the way we work has changed, too. Naturally enough, it is the product of a specific time, of con-

striving to put into effect a form predetermined by a single architect.   We find it a more

frontation, reaction, and of specific personalities and contexts.

worthwhile approach to determine form at the latest possible stage.   There are naturally

certain elements that have to be fixed at each stage. But only those that it is absolutely nec-

Only later do we - perhaps - become aware of the

essary to fix, and not the whole project. In this way we approach the end-product step by

problems. But the originality and the strength of architecture tend to belong to the first phase. Subsequently, it is easy

step, become acquainted with as many aspects and elements of the project as possible,

for our work to be weakened by "blandness of intellect."

work out answers piece by piece, and on completion we are able to recognize the many

aspects and separate parts of the brief that have combined to form a "single entity." This

Our original designs are the result of phenomena we have not yet registered, of problems we do not yet "know." And it

approach presupposes that all those involved in the design of a project are willing and able

is an elevating experience when, from time to time, we perceive what wanted to find concrete expression through and in

to contribute the knowledge that they have and that the architectural form can still be

our work. The realization can come in a split second: "so that was it" - an "intuition surpassing all conscious expecta-

changed, differentiated, and modified during the design stage.   Determining form?

tions." It is a pity it happens so rarely.

Finding form?   We mean: looking for form or - to go even further - seeking out our task.

This approach allows us to look at each part of a project individually. This means the individ-

One of the tasks of art is, no doubt, to point to things that have not yet been consciously assimilated, things that are not

uality of the project in hand, the functions it must fulfill, its various aspects and components

yet known - and this is where, for me, architecture and fine art share common ground. Through a painting or building

and its time and place ... and not so much the individuality of the architect.   The col-

these lesser-known aspects of life can be transferred into the part of our world we are conscious of, or believe we are

umn happens to stand next to a stairway, a window, or a wall, etc., or a tree grows close to

conscious of. Architecture should actively participate in this process, and in fact it does, even though we are oftentimes

a hill, a stretch of water, or a path, etc. Each part is self-sufficient, needs its own lebens-

unaware of the process itself.

raum - assumes its function within the whole and has equal status.   A varied, complex,

and functional system - outward appearance is not the principal determining factor.

But if one is aware of the process, one can reflect on how it might be encouraged or obstructed.

In this context it is clear that architecture should remain "open" for as long as possible; that it should not be isolated too soon - not even in its formal aspects - from factors which are as yet unknown and cannot yet be known. (We may certainly assume that there are many such factors.) And we should not allow the freedoms and resources that were created on the way to the modern age to be completely consumed by the powerful forces of the "system," or social norms, or even architectural norms. Some freedom must be preserved for the surprising to manifest itself and find a niche. And when a job comes our way all "wrapped up" like a parcel, we should undo it - we must simply create the freedom (for example by rejecting the claims of others); freedom for the "here and now," even if, initially, we have some difficulty finding it.

We must always be aware of forces which limit invention. Form is one. If we commit ourselves too soon as regards form, we isolate architecture and prevent it from developing further. To this extent, formalized modernism opposes the real message of modernism.

We should also critically appraise and challenge the many types of organization that exist to produce architecture - the organization of "the system," of office routine, of the construction process, the organization of the engineers' working methods, even if this risks leading to problematic confrontations. We should discard routine, and the professional shields and armour we have created, at least from time to time. By doing so we can ease the transition of the new and the weak into the visible world. Devoid of our armour, we ourselves will no doubt become more open to attack and more vulnerable. And some people who serve "the system" without question will want to exploit this situation. From time to time we will get into awkward positions. And we can only cope with them relatively easily if we ourselves do not attach too much importance to the norms - social or architectural. In other words, there must be a touch of anarchy in our attitude.

Our situation is similar to, though not the same as, that of painters or writers. On the one hand, all art forms are a means of giving expression to things that have hitherto gone unrecognized. On the other hand, works of architecture are closely

Techniques and Materials

Techniques and materials have their own structures and are subject to their own laws. Cast steel, for example, is supplied in complicated shapes; when rolled it arrives in the form of long straight lines or in thin sheets that are flat, folded, or pressed, but always ready for use in the form in which they are supplied. Steel constructions are therefore efficient, sharp-edged, provided with a planar outer skin and with structural differentiation rather than plasticity. Space created with this material tends to be open and unlimited. On the other hand, apparently shapeless clay was pounded into thick close-set walls. This resulted in massive structures with a soft plastic quality, smaller openings, and enclosed spaces. The connection, however, between the architectural result on the one hand and paper, pencil, drawing triangle, and modeling material on the other is less immediately apparent. If we resort to the drawing board at too early a stage, or if our drawings are too precise and definitive, we may crystalize concepts that are still at the development stage and so bar the way to further alternatives. It therefore makes sense for us to experiment initially without drawing or modeling material, and then to use a 6B pencil, charcoal, or a soft felt-tipped pen and a sheet of thin white paper for the first sketches; only then should we move on to more exact and durable drawing techniques and materials. In rough sketches we can capture ideas of which we may not even have been consciously aware. There are materials and techniques peculiar to each design stage. All material used for the purposes of architecture is subject to its own laws and has its own history; the T-square, the drawing triangle, and hard pencils produce isometric drawings and three-dimensional rectangular buildings; architectural shapes that, due

linked to practical functions, and the materials used in architecture are more recalcitrant than words. For instance, they

to their history, correspond to a certain

cannot convey messages in the same concentrated form, and previously unexpressed ideas, etc., cannot be illustrated in

stage of developing technology and of

the same complete way as in a picture.

an awakening consciousness. The

three coordinates, however, are not

But in architecture, new dimensions can open up at an early stage, perhaps precisely because of this awkwardness. And

the only means of creating space;

all the material objects in architecture, from different areas of reality, and the fact that we work together

rather they are a special case with the

on a project for many years and with many different people, result on the one hand in images that are no

capacity only to produce a relatively

doubt less sharp; but on the other hand, they also make more complex images possible.

primitive pattern.   Cardboard mod-

els give rise to flabby, two-dimensional

At present there are about 100 architects working in our office. And it is not the case that one of us is the creative archi-

and insubstantial buildings. Wooden

tect while the job of the others is to execute the creations of that one. In principle, everyone involved in the process of

blocks result in a blocklike architecture,

giving tangible form to a piece of architecture ought to help ensure that the process is a success.

while modeling clay engenders rela-

tively free plastic shapes.   The

Added to this is the fact that we work with much younger architects. Being young, they are closer to the "here and

design for the Olympic Park in Munich

now." They are less burdened with history. On the other hand, younger people are more likely to be intolerant. All too

was to a large extent developed on the

readily, they regard that portion of the truth which they perceive as all there is. And they find it hard to accept what is

basis of a sand model. The sand came

different, because of course their own perceptions are thus questioned. Nevertheless, these younger architects seem

closest to the deep gravel actually on

more willing to take risks. Probably they know and recognize fewer hazards, while with experienced architects, experi-

the site. Of all materials, shapes made

ence soon and imperceptibly becomes routine. And routine, of course, means isolating oneself from what is different and

with sand are the least predetermined

new.

by their structure and therefore the

most flexible for landscape design.

In my opinion, those who work in an architectural practice should be carefully selected and carefully grouped.

Behnisch

Diversity

We cannot always succeed in creating innovative architecture, but we do succeed from time to time, though the times

Diversity is not the same as abundance, which can

are in fact extremely rare. And these individual achievements are not necessarily the ones that win the highest acclaim

indeed be very arbitrary. Diversity implies more: it

in magazines.

also comprises unity. Unity also implies more than

restriction to a single unit. Unity can only be per-

Nor is it true that the innovative element is always in the same area of reality. Sometimes it may be in form, in the orga-

ceived in diversity; without it diversity cannot exist.

nization of form, or in the way things relate to one another and to the whole. At other times it may be a question of

The many folds of a single garment ... an image

which things, from which area of reality, arrange themselves in relation to one another. For this we use terms such as

that gives visual expression to this concept.

fragment, or collage, or montage - in the liberal arts, of course, these things were investigated 70 years ago. But these

The world we live in is monotonous? This is hard to

means, regardless of what we call them, are not the essence. Rather, they are an "expression of an intuition surpassing

believe. It is more likely that the way it is perceived

everything previously perceived or expected." -

is monotonous and that it is made monotonous.

Diversity is obscured by a single consideration or a

In others again it may be something technological that sparks an awareness, and so on.

small number of them: for example, returns on

money invested. Or quite simply by the way the

The "aesthetic norm," which covers what is known - both old and new - is violated by such new architecture. And when

system works. The architect who allows himself to

seen in this light it appears perfectly normal that one observer should reject the new, while another is willing to accept it.

be influenced primarily by these considerations and

who disregards the many other aspects will pro-

I feel a certain uneasiness about buildings designed in our office which are immediately praised by everybody. Because

duce monotonous work.   Such interests which

that must mean there is relatively little that is innovative about these buildings, and that they tend to confirm what is

are indeed powerful, and often monumental, hardly

known and expected. Other, less conventional buildings, which reflect more of the "here and now," attract less attention.

need much promotion from us: their claims are

powerfully represented by other parties.

The first of these categories includes the German Postal Museum in Frankfurt. It was designed and built to a very high

There are other considerations that are in urgent

standard, and it was published in all the architectural magazines. As far as that is concerned, we can be pleased. But, pri-

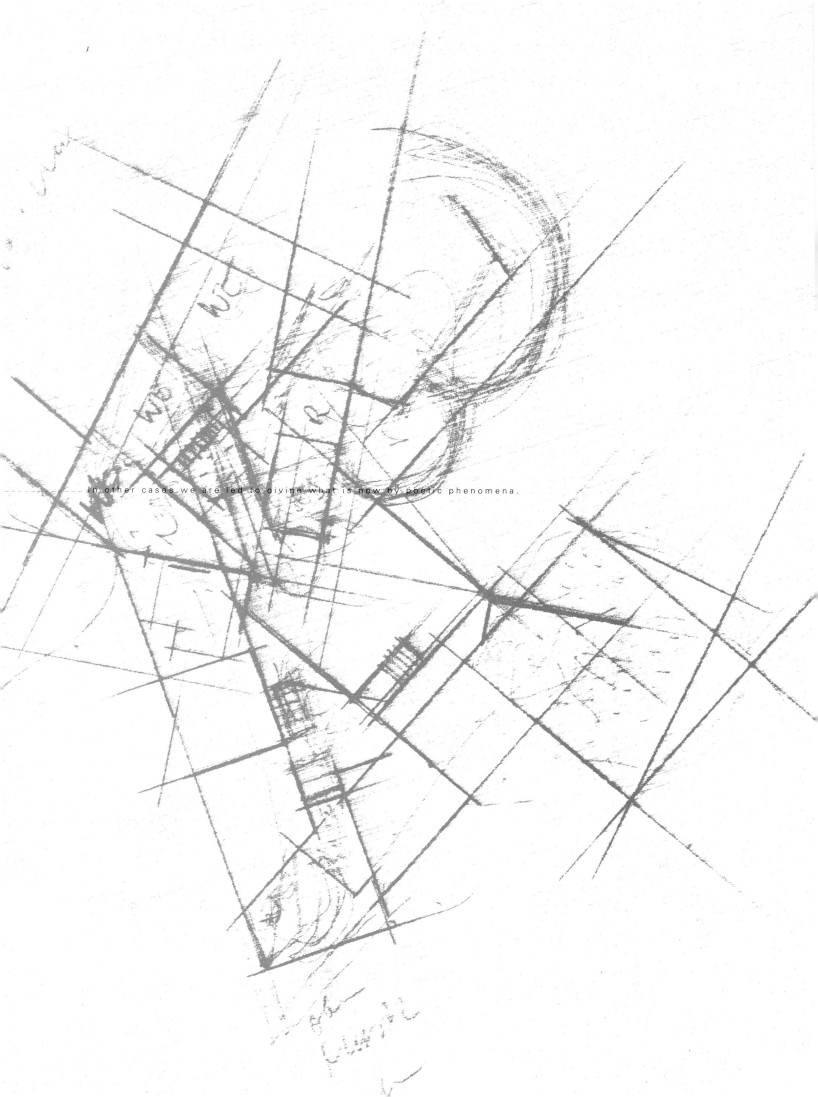

In other cases we are led to divine what is new by poetic phenomena.

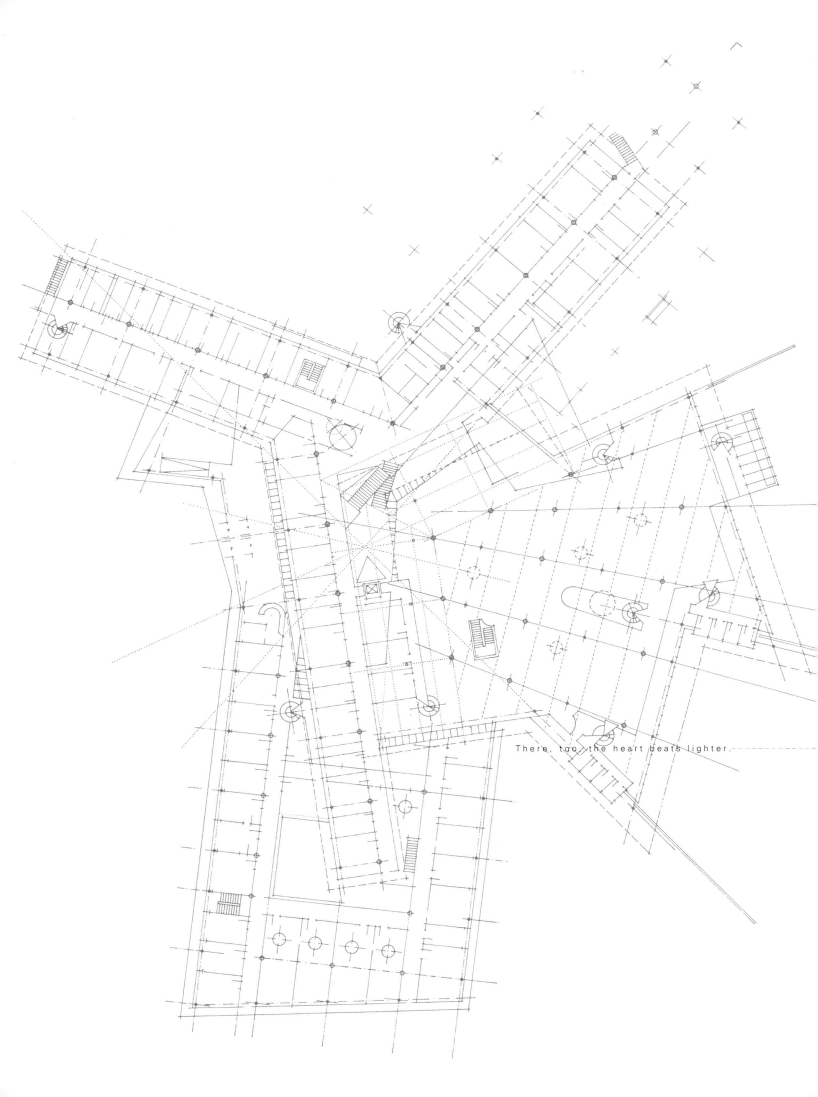

There, too, the heart beats lighter.

marily, it confirms the spatial and formal thinking of the 1920s. It is a building in which one meets many old acquain-

need of our commitment: ecology, for example, our

tances. Yet - and this speaks for it - they are developed in the language of architecture and space, in poetic terms, in

fellow-men, children, people, working methods, com-

accord with the possibilities and the awareness of our age.

munal living, and many others. We can uncover and

investigate as many as possible of the almost unlimit-

The building we designed to house the library of the Catholic University in Eichstätt is quite different. Even today, I can,

ed number of facets of a brief - which we receive in

at best, sense what makes this building so unique. Seen in its individual elements it seems rather awkward, but as a

the deceptive guise of a single concept, e.g., a hospi-

whole ... The best explanation of this came from a lecturer who works in the building. One morning, she said, she was

tal - facets that otherwise remain unrepresented. We

on the way to her workplace in the library, in a thoroughly bad mood and feeling rather depressed. Then she entered the

are in a position to enable hidden forces, neglected in

building, and saw the interplay of light, its gaiety and levity; she could look right through the building and see the

the reality of our society, to find expression and to

romantic River Altmühl, and her heart became lighter.

assume their visible form.   The more such

aspects we can identify, the more richness we will

Or the building for the "Diakonisches Werk," the Lutheran Church Charity, in Stuttgart. In this building the light really

recognize in the brief and the greater the diversity of

does now shine on an empathy with the weak.

the resultant architectural form. Additional techniques

of harmonization - be they mathematical, geometrical,

Or the Lutheran Academy in Birkach, a suburb of Stuttgart.

formal, or of any other type - become superfluous. It

is also certainly true of architecture that it assumes a

One could comment on every project in this way. And as I said, some conform to aesthetic norms while others race

special quality if it is constantly new, different, and

ahead of them.

many-sided, or if it can never be definitively under-

stood or interpreted: architecture as the mirror of the

Given such approaches, it must be accepted that we enjoy experimenting. A phenomenon or a feature that we were able

diversity inherent in our environment and as the

to emphasize in one project need not necessarily be repeated in the next: it already exists, in architecture and in our con-

reflection of our concern for it.

sciousness.

Library Building of the Catholic University, Eichstätt

That may sound rather egotistical, rather as if we were mainly interested in our own pleasure. But that is not the case.

The Library was to be built on the river bank outside the old

How could we produce good work without committing ourselves and becoming enraptured by what we are doing?

town.   It is from this location that the project derives its

external influences - less from the town; i.e., it is less

So far I have spoken of only one aspect of our work - the design process - but it involves much more: that our buildings

ensconced among the other Baroque buildings, but there is also

should be usable, that there should be a reasonable relationship between cost and benefit, that we work together with

just less restriction in the Library, less constraint, less geometric

our clients for several years and want to please them, that we have to earn enough money, etc., etc.; this is also the

order, and instead more openness, more chance for the building

basis from which special and original things can grow.

to find its own identity, more consideration for the forms of

Nature, more of a "natural" order.   Thus, also, the choice

Experimenting in this way demands effort. One cannot be lazy nor self-satisfied. But it gives satisfaction and brings

of materials, of constructions, and the intended forms reflect

pleasure. **Because through our work we get to know the world.**

this freedom. "Weak" natural materials and "adequate" con-

structions were better suited to the surroundings.   The

building is not a monolithic or formally harmonized unity; rather

it is a complex of many individual forms. Its harmony is intrinsic,

by virtue of the fact that less constraint is exercised, that there

is a tendency to let each individual form be itself – in this, too,

resembling the surroundings in which the building stands.

Preceding pages (drawings)

64. *"At first we tend to react intuitively to conditions outside ourselves"*
Hysolar Institute Building. University of Stuttgart, Stuttgart-Vaihingen, Germany, 1987
partial plan study
pencil on vellum

69. *"In other cases we are led to divine what is new by poetic phenomena"*
Secondary School on the "Schäfersfeld," Lorch, Germany, 1980
plan study
soft pencil on vellum

70. *"There, too, the heart beats lighter"*
Library Building of the Catholic University, Eichstätt, Germany, 1987
plan
ink on vellum

*Hysolar Institute Building, University of Stuttgart, Stuttgart-Vaihingen, Germany, 1987
view from interior to solar panels (preceding page)*

*Library Building of the Catholic University, Eichstätt, Germany, 1987
atrium and detail of interior curtain wall*

BEHNISCH, Günter. German. Born in Lockwitz bei Dresden, 12 June **1922**. Studied engineering at the Technische Hochschule, Stuttgart, **1947-51**, Diplom-Ingenieur, **1951**. Oberleutnant, German Navy, **1939-45**; prisoner-of-war in England, **1945-47**. Married Joanna Fink in **1952**; children: Sabine, Charlotte, and Stefan. Practiced with Bruno Lambart, Stuttgart, **1952-56**; practiced on his own, Stuttgart, **1956-66**; formed company, Behnisch & Partner, Stuttgart, **1966** (partners: Fritz Auer, Winfried Büxel, Manfred Sabatke, Erhard Tränkner, and Karlheinz Weber). Regional Director, Bund Deutscher Architekten, Baden-Württemberg, **1965-68**. Professor, Technische Hochschule, Darmstadt, since **1975**. Address: Behnisch & Partner, Mendelssohnstrasse 22, 7000 Stuttgart-Sillenbuch, Germany.

Experience

90-91; *5 – 9*   *a fantastic wall lit from the sky*

illuminated from above

this great chamber where the painting is

the dimension of the painting and the geography of the boundary

like a giant tokonoma in the space of the most precious

90; *1 – 4*   *almost like a drawbridge*

from the street all through the house to the garden

each private realm had its own garden

the landscape as I found it and the landscape we made

91; *18 – 21*   *between earth and sky*

marking the passage of time and day on the ground

the ground, the shadows and the sky are reflected

a reflectivity that extends space

91; *10 – 17*   *build in a forest*

the light and shade and random patterning of the leaves in the forest

extend the sense of the landscape

a great leaf that protects the family from the elements

down the site, through the trees

allows the forest to enter the house

one with the ground and the sky

rooted, in the forest

adele naudé santos 1992

Naudé Santos

Atrium, detail
Ichibancho building with Imai
Tokyo, Japan 1988
page 80

Window, detail
Mother's House
Capetown, South Africa 1969
page 81

Column, detail
Beach House
Ninomiya, Japan 1988
page 82

Court, detail
Center for the Arts, Albright College
Reading, Pennsylvania 1990
page 83

Roof, detail
Beach House
Ninomiya, Japan 1988
page 84

Forest, detail
Beach House
Ninomiya, Japan 1988
page 85

Adele Naudé Santos – Excerpts from a Conversation with Michael Meister   *I was taught design from an experiential base. I start a project by thinking about the purpose of the endeavor and about ways in which one can resolve activities and experiences in space.* **As I design, I imagine space. I imagine experience. I imagine a sequence of moving through things, I imagine journeys. I think about a series of narratives which have to do with the experience of space.** *This approach makes more sense to me than a series of formal propositions.*

My earlier work was very much involved with developing ideas of space, but was also preoccupied with the issues of the plan — trying to find the poetic in the plan. As I look back on the evolution of my work, by the time I arrived in the United States and started building again, I always started design with the cross-section. I did not start with the plan. I found myself thinking much more in section — three-dimensions. This was partly due to the fact that I was dealing with urban situations where I had to solve problems that were considerably more complex. **I was involved with the idea of cross-section; the sequence of spaces, and the quality of light.** *If you consider a recent building of mine like Tokyo Fantasia, the cross-section is critical. You can see that it was started with the idea of the cross-section rather than a plan. I think that was because I had been developing my skills spatially, and cross-section is all about space.*

The whole question of how I design and the method I've developed over the years has to be predicated on my belief that no architectural or urban design project has only one or two ideas. There is always a series of ideas and one has to make these layers reasonably explicit when designing. My way of doing this is to record the concepts that I want to incorporate in a series of diagrams. There is no hierarchy to these, just layers of ideas. When I am doing a competition it's a very easy way of giving the jury access to my thought process. This is particularly true in the area of housing where one is dealing with social and spatial issues, and issues of the economy and technology, issues of the street and urban space, play and leisure, and security. All of these things have to be solved. If one can explicitly state these issues in a way that is acceptable to people, you can begin to understand the layers of meaning and the problems which you've set yourself to solving. This applies equally well to the single building; when one is concerned about light and space, there is always some central idea that has a narrative. **There is always some attitude toward the street and vistas, and sequences of moving through space, hierarchies of space, and ideas of human experience.** *Usually I set these down rather explicitly in a notebook. Sometimes I represent them. Sometimes they are the first diagrams that I make as a way of thinking. It's a self-checking process that helps me record to myself, my staff, and to other people the complexity of the issues.*

Design is a complex process and I think that good architecture is architecture where there is a multiplicity of ideas that coincide and coexist, as compared to a lot of the simple-minded and gratuitous gestures that much of today's architecture is about with only one or two formal strategies. I'm very committed to the idea that architecture is about its final result. **There are forms and aesthetics, but a lot has to do with the nature of space which has to do with the interior of architecture.**

A lot of buildings are designed from the outside in. Certainly, when published they are mostly about exterior form and very little about the process by which the building came to be: its program, purpose, spaces, arrangements and everything else. I've often said that to solve the pragmatics of architecture is really easy – buildings have to work – but to transform the pragmatic of architecture into the poetic dimension, that's the real trick.

If architecture is about experience then the making of architecture is also about experience. It is a process that at many levels is playful. *It's about imagining experience and in the end it has a lot to do with inventing things, with making unusual places and spaces, with elements of surprise. A lot of my work has elements of surprise. I don't try to do the obvious. I am always trying to rethink things, to reformulate things. The process of doing so each time creates a unique experience for me and, in that sense, it evolves.*

I believe in collaborative ventures because architecture is so involved with the other arts; with landscape and with environmental art. These collaborations bring about projects that are born of the interface of different kinds of creative minds.

What I suppose I'm trying to get at is that **one must lay aside all of one's preconceptions** *— which I had to do on the Albright project with Mary Miss — and say, "This is going to be an adventure. I don't know where this is going to end; I certainly know the questions we're beginning with, and out of this may come a series of forms and ideas that I've never played with before." I have to allow a sense of adventure to be there, and know that some surprising things may be invented. I've always tried not to take a lot of baggage along with me, in a formal sense such as "I'm a post-modernist ... a deconstructivist," ... whatever that is. I am open to the particularities of the conditions; where the project is, what culture it's in, what its uses are.* **In that sense my work is often able to grow in surprising ways; the language is evolving.** *Yet it always refers back to a series of themes which I will continue to develop for the rest of my career.*

One is **the relationship between building and landscape;** *the creation of landscaped exterior rooms related to interior rooms and the whole sense of an indoor-outdoor continuum as part of a spatial strategy.*

Another is the idea of how we use natural light to transform and enhance space and change the experience of the house from morning to evening with the passage of the sun in the day. **I am interested in the idea of sunlight because it makes spaces cheerful and enhances the sense of enjoyment of the space,** *particularly when you can bring in light in subtle ways — when the source is invisible.*

Another fascination of mine is spatial illusion, the idea that you can, through the manipulation of space and light, create spaces that feel larger than they are. In my mother's house, the idea of creating an artificial hill over the garage area prevented one from being able to see the street and led to the landscape of buildings beyond.

I believe in context. I believe that one has to respond to context, be it the natural environment or the man-made environment. **There are many clues in a particular context, and as an architect one has a responsibility to the wider context in which one builds.** *I try as much as possible not to presume a language or a stance. I have to retain some level of design flexibility without prejudice when dealing with a place. If I believe that this is true, which I do, buildings are contextual. I think that I am not taking stylistic "baggage" with me where I go. Although obviously my buildings have a series of philosophical attitudes and comment. Someone studying the work could understand these, could see the hand. But what I build in Japan versus what I build in San Francisco and Philadelphia are taking their clues from the place.*

I don't tend to think about buildings as a series of isolated objects, I think about a building as if it were a part of the city, as a continuum. If you consider housing, for example, you are dealing with a very interesting set of environments that go from the most private of spaces, the bedroom of one person, to the collective living spaces of the family, to spaces in which the family and neighbors share things and so on. It is an attitude toward city making and space making that grows naturally from a social plan. **I always start with the social issues because that's where my ethos is.** *I think that architecture is about people and space and place-making. It's also about visual enjoyment; architecture is indeed an art. Yet if one errs too much in terms of formal presumptions, you leave out the guts of what architecture is about.*

Mother's House, South Africa   *The house is viewed as a microcosm of the city. I was literally bringing my training in urban design to my training as an architect and my interest in the design of prototypes. The prototype has always fascinated me, the logic and the idea of the prototype as a way of thinking about something.*

So when I began to design a house for my parents, I started to rethink the fundamentals of what a house is. I began to think of a sequence of spaces and places within the house that could be viewed hierarchically. From the public domain to the street I made a very slow procession up to the house itself <u>almost like a drawbridge</u>. The bedrooms were houses within the house, and corridors became streets for art. These corridors were paved in blue brick <u>from the street all through the house to the garden</u>.   1 , 2

I also rethought the way in which light was developed, the whole strategy of getting natural light into the house. This related to light cast onto walls which would display art, which was part of the procession, which was part of the street, which was part of the house. This way of thinking also helped me to redefine the outdoor space so that <u>each private realm had its own garden</u>. The gardens allowed each person to feel a sense of privacy and independence within the house.   3

The other important theme of this house is spatial illusion – of trying to make the space feel bigger than it was. The house is also very much involved with the inexplicable relationship between indoors and outdoors; between <u>the landscape as I found it and the landscape we made</u>; the house we created and all the edges between.   4

Ichibancho Building with Imai, Japan   *The project was a headquarters building and a gallery for paintings commissioned from the painter Imai. I knew the work of the painter, who uses gold leaf and silver — his work is very much about landscape and nature. I had an idea of <u>a fantastic wall lit from the sky</u> in a very subtle way. My idea was to make one glorious room with this fantastic painting that would stretch up from the second level to the sky, and be <u>illuminated from above</u>. The three-level atrium space which Imai filled with paintings of the four seasons allows the three office floors of the building to view parts of the painting. The public is invited into the main chamber below where they are able to see the entire space.*   5 , 6

The whole building is about this painting — the ways in which it can be viewed — and about a staircase with landings that refer back to <u>this great chamber where the painting is</u>. The only wall that is not orthogonal in the whole complex is the wall of the painting: this relates to <u>the dimension of the painting and the geography of the boundary</u>. The wall is tilted toward the entry, so as you arrive the fact that it's not at a right angle to the rest of the space enhances its importance. It's _like a giant tokonoma in the space of the most precious_ – of the painting.

7 – 9

Ninomiya Beach House, Japan   The house started off as being a dialogue about how you would _build in a forest_ — particularly a protected forest that is precious in a context like Japan — and how one could relate the building to _the light and shade and random patterning of the leaves in the forest_, to the vista of the bay, to the sloping topography; how one could set a building into this beautiful place and _extend the sense of the landscape_. The project is really an essay on building in nature. I started thinking about the roof of the building almost as _a great leaf that protects the family from the elements_. I saw the profile of the roof changing in cross-section like a leaf going from the chimney to the outer edges where it begins to flatten out.

10 – 13

I saw this roof being made of aged copper to blend into the landscape of the trees. I saw the sequence of entry from the street to the house as being very much what you would expect in Japan, where entry is not direct and the front door is not evident. I wanted a procession from the outside to the inside, as the house steps _down the site, through the trees_. After passing through a private entry garden, one opens the front door to a view of the ocean beyond.

14

I began to think about linking the elements of the house in a way that was spiritual; where the place of fire, which would be winter, would be the most intimate part of the house and would have a linear relationship to the place of summer, — the water, the pool, and the pool to the forest and the ocean beyond. Along the line between these two worlds of winter and summer is a giant skylight which _allows the forest to enter the house_. Inside you are always viewing the forest. The columns that hold up the roof and skylight are intentionally tree-like – a sort of man-made equivalent to that which you find in the forest. Although the building may be seen as an object, it is _one with the ground and the sky_, the trees and the ocean; _rooted, in the forest._

15 – 17

Center for the Arts, Albright College, PA   One of the things that I like about this project is that the shade roof which articulates the court at the sky was primarily the responsibility of my office and the plaza at the earth was the responsibility of Mary Miss. There is a real dialogue _between earth and sky_, it is beautiful when the shadows from the roof move like a sundial _marking the passage of time and day on the ground_ and the glass. There's _a reflectivity that extends space_ — it becomes almost magical as _the ground, the shadows and the sky are reflected_ in the glass around the rotunda — it's something that's difficult to imagine until you are there.

18 – 21

NAUDÉ SANTOS, Adele. South African. Educated: Architectural Association, London, England, Diploma, **1961**; Harvard University, Cambridge, M. Arch. in Urban Design, **1963**; University of Pennsylvania, Philadelphia, Master of City Planning, M. Arch., **1968**. Partner, Adéle Naudé Santos and Antonio de Souza Santos, Architects, South Africa, **1968-74**; Partner, Interstudio, Houston, **1974-78**; Principal, Adéle Naudé Santos and Associates, Philadelphia, San Diego, **1979-** . Visiting Assistant Professor, School of Architecture, Columbia University, New York City, **1966-67**; Studio Critic, School of Architecture, University of Cape Town, South Africa, **1968-72**; Visiting Critic, School of Architecture, Rice University, Houston, **1972**; Graduate School of Design, Harvard University, Cambridge, **1973**; Associate Professor, School of Architecture, Rice University, Houston, **1973-77**; Visiting Associate Professor, Graduate School of Design, Harvard University, **1977-78**; Professor, School of Architecture, Rice University, **1979**; Professor, Graduate School of Design, Harvard University, **1979-81**; Visiting Professor, Department of Architecture, Miami University, Ohio, **1981**; Visiting Professor, School of Planning, University of Cincinnati, Ohio, **1981-87**; Chairperson, Department of Architecture, University of Pennsylvania, Philadelphia, **1981-87**; Professor, Department of Architecture and Urban Design, University of Pennsylvania, Philadelphia, **1981-89**; Founding Dean, School of Architecture, University of California, San Diego, La Jolla, **1990-** . Research: "Housing in Traditional Tribal Villages of the Twsana in Botswana," Rice University Research Grant, **1975**; "The Single Family House in America: Changing Social, Cultural, and Economic Factors," Research Grant, National Endowment for the Arts, **1976**; "Open Space Choice for Blighted Inner City Neighborhoods: A Philadelphia Case Study," Research Grant, National Endowment for the Arts, **1984-85**. Address: Adele Naudé Santos and Associates, 2947 First Avenue, San Diego, California 92103, U.S.A.

ALDO ROSSI

Architecture, furniture
and some of my dogs

A Selection of Drawings and Lithographs
From the Notebooks of Aldo Rossi

1989-1990

In this notebook we have shown images and examples which demonstrate that alternatives to the kind of mass production which attempts to standardize the world are possible. The proposal of bizarre things or even a more complex research, which today we have just begun, could be further alternatives.

Furnishings must become more architectural, and that which we call furniture, objects and domestic monuments, should return to our lives as an integral part of our affection.

Milan, September 1990

In the course of time, situations and emotions in which we believed are destroyed or realized. Sometimes I see time as a three-dimensional object, in which fragments, whose original meaning we have lost, are kept with the fragments of a wonderful structure.

But we cannot piece the broken parts together again and we are not interested in understanding the forgotten. And architecture?

Milan, February 1993

Aldo Rossi

I love this dog. 1990

Penna e acquarello/Ink and watercolor

26 x 21.3 cm

Il caffé del mattino. 1990

Penna e acquarello/Ink and watercolor

29.5 X 21

24 Marzo, il caffé del mattino. 1990

Penna e acquarello/Ink and watercolor

26 x 21.3

Impiegato con busta gialla in un ufficio con i miei mobili. 1989

Penna e pastello/Ink and pastel

42 X 29.7

Interno e piazza. 1990

Tecnica mista/Mixed media

21.6 x 35.6

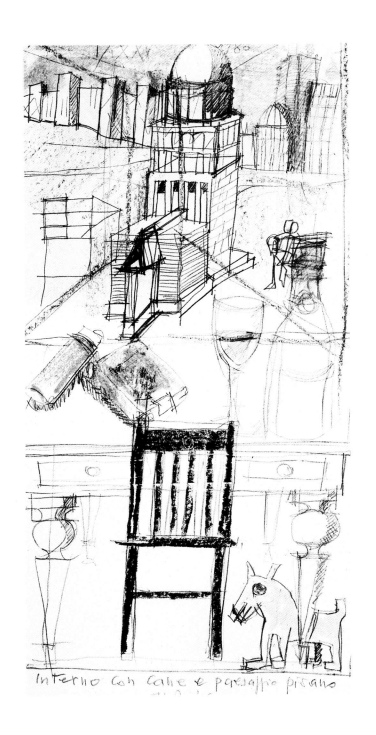

Interno con cane e paesaggio pisano. 1990
Penna e acquarello/Ink and watercolor
21 X 44.5

Senza titolo (detail). 1989

Acquarello/Watercolor

70 x 50

A Conversation
Aldo Rossi and Bernard Huet

Bernard Huet: For a long time, the public knew only one Aldo Rossi, the theoretician and the author of the famous book *The Architecture of the City*. Pretty soon, however, we discovered in magical architectural drafts and powerfully autobiographical imprinted images the poetic world of Aldo Rossi, which lies relatively far away from the conventional association with architecture. One day it became news: Aldo Rossi does not only sketch theoretical projects, he even builds them.

These three areas, in which you have been simultaneously active at specific points in your life, represent to me three insoluble, integrated, complementary aspects of Aldo Rossi's contribution to the architecture of the second half of the 20th century.

I would like to know how you devote yourself to these three aspects in a time in which we increasingly experience the return of the totally one-sided professional architect (whom some call a manager-architect) and which part they play in the creation of your work?

Aldo Rossi: I believe that in the life of an artist, a scientist, and an explorer there exist side by side constantly changing and contrasting possibilities of occupations. Sometimes, at a given moment, one of these occupations dominates the other. The author Aldo Rossi, the painter Aldo Rossi, or the architect Aldo Rossi, consequently does not exist. I simply see these diverse aspects in their entirety—like all artists, I think—and in this sense especially, I like those opportunities in which I am able to express myself in the same way as a technician, an artist, and a writer. Certain moments of my life collide with a sum total of circumstances, which one could call "correspondences" in reference to Baudelaire. These relationships between people, these connections between historical events and personal events, are important, in order to understand the reasons for one occupation being preferred over another.

When I began to concern myself with architecture, writing played a remarkable role. My training is basically literary, and so I believed that writing was decisive in escaping the catastrophic situation in which architecture found itself in the 60s, when I completed my studies at the Polytecnico. It seemed important to me to work out a theoretical foundation, and undertake a complete separation from the Modern, not only from a historical perspective, but also from a professional, architectural production perspective (and for me, of course, this was the architectural production in Milan and the entire European production), which referred itself to the Modern and eliminated every theoretical concept in architecture.

My preference for literature and intention to deepen my then relative interest in architecture in a theoretical rather than a graphic way are the two reasons which propelled me to write essays in Casabella and later in books, which you know have not only made me famous in France, but in the whole world. I must add that I never had a special inclination toward architecture, and since we are already talking about circumstances, I would have been an equally good soldier or actor—had I learned one of these trades. Architecture for me was no clear choice. I studied architecture like I could have studied medicine.

After I completed my studies, and while working as an architect, over time, I have become more preoccupied with architecture and with other areas, but even today, when I write an essay on a recently deceased friend, I feel a greater pleasure in writing than in the profession of architecture.

Without wanting to elevate myself to the ranks of great artists, I think that it is a characteristic quality of the human mind to develop the subject matter to which it is directed. If Picasso had written he would have been a great author, as Dante would have been a great painter had he painted. There is no special intrinsic quality of the mind which is tied to a specific occupation; rather the practice of the profession develops the subject, as little as the mind may be prepared for it.

BH: One could think that you are currently dedicating yourself to the realization of a number of projects around the world, and do not have the time or opportunity to develop any new theoretical notions. There was a time when one could see a particular abstraction in your projects, which remained as rough drafts, or were realized like those of Gallaratese. This gave the work an exemplary, demonstrative value.

Today that no longer seems to be the case. Along with its maturity, your architecture has attained a density of scale and material, rendering it more subjective (in which I see a transformation of the celebrated notion of analog architecture to which you referred during the late 70s), so that it may at least appear to be almost pragmatic. Nevertheless, every time I see a sketch of yours I am surprised to notice how much your architecture is influenced by the implicit application of theory.

Can you explain how your most recent works fit into the continuity of your theoretical reflections, most of which you constructed almost twenty years ago?

AR: I believe that I have created fundamental architectural principles for my colleagues and myself, which allow one to design and build relatively easily. Parallel to this, I am teaching or have taught these fundamental principles to a number of young architects.

The commonly raised reproach that there exists a school of young architects that imitate my style throughout the world and who build like Rossi only appears to anger me, because in reality I do not dislike it. I would even claim that it makes me happy, because, basically, I have achieved that which I wanted to. I am convinced of the fact that one can develop one's own personality upon having acquired the fundamental elements of architecture. It is as with language: if one does not have a good command of the basic elements, if one does not learn the most important rules of French, one cannot speak French. Among all of those who speak French, there will be geniuses like Racine, but they are rare. Starting with any language, each can develop his own style in his own way. And, when one shows me so-called copies of my buildings in Japan or in Latin America, I do not see them as copies of my work. It seems to me much more that every architect develops his own specialty and that in a certain way he is even better than I am.

Let us take an example close to my heart. Palladio has created a type of Venetian architecture, which is, as one well knows, very closely related to the "place," with the "genius loci," the spirit of the place. So one has the Venetian Palladio of the villas and palaces, and then one has the Palladio which can be seen in the entire world—from Louisiana to Russia, from England to France—where a beautiful, wonderful Palladian architecture is being developed. I believe that certain English Palladian architects like the Adams Brothers can surpass Palladio in perfection. They elevate the Palladian architecture to its highest level, but in spite of this, there is still a real difference between this perfect Palladian architecture and the Palladio from Vicenza, or the Palladianism of his Italian imitators, which leans more strongly toward the Baroque. With this example, I would like to demonstrate that once the fundamental principles of architecture have been created, they will remain and develop themselves over very long periods of time. This is in part what the Modern (modern architecture) wanted to attain; however, its notorious failure was due to the fact that it chose to induce a rupture rather than represent continuity.

BH: What you are saying seems very important to me in order to understand your work within the language of architecture. What is indeed initially impressive is the consistency, the togetherness and continuity of your work, with which you have proven yourself against wind and storm, without making any concessions to trendy showmanship.

At a time in which difficulties and longwindedness are seen as virtues, your architecture extrapolates its strength and credibility from a simple language and an immediate style. A simplicity which, nevertheless, causes a complex perception of identification within the observer. In view of your rough drafts, or of your constructions, one is often gripped by a strange feeling, a mixture of familiarity of the seen and the already recognized, and the strangeness of a rather odd poetic vision. The basis of your language forms a very small number of terms and commonplaces, which, along with the result of variation and the subtle shifting of context, can be incessantly referred to and repeated. The catalog of inventions by Aldo Rossi would appear easy to draw up. In reality, everything of yours is a lot more complicated.

Regardless of the language problems which your work presents, there are two aspects which I would like to discuss with you. The first arises out of the question of typology. You have said that your architecture relates to consistency, which in my eyes results from both the archetypes of didactic architecture and the typology of the buildings in the classical sense of the word.

Beyond that, through your images one is well acquainted with the arsenal of your poetics, which obtains its substance from everyday objects (the factory chimneys, bathing cabins in Elba, the coffeemaker, etc.). In this respect, and within certain boundaries, it may not be wrong to compare your way of thinking to that of Robert Venturi. When one imagines to what degree everyday objects originate from an exclusively typological universe, then I believe that your typological and poetic advances agree with each other.

AR: When an architect claims that typology is a rigid affair and that it does not agree with artistic freedom, then he is demonstrating his ignorance and stupidity. Typology is a technical term, which has always been used in architecture to define specific types of buildings and the various ways in which they are built. The typology of the palace is gradual, established over the course of centuries. The Renaissance palaces follow this typology, and yet Renaissance architecture is exceptionally manifold. Milizia said of the architects who have not been able to complete their work: "They did not grasp the general idea of the work," and this according to the typology.

To me this debate seems to rest upon an irrelevant and antiquated misunderstanding. When I should build a room I have to know its dimensions, whether it is square or rectangular, whether it faces a corridor or not. There are specific aspects which the architect must consider, which, incidentally, exist in all fields. I do not horseback ride, but as far as I know, one distinguishes between several riding schools—American, Italian, French, etc.—which by no means lessens the value of the horse or the rider.

For me the reflection upon everyday objects takes on a great meaning. I always tell my colleagues and students that, most importantly, they must observe these objects, since one is taught the most by observation.

Anybody who visits Paris can, for example, visit a museum or just take a walk. It is also the latter view which suffices to enrich one's own personal architecture. In a specific way the observation transfers itself to the draft, which I believe answers your question of how, starting from a consistent and fundamental ground position, one arrives at building different houses in Japan, in the United States, in Germany, and elsewhere—since the final observation always enriches a project and becomes visible within it.

Let us take, for example, the experience which I had with the hotel "Il Palazzo" in Fukuoka, Japan, which is very important to me. The relationship between the Japanese architects, who liked my architecture very much, and who would have gladly approved if I had been more "Aldo Rossi" for this project than I was, and myself, who wanted to become a little bit "Japanese" (not due to a preconceived idea, but rather as a result of observations), very quickly developed into a dialectical one. Many of the typical Japanese objects surrounding me, which I liked, inevitably found themselves again within my creations, as it always happens when a real reciprocal exchange of interest occurs.

To return to our subject matter (typology): It is nearly the same with the farm houses in Louisiana (which perhaps you know more about than I do), which one recognizes by their typology and colonnades, above all, because one knows of Palladio, even though these Palladian houses do not really have much to do with Palladio.

BH: In your answer you did not touch upon the problem of invention. You know, a generation of contemporary architects have been encouraged by a certain trade press to place their work in the perspective of a "new" architecture of the "Modern," without revealing why they are fundamentally new, or which "modernity" it represents.

What place does the problem of invention take in the context of your work?

AR: For me, invention represents a way of living and may not be a problem. I cannot and will not pose myself the problem of inventing a new architecture. I create an architecture, and with this architecture express a few things, but I have never posed myself the problem of invention, and I also will not in the future. Each of us invents when he is expressing his own sensibility.

BH: I understand your answer as a fundamental position, but nevertheless I do believe that one can discover architectural spaces and arrangements that approximate an invention if one analyzes certain projects of yours. For example, I would like to speak about this cylinder-shaped room, which is open in its entire height, and is lit from above, which one knows in draft form as the Congressional Palace in Milan, and which was realized as the foyer of the theater in Genova.

Could one not view this singular room as a true Aldo Rossi invention?

AR: No, for me it is a matter of the result of an observation. Hundreds and thousands of people can see the same thing, yet each perceives it in his own unique way. It is a little bit like love: One meets many people and nothing happens, and then falls in love with one destined person. I have had the idea with the "sky light," with the light that falls from the sky, for a long time, and I have often mentioned it in my lectures. I remember that the large glass-roofed courtyard of the University impressed me the most of everything that I saw in Zurich. Some time ago, while in Colombia for a lecture series, I visited the tourist attraction Christ Cathedral. It is about former mines given up by the Indians, which the Spanish Conquistadors secured and completed. They used the light that fell from above to place a large wooden Christ (figure) against the wall, so that the sun's rays would illuminate the statue at dawn and dusk.

Thousands of people have seen this installation. It especially impressed me because here architecture reaches the level of the sublime, so that one no longer talks about architecture, nature, or religion. I do not know which general or soldier of the conquerors' army had the idea to use the light of the mine in this way, but he created great architecture. So the idea of the "sky light" is not an invention of mine, instead it goes back to an observation, which I have given a special meaning within my structures. I probably got the idea of the light falling from above before I visited Colombia. The top of the Chapel of Giussano is in its upper part nothing but light, as if death came from heaven and not from earth.

BH: If I understand correctly, everything is already available for you. So there remains nothing to invent, because it suffices to carefully observe and to give new descriptions to the existing.

But this retranscription is not readily available?

AR: Right, that is not easy!

BH: I would now like to talk about the relationship between the sketch and the realization of a project. You belong to those who speak mostly of the sketch as the central point of architecture, but thereafter follows the transition to the execution of the building. For many architects this transition can result in a loss of substance. It can be that the poor quality of the execution changes the quality of the sketch until it is unrecognizable, or, as often happens these days, that the execution merely resembles a mechanical and abstract enlargement of the model or sketch. If one follows the history of your sketches, one discovers several that were realized practically without any changes. On the other hand, there are models which were noticeably altered, due to various economic, technical, or functional reasons. Your apartment house in La Villette, for example, was a project which experienced a series of changes from the initial sketch for the competition to the finished building, whose history might be interesting in understanding the acceptable and the changes accepted by the architect.

To put it differently, one would recognize from this what is essential and what is incidental in architecture for you. Every project has its history, which is part of the history of all projects?

AR: Let us distinguish between two things: First of all, I agree with what you just said about the history of all projects. That is right, the history is also a part of the project. The very big projects like the Louvre or Saint Peter's Cathedral all have a very long history, which amounts to a textbook on architecture. Even though I built neither the Louvre nor Saint Peter's, I am naturally interested in their history. But in the same way, even the most modest building has its own history, which is not merely of a technical nature; the succession of various masters, legislators, owners, and epochs is part of it. Let us take the town hall of Borgoricco, which was realized according to the model in spite of everything. This small city in the Veneto experienced so many vicissitudes—a series of municipal councils and administrators, who wanted one thing and its opposite—and in the end all of this creates the history of the building, and this is for the best.

As far as the relationship between the sketch and the completed building is concerned, I believe—and am proud of it—that there exists in most cases an almost perfect correlation between the two. If one looks at the Casa Aurora, the headquarters of the GFT in Turin, one sees that the photographs of the completed house are identical to the initial sketches. Likewise, there have been no changes with regard to the architecture in the town hall of Borgoricco or in the latest projects I realized in the United States; sometimes there was a technical improvement, but that is tied to other considerations. Increasingly, an architect today must be a technician, he must always understand the problems better and, I believe, have obtained a certain maturity in the comprehension of these things. Architecture strikes me more and more as a collective work, which requires effort in every part of the construction from specialized technicians, but it does not mean that I give up my role. At the moment, I am preparing the construction drawings for the Congressional Palace in Milan.

First I tried to find and determine a structural type for the roofing (very significant due to its dimensions), and then I could work with the engineers, who restored order to the structure. I do not believe in the architect who rules everything, except in the sense that he must be capable of imagining what is possible and therefore also of discussing it. It would be absurd to do without the high-level technology we have at our disposal today.

BH: All the same, I have a personal explanation for your way of working. It would be a mistake to accuse you of sketching your projects in Milan and then sending them abroad without caring too much about the execution, for the completed building ostentatiously carries your signature. Nevertheless, something remains a mystery to me. As I already mentioned in regard to La Villette in Paris, but which applies equally to the Friedrichstrasse in Berlin, sometimes sketches must defy a building's execution, which goes against the fundamental idea of the sketch. The typology of the public housing "with a foliage-covered arcade," for example, which you favor, is unacceptable in Berlin as in Paris. The first surprise is your ability to take on the typological changes and at the same time maintain the architectural idea. Similarly, you appear to give little notice to drawn details (this does not mean that the details are irrelevant to you), and to handle the measurements and exact proportions of the individual parts of the creation very generously in the building phase. In this you distinguish yourself from the widespread practice of the "art architects," who demand a manic control of all the parts of a building. The detail is for them clearly the mark of architecture. One can rightly object that this tendency is all the more paradoxical, in that the division of labor in the organization, the interdisciplinary teams, and the use of industrial serial products (steelforms, paneling, etc.) all reveal the unavoidable conditions of contemporary architectural production. The exemplary in your work lies in the correct assessment of these production features.

Your projects demonstrate such elemental and essential architectural qualities that the adaptation to a construction system, the details of the execution, or the scale of the building cannot alter the idea of the work itself or its intrinsic poetry. Is this your relationship with the execution?

AR: I think that is exactly how it is.

BH: I could, by the way, bring up numerous examples from the history of architecture that follow your direction. Several important works by Michelangelo were built or finished according to more or less exact handwritten indications long after his death.

The poetry of the artist is so powerful that it can free itself from the authenticity of the detail.

AR: I think you have already answered the question, but I would like to add something. First of all, what you said about the serial production of building parts belongs for me to the basis of architecture: I consider myself a real contemporary architect, because I use modern technology, as it must be used. While I was studying at the Polytecnico in Milan, we were asked to draw individual parts of metal panels—I do not think that is done in any school anymore—and I remember that I failed several times, for it is a difficult assignment: The system must be air-tight, function well, etc. Honestly put, I considered it an aberration.

I have always refused to do it, because there are many specialized businesses in which technicians and engineers spend their lives conceiving of and producing metal paneling. I will not mention any names so as not to give publicity, but is it not ridiculous that in today's world an architect is occupying himself designing metal panels? As if one could study the ventilators of a Mercedes motor!

The designer builds the parts so they are bought when they are needed! In this respect, I believe I have a definite modern attitude. Architects who occupy themselves with the technology of laying floor tiles, or with the individual parts of metal paneling, appear archaic to me. And when an architect has to control the realization of his project to the centimeter, then, as you say, he is a little limited and surely has no generous view of his own architecture.

To answer your question, it is enough to recall Alberti, who perhaps never saw any of his houses built, or Michelangelo, who sent his indications of the approximate height of the columns of the Laurentian library to Florence by letter. In the wonderful collection of Palladio's sketches—which I was able to look at thanks to the kindness of the Royal Institute of British Artists—one sees that he did not draw any details anymore. He limited himself to the sketches, or referred to several of his realized projects, which rendered the spirit of buildings like the Casa Aurora, for example. This will not change if one alters the columns by two centimeters.

So I approach the execution with a certain lack of constraint. But it is not true that I simply send a sketch to Japan. I followed the project in Fukuoka, for example, with special care. What does it mean "to follow a project"? If one wants bricks or supports that are produced in this or that manner, one must know exactly what one is looking for; and since I had absolutely no idea how the Japanese produce bricks, I tested two or three samples and finally selected one type, which was of better quality than the brick from Lombardy.

BH: I wanted to ask you about your relationship to construction systems. In this area you have always defended yourself by pointing out that you studied at the Polytecnico in Milan and therefore consider yourself an engineer. I think your response is autobiographically correct, but it does not explain the place the construction system takes in your interpretation of architecture. I dare to make the hypothesis that your approach to the construction system, except in the case of unusual buildings such as the Congressional Palace in Milan which you have spoken about, is of a purely typological nature. For you the construction systems represent an ensemble of conventions and commonplaces that are inseparable from the system of architectural forms. Support walls, beams, columns, and roof frameworks are integral parts of your language and therefore have no buildable independence.

In my eyes, this interpretation contradicts the (currently in France very strong) trend, which favors the exhibition of structures and the constructive decoratism as expressions of the modernity of architecture. How do you view the appearance of this fashion?

AR: First of all, I do not believe that the essential purpose of architecture is achieved through this. The development of technology leads to ever simpler structures, to ever clearer decisions. The exhibition of structures and technologies is always limited by time, and in relationship to the future is often already surpassed. Let us take an example that is known to us, since we unfortunately—like all architects nowadays—spend a lot of our time at airports. Let us compare two big European airports: Paris and Frankfurt. I do not know how old Roissy is—ten years maybe? In any case, one wanted to discover the future and truly developed it muscularly, a "body building" of structures, gates, and elevators. When one came to this big Parisian airport at the time of its construction, one felt transported into the future. Ten years may have passed, and honestly, with all due respect to the French technology, the airport "functions poorly," it is ugly and has aged. The airport in Frankfurt is extraordinarily simple—no exhibitions, completely ordinary structures—and although it is of the same time, it is a modern airport that "functions." What I want to say with this is that the technology must always be the available technology and not a fake imitation of the future.

It is the old futurist idea of Marinetti, for whom Milan was a truly modern city, because it reverberated with the track noises of the streetcars. Today this image of the streetcar and its noise on the tracks reminds us of the past. There is nothing worse than looking into the future, and it is the fate of all science fiction to exhibit in a theatrical manner structures which are simplified and quickly surpassed.

BH: I just noticed that in your defense of the building of La Villette, you unconsciously used the same arguments that one knows from Adolf Loos's quill, from his answer to criticisms of the famous office building on Michaelerplatz in Vienna. Do you remember what he wrote? I will quote him roughly: "I did not want to make a manifesto to the avant-garde with this house. I simply built a house, as the old masters did." Loos's modernity lies in the demand for a continuation in the authenticity of a forgotten tradition.

Is it actually true that you responded to a journalist who asked you where you place yourself, if you are modern, or, rather, postmodern: "No, I am not postmodern, for I was never modern."

How do you explain your relationship to modernity today?

AR: Yes, but what is modernity? I believe that this invention of the "modern"—as applied to architecture—is a critical distortion which is tied to a particular moment of the history of architecture. Does one today ask of painting, of poetry, of cinema, if the work is modern? If a film is modern or not? Stupid critics in painting, who asked themselves if Picasso or De Chirico was modern, also have no sense anymore; the question is if it is painting and of the particular way the painter chooses to express himself. In contrast, the absurd problem still poses itself for architecture. Does one ask if the patient or his physician is modern or not modern? First of all, it is about a physician who practices today's medicine, whereby he can naturally choose certain cures over others. When I replied that I could not be postmodern, because I have never been modern, I only wanted to say that I am an architect and I practice my profession as architects have always done. It might be more intelligent and logical to inquire about styles, I mean if a particular architect tends toward the Baroque or the Renaissance. This is the difficult question today; because the boundaries of styles are no longer clearly drawn. To explain it again with medicine: it is really absurd to ask if a certain physician is modern or postmodern, but one can ask, instead, what kind of medicine he practices.

BH: As you speak, I cannot help but think of Roland Barthes when he declared, "Suddenly it has become indifferent to me, if I am considered modern."

To which history are you referring when you say that you have never been modern?

AR: I am referring to the journalistic usage of the term "modern," which goes hand in hand with a certain "modern" history of architecture, whose relevance I dispute. I am convinced that there is a certain continuity through time in architecture. It is evident that Greek architecture precedes Renaissance architecture, which, in turn, precedes that of the 20th century, and so on.

But let us leave this question, which arises out of intellectual discourse, limited to journalistic and university circles, and which loses all meaning in a country like the United States, because such superfluous questions, as you know, occupy barely a handful of New York critics. In some states one sees Georgian houses, in others glass buildings. American architecture is a conglomerate of all of this.

BH: Naturally this is not a question for mass architecture. For the architectural elite, it is different, for it must always pursue an art of "distinction" to persist as an elite.

To a certain degree you belong to them?

AR: No, for I do not believe that there is an architectural elite. To return to my previous example: What does it mean that in a big country like America all different types of architecture exist next to one another, without anyone getting agitated about it? Basically, the illness of the modern—at least, one of its illnesses, which caused the ruins of great parts of our cities—is morality, that is the intrusion of the moral question into architecture. We are unfortunately still today suffering from this illness. And when I say that I am not modern, I am declaring my rejection of morality in architecture, a morality which does not rage in other artistic disciplines. At this point we do not want to debate any academic or philosophical questions, but whether one finds a Doric column beautiful or ugly, whether one likes it or not, this is a judgment which has absolutely nothing to do with morality. For many years I have been accused of liking the Stalinistic architecture, because I considered the buildings of Stalin's era great—and still do. Stalin had buildings erected with columns and the entire Soviet architecture should be damned for using columns and gables, whereas in the predominantly democratic Europe an architectural production (incidentally very ugly), because it uses glass and flat roofs falling to all sides, is considered democratic! Here my polemic begins. Of the so-called "modern" architects I was mostly influenced by Mies van der Rohe, although especially in the final years of his life he built a lot with steel and glass. On the other hand, a Renaissance palace can also have a very permanent influence upon me. For me, architecture is a whole, and I take the good wherever I find it.

ROSSI, Aldo. Italian. Born in Milan, 3 May **1931**.

Educated at the School of the Somaschi Fathers, Como,

Italy, **1940-42**; Collegio Alessandro Voltas, Lecco,

Italy, **1943-46**; studied under Ernesto N. Rogers and

Giuseppe Samonia, Polytechnic of Milan, **1949-59**, Dip.

Arch., **1959**. Worked in the studios of Ignazio

Gardella and Marco Zanuso, Milan, **1956-57**. Since **1959**,

in private practice, Milan: in collaboration with

Gianni Braghiera from **1971.** Teaching Assistant to

Ludovico Quaroni, Scuola Urbanistica, Arezzo, **1963**;

Visiting Instructor from **1965**, Professor of

Architectura Composition, **1970-71**, and Member of the

Council from **1971**, Polytechnic of Milan; Professor of

Planning, Eidgenössische Technische Hochschule,

Zürich, **1972-75**; Professor of Architectural

Composition, University of Venice, from **1975**; Mellon

Professor, Cornell University, Ithaca, New York, **1976**

Visiting Professor, Cooper Union, New York, **1976**;

Professor of Planning, Yale University, New Haven,

Connecticut, **1980**. Editor, *Casabella-Continuitá*,

Milan, **1955-64**; contributor, *Societa*, Milan, and

Editorial Board Member, *II Contemporaneo*, Milan, **1959**.

Director of the architectural section, XV Triennale,

Milan, **1973**, and of the Biennale, Venice, **1983**;

Director of the International Seminar on Architecture,

Santiago de Compostela, Spain, **1976**. Pritzker Prize

for Architecture, **1990**. Address: Via Maddalena 1,

20122 Milan, Italy.

Lost Colony W.G. Clark

I can only imagine what it must be like to be an architect in a country where the built form allies itself with and springs from ancient traditions and meanings that are shared and understood by everyone; where the language of the architect and the builder is the same and buildings are of the place and not just built upon it in obscure and alien reference. Our architecture, like our culture, was transplanted and imposed upon the land. Any colonial architecture is odd, representing traditions of another land with the quirky hybrid adaptations to the conditions of a new place. Ours is particularly rich because of the many cultures represented, but this richness, for me at least, nevertheless lacks a profound sense of belonging. So "traditional" American architecture has never stirred me. It is not that I don't find it interesting or beautiful, nor that I think it is not a legitimate representation of our cultural past. It is just that I am more moved by things that have sprung from this land, forms subjected to our early sense of economy, inventiveness, and questioning. We transcended colonialism. Our independence established a home and that home was founded on more than just a separation: it was founded on an ideal. So naturally one looks for a true indigenous expression of this ideal, one rooted in our own traditions of simplicity and practicality, at home in our beautiful, stolen place.

Modern architecture has always seemed to me to come curiously close to being this: as if our own Declaration had finally made its way to architecture, or that more likely, those ideals of our early country were born of the same spirit that generated modern architecture. Its concern for spareness, honesty of expression, and modesty appeals to our American sensibilities, as if we invented it to replace an unnecessary and obnoxious posture, not unlike learning to fire from behind trees. While I find this exciting and hopeful, it is disturbing that the imported models of modernism, no matter how based on principles that would seemingly be at home here, are as alien to our land as the traditional models. It is as if modernism's sought-after universality ironically made buildings for nowhere, unrooted and insignificant with respect to place, ungrounded in terms of form, tentative and ill at ease in our landscape.

It would seem as if we are in a hopeless position, that our architecture has not developed a legitimate character as strong and sure as that early ideal that we think of as young America. We have also failed to establish a respectful settlement. We have been so intent on development that we have ignored the more serious objective of the realization of ourselves as a model civilization. We seem lost.

Of course we are still only beginning. We are still basically an uncivilized nomadic culture, moving about, using the place and its resources, seeking momentary transportable wealth and satisfaction here and there, staying in no one place long enough to develop either an understanding of it or a veneration for it. It will take thousands of years to come to terms with this place and for our architecture to assimilate its character and its ideals. It is hopeful to realize that the real traditions are yet to come, that the ones we've been working with were provisions for the voyage. We need to learn to plant corn. We are still a young country in search of native form. The confusion and disarray that appear to be lost-ness and misadventure may simply be that initial awkwardness and stridency that always accompanies new things. I prefer to think that maybe we are not bereft of a genuine architecture, but merely fumbling around at the beginning of one.

The American architecture that I admire is almost invariably that architecture which has sprung naturally from local conditions and customs. It is interesting that these buildings are more often generated by poverty than by wealth; thin shacks and sheds with an insubstantial beauty which seem so casually and effortlessly at home. It is also wonderfully troubling that the more naive and innocent these buildings are of architecture, the more profoundly suitable they seem to our land. More troubling still is the recognition that those buildings that seem to be the most beautifully and surely placed were done so with more regard to economy and practicality than to any notion of a response to the landscape. This is probably because their placement was based on a more profound sense of appropriateness and fit than formal architectural language can address.

Another kind of American architecture which has a more substantial beauty blurs the distinction between landscape and architecture: the earthen architecture at Mesa Verde and Pueblo Bonito, which involves ambiguity between the buildings and the setting, and it is difficult to tell which is which. At certain fortifications, emplacements, bridges, etc., where the earth has been shaped to specific duty, it is hard to tell where the earth stops and the building begins. In ruins, where the intended use of the building has departed, it is often unclear whether the structure is landscape or architecture. Conditions are reversed and a missing roof allows sunlight and vegetation inside and the building becomes a garden. These places, in their reductive, earthbound condition, are very satisfying, as if they offer us a primitiveness that we need, one not found in our transplanted formal models.

One of our first attempts at blurring the distinction between building and the land was the design of a visitor orientation building for Middleton Place Gardens in South Carolina. This building separated a parking lot from a long reflecting pool at the edge of the formal gardens. It became clear that the normal, closed, air-conditioned, media-dependent visitor center would make acclimation difficult and even cruel, given the climate and the long walking tour. We also did not like the idea of a visitor seeing in advance photographic or film images of what they were about to see. So all information was limited to that which they could not see for themselves such as history, information, and overall site relationships. This information was reduced to ten white panels and housed in an open-air structure with offices and services adjacent. These small buildings were inlaid into ivy-covered geometric earth-works. This was done to obscure the buildings and parking from the gardens. It was also done to ground the buildings and to make them read as part of the landscape.

Later, we were commissioned to design an inn for Middleton Place. The site was in a forest along the river and it contained a clearing and a remarkable embankment left by an old mining operation. The inn was designed to fit this embankment and to stretch along it like a retaining wall. The building became a boundary between the forest and the clearing. Its walls were to be covered with ivy in order to make it unclear upon approach whether it was a building, a topiary, or a ruin. The L-shape of the building appears as a fragment, enclosing a space and relying on the landscape for completion of the composition.

The project for the New Orleans Museum of Art Competition proposed the new addition as a place floating in a lagoon. We wanted the addition to become a setting or a surround for the old museum building. Since the addition was placed between the museum and City Park, we tried to make it belong to both. The roof of the auditorium was designed as an amphitheater for park concerts. Sculpture courts and a grove of trees were added to make the building read as a place. Bridges and an open-air passage through the building made a path connecting the museum and the park. This all played upon water imagery in this city so bounded by that element.

preceding pages (photomontage)

116–121 "insubstantial beauty, substantial beauty; shacks and sheds, landscape or architecture"
photomontage of American rural structures on southern landscapes

Similarly, our unsuccessful entry for the Arizona Historical Museum Competition involved making the building a path. In this case we buried the museum so that its roof became a promenade and entrance to the desert park beyond. The earth from this excavation was used to form and cover the auditorium and classrooms. This was an attempt to make the building a subtractive part of the hillside, merging with the earth by an indistinct boundary. It was also a way to reduce the apparent size of the building and to make it of less importance than its hill site.

The Reid and Croffead houses are not so much about creating an ambiguity between architecture and landscape as they are about marking a place. The Reid house was designed to rise above its farm-site clutter. It is made of cheap materials, block and plywood, in sympathy with the very modest and inexpensive houses and outbuildings that are its neighbors. The Croffead house enjoys a site at the confluence of two rivers; this site is divided by a line of live oaks which extend through the neighborhood. The house was placed tightly in one quadrant of the site in alignment with neighboring houses. Its loggia is canted to be parallel with the trees and to provide views of them from the internal staircase. The house is an object which ends the neighborhood pattern and begins the open views of the water along the bluff's edge. The main chamber of the house is two storeys high, enclosed by the chimney at one end and by a projected window and tree at the other.

Finally, we were initially asked to comment on our theory and methodology. I am unaware that we have either. I don't believe that either is necessary. We do know that all building involves the use of a place and that all architecture, regardless of program or cost, must become that place. The things that we admire most accomplish this either through an architecture of innocence or through an architecture of emplacement which seeks to make the building and the place one thing. This makes the job quite difficult since it is probably impossible for an architect to achieve innocence, and just as unlikely that one can achieve that profound engagement of building and land which seems so maddeningly easy for primitive man. But I think we all crave an ancientness which we never had and an innocence which we have lost, desperately, if futilely, seeking their realization.

CLARK, W. G. American. Born in Louisa,

Virginia, 14 May, **1942**. Educated: School of

Architecture, University of Virginia, B. Arch.,

1965. Private practice, Charleston, South

Carolina, **1974-84**; Partner, Clark and Menefee

Architects, Charleston, South Carolina, and

Charlottesville, Virgina, **1985-** . Visiting

Professor, Graduate School of Design, Harvard

University, **1987**; Professor and Chairman,

School of Architecture, University of Virginia,

Charlottesville, **1988-90**; Professor, School of

Architecture, University of Virginia,

Charlottesville, **1990-** . Visiting Critic:

University of Pennsylvania, North Carolina

State University, Ohio State University,

Harvard Graduate School of Design, Virginia

Polytechnic Institute, University of Virginia,

Georgia Institute of Technology, Smithsonian

Institution, Rhode Island School of Design,

Syracuse University, University of Florida,

Rice University, University of Maryland,

Clemson University, Architectural League of New

York, Yale University. Exhibitions: "40 Under

40," The Architectural League of New York,

1986; "Emerging Generation in the U.S.A."

exhibit, GA Gallery, Tokyo, **1987**. Address:

Clark and Menefee Architects, 404-B East Main

Street, Charlottesville, Virginia 22902, U.S.A.

Sometimes I wish I had been an art historian

I felt I had to leave things ou

I was unsure of myself

Interview with Denise Scott Brown and Robert Venturi

Phillipe Barriere and Sylvia Lavin

L'Architecture d'Aujourd'hui:
Your practice has gained considerable acclaim for having introduced an historical dimension to the matrix of modern architecture. But of the many ideas of history, not much has been said of the one you have in fact introduced, nor of how you came to develop your particular conception of the past.

Robert Venturi:

Let me begin by saying I think the recent past is the hardest thing to understand. You have to try and remember now, how out of fashion history was among architects when I was young. I have always loved history, and if I hadn't been an architect, I would have been an art historian. ███████████ ◀ ◀ ◀ —no more dealing with contracts, public relations, marketing, insurance, partners, codes, bureaucrats, lawyers, clients, and meeting the payroll. I was just born with an interest in the history of architecture. I studied at Princeton—by accident but also by luck—where history in the architecture curriculum was OK, unlike Harvard, which at the time was the place to be. Going to Harvard in those days was like going to Divinity School—a place where you got the Word, and once you had the Word, you had to go out and propagate it. But at Princeton, we studied Modern architecture and everyone agreed Modernism was the appropriate current style—of course we didn't use the word "style" then, but "Modernism" was understood in the context of history. The Department of Architecture was even within the Art History department.

You've probably never heard of Donald Drew Egbert, who is the biggest hero of my life. He taught the history course in Modern architecture at Princeton. Unlike Sigfried Giedion, who used history to prove a point, Egbert implied that Modernism, within the context of history, could evolve into something else: it was not an end in itself, but a phase within an evolution. I think this is the reason why innovators came out of Princeton in my generation and after.

Also, at the American Academy in Rome, I had two years to just look at history. In our day we had a bias toward the Baroque and piazzas. And we looked at form and space rather than symbol and meaning. But during my last months in R o m e , I realized that Mannerist architecture was what really meant most to me, and I reexamined a lot of Italian historical architecture for its Mannerist qualities. This was important when I came to write *Complexity and Contradiction* in the following years.

To this day Denise and I essentially look at old architecture and everyday architecture. We don't look much at what other architects are doing, and don't keep up much with what's going on.

AA: How did you come to meet Louis Kahn?

RV:

Well, when I got out of school, ███████████ and didn't find myself until I wrote *Complexity and Contradiction*. In a way, I did find myself relatively early, but in another, I haven't found myself yet—you shouldn't find yourself entirely until the moment before you die. I had a summer job with Robert Montgomery Brown, who was a local modern architect. Louis Kahn—whom no one had heard of—was in an office on the floor above. I would see him in the elevator. I also saw the five or six young people who worked for him. They never talked to me because I was young and naive, but Louis Kahn did; he was very kind. And when I returned to Princeton to finish my Master's thesis I asked Kahn to be on the jury along with George Howe.

AA: Was that when you won the Prix de Rome?

RV:

I got that several years later. Kahn was on the jury and I think he liked what I had done, so he took an interest in me. I then went to work for Stonorov, who was one of the few Modern architects in the city at that time. I worked there for a year, mainly designing an exhibition of the work of Frank Lloyd Wright, which was to open in Philadelphia and then to go to the Strozzi Palace in Florence. Louis Kahn also recommended me to Eero Saarinen, whose office I was in for 2-1/2 years. I was not particularly at home there, but I made some nice friends and I learned a lot about the running of an office. Then I came back to run my family's fruit and produce business because my father had become ill. For a year and a half, I worked in the family firm—horrified that I might be caught in the business for the rest of my life. At that time, I would visit Kahn's office for sustenance, and he was a good friend. Then I did win the Rome Prize. I applied for it three times and the third time, I got it. People said, "Why do you apply a third time, don't you know when you're not wanted, can't you take a hint—have you no pride?" But the secretary in the New York office at that time, Mary Williams, was a very nice person and encouraged me to reapply.

AA: When did you start the research that led to "Contradiction"?

RV:

That was in 1954, when I went to the American Academy in Rome for two years. When I came back I worked for Louis Kahn and also taught at the University of Pennsylvania as his assistant. Later, probably in '61, Holmes Perkins, the Dean of the Architecture School at Penn, asked me to teach a course in the theory of architecture. In a way that course was a preparation for *Complexity and Contradiction*. Denise helped me with the course and the notes evolved into the book. It was finished in '64 and published in '66. In one sense the book was a reaction to the ethos at Penn at the time. Under Holmes Perkins, Penn was an orthodox, Harvard-oriented, Modern school. ██████ ████████ of the course for fear of being accused of corrupting the morals of minors. So I decided that what I was leaving out of the course I'd put in a book.

AA: Denise described your course as a professional architect's view of theory. She said you discussed your own theory briefly at the end of each lecture, and that this became the book itself. Where did the material in the first part of the lectures come from?

RV:

Ironically, from Holmes Perkins; so he was instrumental in promoting the book. He must have sensed that no one from Harvard had the background in history or theory to teach this course, while someone who had been to Princeton probably did. But even at Princeton I had not had a course on theory; I had no idea what to do. It was Holmes who suggested I look at Guadet and use his system of dividing architecture into elements for the purpose of analysis. And that's just what I did. I put together a course with fifteen lectures, each devoted to an element of architecture: space, details, form, structure ...

Denise Scott Brown:

... scale, decoration, light ...

RV:

I did not include symbolism. No one mentioned symbolism in those days—not even at Princeton. Denise and I did that later. And as she said, at the end of each lecture I added my own twist—on scale, light, or whatever.

AA: Tell us about Jean Labatut.

RV:

Jean Labatut is very important in my background, and when I had him as a critic I would have said he was more important than Egbert, the historian. Labatut's background was Beaux-Arts; he had placed second in the Prix de Rome in the mid-20's. He had a wide, though not formal, knowledge of history. The most wonderful thing he did was to teach by analogy. He would say something was like something else, employing a rich range of historical examples.

But it was Egbert who was amazing. He deserves more recognition. At the time, he was working on a book on the Ecole des Beaux-Arts. It seems an obvious subject now; in fact, it was very "in" only a few years ago, but in the 40's no one dreamed of taking the Beaux-Arts seriously: it seemed outrageously irrelevant and reactionary. Sigfried Giedion ignored the Beaux-Arts, except in his references to Labrouste, who used cast iron; for Giedion, the Beaux-Arts was not a "constituent fact" of history, but only a "transitory fact." Sadly, Egbert eventually stopped work on this book and never finished it. He went on to another book, *Social Radicalism and the Arts*, which is well known in Europe but less known here in the USA. But Egbert's writings on the Beaux-Arts were published after his death by his former student, the distinguished historian David Van Zanten. In choosing to be unfashionable, Egbert had been heroic.

AA: So during that period of time did you have conversations with Kahn regarding your research and your own theory of architecture?

RV:

Yes, we did talk a lot.

AA: What was his reaction?

RV:

Well, Kahn respected the Las Vegas direction Denise and I took, but could not accept it for himself. Also, although his later historicism may have derived from his Beaux-Arts training with P a u l C r e t at Penn, I think a lot of it came from me. Someone should consider the subject of students influencing masters.

DSB:

It was certainly true with Louis Kahn. I watched him over the years, first as his student, then as his colleague, and I saw ideas I had suggested incorporated in his work, and heard things I'd said repeated by him.

AA: Is that good or bad?

DSB:

Well, it would have been nice to have been acknowledged.

RV:

It isn't good to adopt the ideas of a young person who has no standing and to present them as your own—without acknowledgment.

AA: That's what happens, though, when you're working in an office sharing ideas on the same project.

RV:

There's nothing wrong with that kind of give-and-take; in fact, it's wonderful, but there should be proper attributions in the end. Especially if you're dealing with young people who are original, because they already have a terrible fate before them. To be original is punishable. In the end, of course, the older person can't forgive the younger person.

AA: There's always something that strikes me about the Philip Exeter Library. The refectory building is very much a Venturi design. It comes directly from Vanna Venturi's house, a slanted roof on both sides of a central chimney.

RV:

I don't remember that aspect of it. I don't want to talk about this too much because ▮▮▮▮▮ and I want to be positive.

DSB:

Perhaps one difference is that our designs distort the systems that they're based on. It's interesting to compare Lou Kahn's work with his students' works. There's a huge difference. The students impose Kahn's system from the outside in, whereas Kahn grows the system from the inside out—it grows out of his particular problem. In our work, the system that grows from the inside is distorted in some way; it gets broken or squashed, to meet some extraneous need or pressure. As an urbanist you must develop a sense of where the system exists, where it breaks down, where it distorts, and how all this should fit together. Lou did not have that sense, although later, he did become interested in Roman plans where some of these combinations did exist; where there was, for example, an arcade surrounding a cortile, and different types of space connected to the arcade and related to it in different ways.

AA: You both grew up in families that were very much aware of architecture.

DSB:

Bob knew when he was 4 years old—maybe before—that he was going to be an architect. And I too, at the age of 5, wanted to be an architect, because my mother had studied architecture. But the next year, I decided to be a teacher, then a writer—in the end I have done all that. People who are "this and that" are very difficult to define. The heart surgeon becomes a hero; the general practitioner—though brilliant—does not. ▮▮▮▮▮ mine is not.

AA: Perhaps we should discuss the period of your early research, the pop art influence in your work, essays that were never published and about feminism in architecture.

RV:

Those are very big subjects.

AA: They could be a beginning.

DSB:

Well, let's take the last one, feminism: architecture has been an upper-class male club and, in many ways, still is, although architects don't intend it to be; but old habits die hard. I think the wave of the future is upon the profession now, but at the top, it's still hard to be a woman in architecture. At least, ▮▮ ▮▮ ▮▮▮▮ ▮▮ ▮▮

AA: Very difficult for any woman in architecture.

DSB:

For instance, when people come to interview us they usually say to Bob, "Tell me about your work," and to me, "Tell me about your woman's problem." That in itself is sexism. You did not do that, but at this stage in the emancipation of women architects, the woman is seen as having the problem.

It has even been suggested that the articles I wrote were in fact written by Bob using my name. Of course, it wasn't so. But the perception has been a big problem for both of us. There's a strange psychology around the guru in architecture, particularly because architectural design ability is supposed to be an inborn talent, not possessed by all; hard work is a necessary but not requisite ingredient for achieving good design.

The unmeasureable side of architecture—design—is the part that scares people, the more so because it's the part we most honor in this profession. If you are not a good designer, forget it. And there's no way to be a good designer except through talent—that's the mythology of architecture.

AA: The development of detail in working drawings is also very important.

DSB:

That is very important, but the profession doesn't see it that way, what's more, the world doesn't see it that way. ⌐ Architects, inside themselves, honor most the part they cannot measure. ⌐ Saying, "I'm not a good designer," is like saying, "I'm not a good architect." Because of that, we architects can't use science to validate ourselves. The parallel is with crossing the ocean. When nautical compasses were invented, sailors stopped putting a beautiful lady on the front of the ship. Once they had science, they didn't need magic to steer them to their destination. Architects still need magic in the part of architecture which involves design, where science cannot help. And so they make gurus. They get the latest journal, where pictures of the latest guru's latest building will help take them across the frightening ocean. But there's no room for a mom and pop guru. And because architecture is still mainly a man's profession, there's no place for a woman guru.

AA: If you had been a man, would you have teamed up with Robert Venturi?

DSB:

It's interesting to consider what would have happened had Bob and I both been men. Greene & Greene have an identity as two men. Hardy, Holzman and Pfeiffer seem to have an identity as three people. It's hard to tell. I think if I were a man, things may have been different but I can't say for sure, partly because the subjects I bring to architecture are unfamiliar to many architects, and uninteresting to them as well.

One reason for this is that Americans don't know much about the influences on me that come from Europe (including the European-Jewish origins of my family) and Africa. I have had an intellectual life in three countries; areas of my thought derive from

it's been very difficult for me.

it's painful,

SEATTLE·ART·MUSEUM

The specialist's work is easy to define,

I felt a sort of shiver; I couldn't tell whether it was hate or love.

You don't quite know; you're always surprised

a childhood and youth in Africa and student years spent in the England and Europe of the 50's. American architectural critics know little of these places and times. The second axis of my thought, which counted a lot when I came to America, was my training in "town planning," as they call it in England, where it was a field strongly allied to architecture. In the City Planning Department of the University of Pennsylvania, I found I was studying social sciences more than architecture. This was just as the civil rights movement was starting. The people I learned from at Penn became my colleagues and greatly influenced my way of being an architect. I brought their perspectives to my collaboration with Bob, finding him to be the only architect in the school sympathetic to what was going on in the Planning Department, and who could understand its relevance to architecture. Perhaps Bob had this insight because his mother was a socialist.

The others seemed to side with Louis Kahn who said the sociologists were interested in 2.5 people; therefore, you shouldn't listen to them. But Bob felt, as I did, that we could learn from the sociologists' critical, skeptical, and disagreeable views of architecture, which were challenging and a goad to architectural creativity (in fact, it was criticism of CIAM's city planning). Every now and again architects and urban designers have to become their own sociologists, because there aren't enough sociologists and those there are aren't interested in architecture. But most of the time I think what we've tried to do is use social insight in an architectural way, and as an aid to artistry. For example, although our discussions at Penn on urbanism and popular culture were largely intellectual and conceptual, ⌐my first reaction to Las Vegas was artistic.⌐ I didn't analyze it as a sociological phenomenon; ▓▓▓▓▓▓▓▓▓▓▓▓▓▓▓▓▓ The strength of the feeling lay in its mixture of both. I've always agreed with the Modernists and Brutalists who felt that the shiver you get from looking at something ugly can be artistically important. It gets you out of an aesthetic rut. It makes your eyes fresh. I think that's what Le Corbusier meant when he said "eyes that will not see." And Ed Ruscha "just looked." But it was great art to look, in the way he did. The freshness of the shiver was what I felt when I first saw Las Vegas. It made me want to interpret and understand the shiver. That's why I invited Bob to visit Las Vegas with me. Later, with the help of Steve Izenour and our Yale students, we used many ways to analyze the strip, based on the sum of our past experiences. This was an exciting time in our lives. Here was a whole new field of discovery. It opened up so many new ideas. Yet it was equally exciting because we could apply traditional ideas to new phenomena, and incorporate the new into the existing body of architecture.

RV:

America is a place where there is a great diversity of taste cultures—and of architectural juxtapositions, combinations, and distortions that should discourage an emphasis on homogeneity. These comings together are a beautiful phenomenon and one of the reasons they're likeable is that they diminish ideology—the idea that there's only one way to do things. Art and ideology don't mix: ideology is the enemy of vitality in art. But ideology is convenient, especially for journalists. It simplifies their job: it's the equivalent of the sound byte.

AA: Some people have said that you're the standard-bearers of Postmodernism. And it's true that your names have served as a reference if not a backing for this movement.

DSB:

There are many reasons why we aren't Postmodernists. One is Bob's interest in architectural history that dates from his childhood and makes his knowledge more profound than that of the Postmodernists. Another is my training in the social sciences and my experience with the social planning movement of the 60's, by which I learned to think in sociologists' terms and to relate social imagination to architecture. A critic of the writer Jerre Mangione said that, as an artist, Mangione has always sought the truth but, because he's a *real* artist, he has made sure never to find it. Postmodernism found truths too quickly; so did some (but not all) Modernism before it.

AA: You think there is a truth to be found?

DSB:

Well, their definition of truth maybe. Modernism cut out history again through indiscriminate borrowing. We try to make our borrowings relevant ones, contextually and culturally, then break with context to meet new needs and to ensure we don't limit the truth by overdefining it.

RV:

When ⟨ Guild House ⟩ was under construction, around 1965, Vincent Scully came to Philadelphia. He had some other business here but he made a point of coming to look at the building, which was almost complete. Later that afternoon we met Penn's Dean of Architecture, Holmes Perkins, by chance on the street. He said, "Vince, what are you doing in Philadelphia?" Vince answered: "I came to see Bob Venturi's Guild House." Holmes' jaw dropped. I loved Vince for that.

Then, about 5 years ago, I drove past the Guild House with an architect of my generation who said: "You wonder now what all the fuss was about." That made me sad. The building was outrageous then; it's ordinary now. But maybe that's a compliment.

AA: How has the structure of your office changed since you built Guild House?

RV:

At this stage we're completing a series of relatively large buildings that got started all at once. This made for a strain, especially during the working drawings stage, which is so labor intensive. Our office had to get quite big. It's smaller now because the construction administration phase requires fewer people. This sequence of work also means that we have completed no large buildings for some time now. We're lying low and people are forgetting about us, which is all right; I rather like it. But presumably the buildings will all be completed about the same time. We're also starting design on new projects and completing construction on a few houses.

AA: It's funny to note that the Laguna Gloria and Seattle Art Museums and the National Gallery Extension show a kind of similarity in the way the layout and the functions are organized inside, yet they all have different skins. In fact, their skins define the difference between the museums rather than the function, which should be exactly the same.

RV:

Context affects the design of the outside. The design of the ⟨Sainsbury Wing⟩ of course evolved out of the existing National Gallery building next to it. A recent issue of the English "Architectural Review" referred to our facade on Trafalgar Square as "picturesque mediocre slime"; you just can't mind such eloquent criticism. The same magazine said in an earlier editorial: "instead we are to be given a vulgar American piece of Postmodern Mannerist pastiche." We are truly hard to place ideologically, and this makes our architecture hard to take. The Modernists, the Neo-Modernists, and the Deconstructivists don't like us because we're not modern, and the Traditionalists don't like us because we're not explicitly traditional. It's good to be in an ambiguous position, I think. It's nice to be not easy to place. It's good not to be ideological.

AA: Yes, but you've always dealt with ambiguous positions. And you're not the first architects to have looked to the past. Plecnik did it too — beautifully. And there is even a certain similarity between Plecnik's striped bank in Vienna — do you know it? — it was the first curtain facade ...

RV:

Yes.

AA: ... and the striped Seattle Art Museum, with its facade treated like a curtain material.

RV:

I hadn't thought of it that way. Yes, like a curtain with an ornamental fringe.

AA: That is also true of other ornament in your architecture, which defines very strong symbolic elements. Could you say more about the relation between pattern, color, ornament, and texture, how they come through in your design and how they become symbolic elements of a building?

RV:

Denise and I have written about this. Do you know my Gropius lecture at Harvard in 1982? It describes some ideas behind our most recent work. One was on the use of ornament all over—on architectural expansion derived more from surface than from spatial quality. This relates to the d e c o r a t e d s h e d, a notion Denise and I learned from Las Vegas. The Harvard article described a kind of ornament I called "representational." Others have taken up that word in different ways but, as we use it, representational ornament refers to historical symbols and how we feel they should be used today. As an architect ▰▰▰▰▰▰▰▰▰▰▰▰ ⌐ 8
Your classical columns shouldn't be structural.

Describing ornament reminds me how difficult it is to create it. I think it's because of my age. When I grew up you didn't use ornament; you didn't even make an issue of not using it; you didn't even think of it. Texture maybe, but not ornament. So, even though I think I have been good at conceptualizing the new relevance of ornament—good at analyzing it—I find it difficult to design. Young people do it more easily. I think Cesar Pelli produced wonderful brick ornament for his ⟨ Rice building. ⟩

DSB:

Maintaining the concept of a building through all its details is one of the most difficult parts of architecture.   I think Mies' statement is an inversion of one by Nietzsche, "The devil is in the details." This may be more true than Mies' statement for architecture today. I think the Modern revolution led to a loss of skill in architectural detailing. The first generation of Modernists were trained in traditional methods; they could transfer their skills to the new architecture and evolve construction and detailing techniques suitable to it. But new techniques for Modernism couldn't be developed overnight— think how long it took to evolve the tradition of Classicism. So several generations of Modernists had neither the training in new methods nor the rules of traditional detailing to help them.

RV:

To some extent, detailing was really forgotten. When Modernism took over too, almost everything became flush; also, the aesthetic of mass production and repetition reduced the demand for variety of detail. In 50's buildings, there are relatively few details. At Princeton, Fisher Bendheim Hall is next to Robertson Hall, designed by Minoru Yamasaki in the early 60's. Although both buildings are about the same size, our set of working drawings contains about 200 sheets, while there are only about 40 for the 60's building. The number and the complexity of details and the degree of ornamentation make the difference. Good details contribute tension to the composition—and also scale. In traditional architecture big scale and little scale are often juxtaposed. Modernism more or less abandoned this idea: almost everything was medium scale. Modernism tended to diminish the differentiation of little and big, yet it was by using this opposition that architects like Michelangelo achieved true monumentality. Detail and ornament are used in traditional architecture to achieve tension, depth of scale, and monumentality. I think our way of using these elements—flattened and abstracted for representation—is significant in achieving a rich referential dimension for our buildings. Plecnik and others at the beginning of this century did just that.

AA: And Asplund?

RV:

Asplund did it. The Secessionists did it too. I think the detailing of our buildings now going up at Princeton and Penn is going to be good. This is unusual for me. I'm usually the one who doesn't stop worrying about details.

AA: You're not sure whether you like it until it's built?

RV:

You always find details that went wrong, that haunt you. I say I've never made a mistake greater than 4 inches in a building. You can understand the massing and proportions via models and drawings, but the depth of a window reveal can devastate the whole building, and you with it.

AA: How should the strong similarity of positions and proportions that the front facade of the Villa Schwob has with that of North Canton Hall be interpreted?

RV:

The blankness of the front facade of the Villa Schwob was inspiring to us. It took a long time for us to achieve this effect in the design of the ⟨ Laguna Gloria ⟩ facade, partly because we were enamored of an earlier design, with a kind of giant order in the front. Eventually, this front had to have no windows and the blank facade evolved. We also learned from the Mannerist facades of the Villa Pio IV and the ⟨ Acqua Paola. ⟩ Very simply, the ⟨ Villa Schwob ⟩ is an example of taking a blank wall and making it positive; achieving at the same time a kind of generous, if not monumental, expansiveness.

AA: It's surprising that you never used that flat side as an example in "Complexity and Contradiction."

RV:

I should have. Of course, there are other examples: I have mentioned the (Acqua Paola) in Rome, where the great framed panel above the arches has an inscription—a beautiful Latin inscription that George Santayana loved to read on his walks on the Janiculum. I like it also because it does sort of involve representation. It's like a piece of paper with writing on it. Our panel at LGAM is a blank page; a blank page where something could be said. The ⟨North Canton Town Hall⟩ project was not quite that because it did have a very big opening in it. North Canton simply acknowledged a contradiction between the back and the front, the monumental and the circumstantial; it contained a big scale within a small building: Louis Sullivan's great and poignant banks inspired me there. The great-scale detached facade also allowed us to contain all the fuss inside—as in the (Villa Savoye) too.

AA: Yes, but surprisingly, in the North Canton Hall you have the blank square in the middle: it is a real tri-dimensional void. In the Villa Schwob the blank square in the middle is only a void of representation. So rather than "avoid" the issue, you replaced the blank of representation by the blank of materiality, and pushed the transgression of representation to its limit. Which is pretty daring in a front elevation!

RV:

That is a very good interpretation. I forgot about that. I had not thought that way at all.

AA: Would it be correct to say that your influences are Sullivan, Furness, Louis Kahn, and the historical influence of Palladio; and that while your main influence is cultural relevance, you are subject to no contemporary influence?

DSB:

Well, that's putting more meaning into the term cultural relevance than we would have put, and there were many other historical influences. But what you've said about a main influence being Palladio is true. Palladio is an important influence on us because his architecture had great influence on America. There is cultural relevance in that.

AA: So he has the first place in your heart simply because he is important here?

DSB:

Not only for that, but it is one good reason.

RV:

Well, speaking of influence and Palladio, one of the most thrilling and relevant experiences I ever had was reading Rudolph Wittkower's book on Palladio. There are two parts to that work. One is focused on the issue of proportion, which does not interest me at all—it never has, not the golden mean nor Corb's modular. But Wittkower's interpretation of Palladio as a Mannerist, and not the orthodox Classicist that Lord Burlington and his followers made him out to be, that was a great revelation. I also learned a lot from Richard Krautheimer who looked at Roman and German Baroque in a fresh way, when we discussed it in Rome in the 50's. I learned especially from Donald Drew Egbert who taught me _____ But I learned the most from history in general.

AA: Can your way of treating ornament be compared with that of Sullivan?

RV:

I should be 1/1000th as good at ornament.

AA: Like Sullivan, you have the same idiosyncratic notion of the function of ornament, which appears to be a very North American notion.

you don't *do* it, you *represent* it.

to look at everything.

we don't refer to an ideal

RV:

I don't know. It's an interesting point.

AA: Especially in the Seattle Art Museum where it's almost as if the ornament were disappearing into the skin of the building and yet simultaneously revealing it.

DSB:

I think that in ⟨ Seattle ⟩ the decoration is maybe doing some jobs that the architecture would do with Sullivan. For example, I think the decoration near the base of the building mediates the scale between the civic and the individual. With Sullivan, decoration fulfilled that purpose perhaps to some extent, but for him I think the equivalent would be the big arch—that is the element that defines the scale in his bank, as the decoration does in our building.

AA: The Modern movement was in part a search for universality through simplicity and abstraction. Whether we think it was successful or not, this search had political ambitions.

DSB:

We think it was very successful, for its time.

AA: Is there any relationship between contextualism and the search for universality?

RV:

As Denise said, we admire the International Style very much. But I would say a difference between them and us is that in the way the Renaissance did, and some of the Modernists did, by implication. In 1590, buildings in France, England, or Italy were different but these were what we would call regional differences. The same universal ideal was good for all time, for all buildings; so the differences were incidental, not intentional, and to the extent that there were differences, the buildings were considered to be flawed. The Modernism of the International Style exploited that idea too—but its universal vocabulary was based essentially on that of an industrial vernacular, not, of course, on Classical orders.

This approach, too, aimed at producing a universal architecture but the ideal was never achieved, owing to the romantic, individualistic, and perhaps egotistic views of its chief practitioners. Within Modernism, Corb was somewhat Indian when he went to India and somewhat Mediterranean when he worked in the south of France. Mies was more universal: the ⟨ Farnsworth House ⟩ and the ⟨ Research Laboratory ⟩ were essentially the same, the museums in Houston and Berlin were in the same vocabulary. In those days, each great architect had, and was recognizable by, his own vocabulary: Mies was Mies, Corb was Corb, although they evolved over time. There is indeed this funny contradiction: they held to a universal ideal, but they all had to be individualistic at the same time. One of the ways to define a great architect was through the fact that he used a personal, recognizable vocabulary. I would say that today the definition of a great architect would be the opposite: it would be in terms of adaptability and use of multiple vocabularies. This relates to our era's ideas on taste, cultures, heterogeneity, and eclecticism, and to the preference of richness over unity.

DSB:

But if the building is a decorated shed, the shed part is probably universal.

RV:

We try to design that way. And there are other things about our buildings that are constant. Almost every museum has a big stairway.

DSB:

In the ⟨ National Gallery ⟩ there's an interplay between universal and unique, contextual and contrasting, modern and classical. They are interwoven.

RV:

That's true. In each case you set up a system, you set the rules, and then you distort them—as Aalto did. And so it's not as if you have no rules, but rather that you combine different sets of rules, and modify them.

AA: That's Deconstructivism; having it both ways.

RV:

In Deconstructivism there seems to be so much breaking of the rules, that in the end you no longer have broken rules, but picturesqueness.

AA: Can you tell us what deviation is?

RV:

Deviation? What do you mean by that?

AA: You said once that today's deviation is tomorrow's convention.

DSB:

¹² The syncopated pilasters and the single column on the facade of the ⟨ National Gallery ⟩ are today's ▬▬▬▬.

AA: Thank you very much.

end of interview

Interview by Phillipe Barriere and Sylvia Lavin.
Original text published in L'Architecture d'Aujourd'hui, *and edited for* Perspecta 28.

preceding pages (photoworks)

126. "I felt I had to leave things out ..." collage, text and photograph
Seattle Art Museum, Seattle, Washington
facade detail at entry

131–132. "The specialist's work is easy to define ..." double-page collage, text and photograph
Seattle Art Museum, Seattle, Washington
facade view from street

137–138. "You don't do it, you represent it." double-page collage, text and photograph
The National Gallery, Sainsbury Wing, London, England
primary facade from street

140. "deviations" collage, text and photograph
The National Gallery, Sainsbury Wing, London, England
facade detail

SCOTT BROWN, Denise. American. Born Denise Lakofski Nkana, Zambia, 3 October **1931**; immigrated to the United States, **1958**; naturalized, **1967**. Educated at Kingsmead College, Johannesburg, South Africa, **1938-47**; University of the Witwatersrand, Johannesburg, **1948-51**; Architectural Association School, London, under Arthur Korn, **1952-55**, A.A. Diploma and Certificate in Tropical Architecture, **1956**; University of Pennsylvania, Philadelphia, under H. Gans, Louis I. Kahn, D.A. Crane, R.B. Mitchell, W.L.C. Wheaton, W. Isard, C. Rapkin, P. Davidoff and B. Harris, **1958-60**, M. City Planning, **1960**; M. Arch., **1965**. Married the architect Robert Venturi, in **1967**; son: James. Worked as a student architect with various firms in Johannesburg and London, **1946-52**; Architectural Assistant to Ernö Goldfinger and Dennis Clarke Hall, London, **1955-56**; to Giuseppe Vaccaro, Rome, **1956-57**; and to Cowin, DeBruyn and Cook, Johannesburg, **1957-58**; since **1967**, Architect and Planner, and later Partner, with Robert Venturi and John Rauch (associates: Steven Izenour; David Vaughan), Venturi and Rauch, and since **1980**, Venturi, Rauch and Scott Brown, Philadelphia: Partner-in-Charge of Urban Planning. Assistant Professor, School of Fine Arts, University of Pennsylvania, Philadelphia, **1960-65**; Visiting Professor, School of Environmental Design, University of California, Berkeley, **1965**; Associate Professor, School of Architecture and Urban Planning, University of California at Los Angeles, **1965-68** (initiated Urban Design Program). Visiting Professor in Urban Design, Yale University School of Architecture, New Haven, Connecticut, **1967-70** (fellow of Morse College since **1970**); Visiting Critic, Rice University, Houston, Texas, **1969**; Regents Lecturer, University of California at Santa Barbara, **1972**; Chairwoman, Evaluation Committee for the Industrial Design Program, Philadelphia College of Art, **1972**; Member of the Visiting Committee, School of Architecture and Urban Planning, Massachusetts Institute of Technology, Cambridge, **1973-83**; Baldwin Lecturer, Oberlin College, Ohio, **1975**; Visiting Professor, University of Pennsylvania School of Fine Arts, Philadelphia, **1982**, **1983**. Advisory Committee member, Temple University Department of Architecture, Philadelphia, since **1980**; Curriculum Committee Member, Philadelphia Jewish Children's Folkshul, since **1980**; Advisor, United States National Trust for Historic Preservation, since **1981**; Policy Panel Member, National Endowment for the Arts Design Arts Program, **1981-83**; Board Member, Society of Architectural Historians, **1981-84**; Capitol Preservation Committee Member, Commonwealth of Pennsylvania, since **1983**. Address: Venturi-Scott Brown, 4236 Main Street, Philadelphia, Pennsylvania 19127, U.S.A.

VENTURI, Robert Charles. American. Born in Philadelphia, Pennsylvania, 25 June **1925**. Educated at the Episcopal Academy, Philadelphia, graduated **1943**; Princeton University, New Jersey, under Donald Drew Egbert and Jean Labatut, **1943-50**, B.A., **1947** (Phi Beta Kappa), M.F.A., **1950**; American Academy, Rome (Rome Prize Fellowship), **1954-56**. Married the architect Denise Scott Brown, in **1967**; son: James. Worked as a designer for the firms of Oscar Stonorov, Philadelphia, Eero Saarinen, Bloomfield Hills, Michigan, and Louis I. Kahn, Philadelphia, **1950-58**; Partner, with Paul Cope and H. Mather Lippincott, Venturi, Cope and Lippincott, Philadelphia, **1958-61**, and, with William Short, Venturi and Short, Philadelphia, **1961-64**; Partner, with John Rauch, since **1964**, and with Rauch and Denise Scott Brown since **1967**, Venturi and Rauch, and since **1980**, Venturi, Rauch and Scott Brown, Philadelphia (senior associates: Steven Izenour, David Vaughan). Assistant Professor, then Associate Professor of Architecture, University of Pennsylvania, Philadelphia, **1957-65**; State Department Lecturer in the U.S.S.R., **1965**; Architect-in-Residence, Academy in Rome, **1966**; Charlotte Shepherd Davenport Professor of Architecture, Yale University, New Haven, Connecticut, **1966-70**; Visiting Critic, Rice University, Houston, Texas, **1969**; Walter Gropius Lecturer, Graduate School of Design, Harvard University, Cambridge, Massachusetts, **1982**. Member, Panel of Visitors, School of Architecture and Urban Planning, University of California at Los Angeles, **1966-67**; Trustee, American Academy in Rome, **1969-74**; Member, Board of Advisors, Department of Art and Archaeology, Princeton University, New Jersey, **1969-72**, and since **1977**; Member, Board of Advisors, School of Architecture and Urban Design, Princeton University, New Jersey, since **1977**, and of the Ossabaw Island Project, Savannah, Georgia, since **1977**. Pritzker Prize for Architecture, **1991**. Address: Venturi-Scott Brown, 4236 Main Street, Philadelphia, Pennsylvania 19127, U.S.A.

process, projects

"*Conceived as a logical assemblage of materials*, and as landscape collage, the building evolved both in model in the office and in sculptural reality in-situ." 150

"Here we have an architecture for a class that *does not want to announce its own empowerment* or prestige but wants to blend in banally." 160

"This is a work *thought through the logic of building*; from the simple care and pleasure of assembling form to the connections between forms and the beauty of material." 170

"The most decisive point of departure is the base material itself, namely wood and the framing thereof, *developed in relation to the resources* of a self-build client." 180

"This taut convoluted architecture is *bound to its own objecthood* as if it were a skin that has undergone numerous reconstructions and foreign insertions." 190

Given a particular place, person and desire to build, how do the endless axes of our inspirations give way to the finite dimensions of drawings and models, and the concrete reality of architecture? Each of the following five essays and accompanying images explores a different tack along this very personal path.

Introduced through a critical matrix of the architect's choosing, these essay-installations encourage a cross-referencing of written, drawn and built material — critique, study and completed work. How each architect represents his or her ideas, from faint freehand pencil sketches to complex models or computer-aided imagery, sustains a particular sensibility, a sensibility ultimately registered in the buildings and the lives of their inhabitants. On these pages, the visual proximity of study and reality attempts to bridge, or collapse, the distance between the making process and the built projects.

Contributing Architects and Critics:

John Keenan and Terence Riley with Barry Bergdoll; Deborah Berke and Carey McWhorter with Peter Halley; Margaret Helfand and Marti Cowan with Paola Iacucci; Patricia and John Patkau with Kenneth Frampton; Thomas Leeser with Hani Rashid.

John Keenen and Terence Riley

Tectonic Collage
Barry Bergdoll

From Pirro Ligorio's Casino for Pope Pius IV in the gardens of the Vatican, to Schinkel's Casino at Glienicke near Berlin, to Mies van der Rohe's pavilion at Plano, Illinois, the small private pavilion for retreat into the landscape has been favored as a laboratory for exploring compositional and tectonic expressions of the greatest magnitude and potential. Despite, or perhaps because of its intimate scale, programmatic simplicity, and frequently improbable juxtaposition of functions, the casino simultaneously invites a freedom in interpretation and a restraint in scale and ambition, which has more than once honed architectural expression and refined syntaxes of design and detailing. For John Keenen and Terry Riley – in practice in New York since 1984 – the luxury of a client attuned to architectural experimentation and dialogue provided just the occasion. In the Mill House "Casino," completed in 1990 near Lambertville, New Jersey, a personal architectonic vocabulary of materials and assembly postulated in a series of earlier unrealized projects was brought to a masterful level of refinement.

Invoking the topos of the casino – according to Keenen "a building type largely forgotten in the 20th century" – in response to the challenge of creating a game room and screened-in porch/terrace out of one of the small existing structures scattered around the grounds of a modest weekend house, Keenen/Riley converted this first opportunity to build a free-standing structure into a primer for a personal architectural syntax. From the Owner's focus on an old stable on the edge of the property, the architects steered their clients to an overlooked and unpromising derelict mill house only a couple hundred yards in front of the main house. This placed their future casino at a pivotal spot in this gently sloping valley of a stream tributary to the Delaware River, and made it the first building one encounters upon entering the rustic wooded glen of the site.

With its multiple entrances, the casino functions, at least symbolically, as a passage between two levels: the yard of the house on the crest of the slope, and a leveled-off terrain around an outdoor swimming pool closer to the stream. Recognizing the potential of this hermetic fieldstone box – a mere 28' x 35' in plan – the architects set themselves upon the challenge of confronting their long-standing interests in a highly articulated lightweight constructive vocabulary of modern industrial materials with the inert mass of an historical artifact, a sort of primitive degree zero of building. But from the first, this unassuming *objet trouvé* became an active partner in a lyrical dialogue of materials, structure, and space. Rather than an inviolate, historical relic preserved with some false sense of piety, the stone base became the support, both literally and figuratively, for a collage that emerged from the juxtaposition of heavy and light, closed and open, masonry and cage, crafted and tooled, rustic and refined. As Riley explains, "We worked and worked the collage until stone lost its privileged position of being preexistent." Keenen/Riley's additions were essentially two: a small but spatially complex volume to the side of the mill house for a new kitchen, toilet, and secondary entrance; and on its roof, a porch/belvedere of interlocking steel and mahogany frames. This porch, reached by a steel and wood-lattice gangway, provides an equivalent open volume to the found, closed volume of the mill house. The two volumes are left as contrasting states of elementary enclosure; on each level services and circulation have been removed to the periphery to create an openwork modernist collage of lightweight planes and sliding spaces in counterpoint to the closed geometry of the masonry and screened volumes.

Collage, with its engineered intimacy between objects from different universes and different orders of logic, in which the eye and the reason of the artist hold the improbable in a dynamic state of equilibrium, governs this composition on every level from evocation to composition and on every scale from the overall massing to the definition of a syntax of materials. The dynamic of the collage – from its place in both the practices of surrealism and the pedagogy of the Bauhaus to the analyses of Colin Rowe and his followers – is to explore the nature of the forms and materials selected in a continual state of realignments and reconnection, developing an autonomous syntax from a voluntarily limited repertoire. The juxtaposition here of the static, hand-crafted, utilitarian artifact and the industrially-tooled rendering of the traditional American screened-in summer porch – with its faint echoes of lakeside boat houses or early modern aviation clubs – has a deftness in resolution that lures the eye into its own internal logic.

The seemingly effortless finality of the casino's disjunctive parti was in fact the result of a long design evolution. With well over a year to design and build, the architects struggled through a series of design strategies with the masonry wall, seeking to dominate it or master it in some way. Initially, the impossible was entertained: a parti which would have allowed the game room to be linked via an internal stair to the rooftop belvedere. At the same time, the rear wall of the mill house was to be heightened to ground and background the new porch in the tradition of Wright or Breuer. As programmatic and compositional disjuncture was gradually acknowledged and then openly embraced – with the recognition that the two components of the program had no necessary link or need to communicate – the threshold was crossed for a new arranged marriage of a far greater intimacy and subtlety. Entirely distinct in circulation, the two components developed as independent compositions, true opposites in every way, while at the same time they were adroitly interwoven to keep the dialogue continually fresh for each new encounter with the building and the logic of its materials and details. Shifted slightly off the central axis, and then slid off the back of the mill house, the upper concrete terrace asserts its autonomy but remains in a permanent, dynamic relationship with the stone base. This dialogue of sliding and shifting volumes and planes in counterpoint to the two enclosures is anchored by the juxtaposition of two strong, shallow curves: that of the cantilevered kitchen wall which projects above the masonry and

Project: Casino
Lambertville, New Jersey

Existing stone foundation of mill house

Casino, Lambertville, New Jersey (left)

concrete walls of the lower spaces to engage a dialogue with the ephemeral zone of the porch, and the asymmetrical sweep of the wing-like, trussed ceiling of the porch pavilion. Both are clad in lead-coated copper to relate to each other as forms in an abstract composition, as well as to evoke in each case something of the way in which the forms were actually made. Molding and shaping is here distinct from the crisp rectilinear language of tectonic assembly for steel and wood or the sterometric piling of the masonry base.

The notion of the encounter, or in structural terms the joint or reveal, between unexpected partners runs throughout the project, from the overall composition to the detailed elementarist vocabulary of joinery and materials which is the only ornament of this constructivist folly. In a sense, all is born from the spatial joinery or the space-in-between, and in particular from the zone of overlap between the stone base bastion and the ephemeral world of cage and screen. The architects capped off the mill house walls and wove an 18" high clerestory ribbon of transparency between the fieldstone walls and the steel-bracketed concrete slab of the upper structure. This clerestory simultaneously lights the game room below and floats the cantilevered platform of the belvedere in the trees. The platform/slab is in fact the only shared element between the two worlds and it is here that in section the interior spatial articulation is elaborated by puncturing a light monitor over the main entrance to the right of the belvedere, which rises to the terrace level as a pure white cube. This in turn is balanced diagonally on the other side by the open interlocking of the kitchen and the steps of the gangway. The interweaving of the two zones is summarized in the joinery of clerestory mullions and the thin stanchions of the railing above, which is rendered as a single continuous detail.

While the interweaving is clearly expressed in this exquisite detail, the overall relationship of the steel frame to the masonry base is less clearly articulated. The architects were eager to assert the relative visual and structural independence of the terrace and belvedere from the stone base. They planted firmly one of the pair of triads of cylindrical piers on the ground, silhouetted before the rear masonry wall of the base and deftly woven behind the scrim of the screened porch. The other set of piers sits more ambiguously. While visually they rest on the concrete slab of the terrace, in actuality, of course, the three penetrate the slab and are grounded firmly on the great exposed steel I-beam which spans the space of the game room below in the cavity of the mill house. The I-beam itself expresses the hybrid nature of this relationship: in part discharging the weight of the belvedere on a cylindrical post entirely freed from the flooring material of the mill house and in part distributing the charge over the length of the mill house's lateral walls. But to carry such an analysis further is to misunderstand not only the local logic of assembly within the collage, but the regional solutions to the problem in this complex interweaving, and the subtle visual adjustments

which accompany every juxtaposition of materials and constructional modes, as well.

This visual and conceptual autonomy of systems of assembly and structure is carried over to the syntax of joinery, which is most responsible for the lightweight and airy aesthetic of the casino. The integrity of each material continues on the level of detail as reveals of space and materials are kept distinct and articulate. For instance, the concrete pavers on the floor of the game room stop three inches short of the fieldstone walls, allowing each material to read independently. This finds its parallel above, where the concrete terrace is "floated" in its metal frame. Distinct sequences of materials are created throughout, sustained as much for a coherent visual logic as for any programmatic language of construction, in the spirit of Louis Kahn, or more aptly Carlo Scarpa, whose bridge at the Palazzo Querrini Stampalia in Venice Keenen/Riley cite frequently as an inspiration for a syntax of materials and joinery, which can accommodate the handcrafted and the industrial in a rapport of mutual respect and enhancement. But as much as a material language is developed for this delicate assembly, its precise proportions and the relative "weighting" of materials were carefully fine-tuned on the site, and in silhouette against trees and sky on this steeply graded slope. For instance, the clerestory was raised in height to achieve the desired effect of a transparency/shadow line – a sort of negative modernist triglyph/metophe frieze – between the rustic masonry and the lightweight metal assembly. The railings of the upper terrace were studied for the greatest possible thinness and the planks of the gangway adjusted, to cast raking shadows on the wall below.

As much conceived as a logical assemblage of materials as it was adjusted as landscape collage, the building evolved both in model in the office and in sculptural reality in-situ. Indeed the actual finishes and treatment of materials were only decided on-site once the collage was almost fully formed and aligned. Throughout the project, Keenen/Riley sustained a high-level dialogue between formal composition and an expressive intuition in tectonic assembly. One is reminded of Colin Rowe's influential call for a strategy of collage in the 1970s, proposing that Lévi-Strauss's analysis of bricolage might open up strategies for modernism that could accommodate the found and the traditional, open a closed discourse to levels of ambiguity and unexpected meaning, and create an architecture that holds in check the autonomy of the object and its inflection to context. In confronting the images of the American summer and its permissiveness and nostalgia conjured up in Keenen/Riley's casino, the most appealing reference to Colin Rowe's notion of collage is the project's receptivity to, in Rowe's words, "pleasures remembered and desired," "a dialectic between past and future," and "a temporal as well as spatial collision...."[1]

It is tempting to see in this lyric juxtaposition a narrative essay on the myth of primitive shelter and enclosure that has been a major preoccupation of

western architectural theory since the Renaissance. With its combination of masonry base and screened cage, in which support and enclosure are interwoven rather than monolithic, one is reminded in particular, as Kenneth Frampton has suggested,[2] of Gottfried Semper's analysis of the origins of building. For Semper, architecture derived from the choice of a site to erect a hearth, which, as the nucleus for family and social assembly, came to organize man's craft activities in the enterprise of shelter and thus building. Lifted off the humid ground by a substructure of masonry and shielded from the wind and elements by a roof, the hearth fire is both protected and consecrated. For Semper, the roof and the structure that supported it were treated as a unit. Finally, the whole was filled in with textiles, initially in nomadic societies from cloth or hides, and eventually in a more architectonic weaving of wattle, brick, terracotta, or potentially even in the language of the American summer, the gossamer mesh of the screened-in porch. Each of the elements corresponded also to one of the crafts that united in the art of building: the masonry base, the carpentry frame of support-roof assembly, and the walls with weaving or textile arts.[3]

Certainly Semper was far from John Keenen and Terry Riley's mind as they pursued the autonomous logic of the collage, relishing both its control over the incongruous and the rigor with which it allowed all materials within a system to evolve in continual cross-reference and adjustment, expressing the nature of the structure, its assembly, and its coming into being. Yet Semper's model of the four elements of building, which retain, through a series of material and technological transformations, their individual character, has the compelling beauty here of heightening our understanding of both the overall composition of the Casino and the logic of its components, whether they be found and invented, or rationalized and intuited, suggesting that both actually and conceptually, the texture of this project is in the interweaving of opposites.

Endnotes

1 *Colin Rowe,* Collage City *(Cambridge, Massachusetts: MIT Press, 1978): 138.*

2 *Kenneth Frampton, "Una casa per i giochi di Keenen/Riley,"* Casabella *572 (1990): 34–35.*

3 *The most cogent summaries of Semper's theory and its evolution are Rosemarie Bletter's entry on Semper in* The Macmillan Encyclopedia of Architects, *vol. 4 (New York, 1982): 25–33 and Harry Mallgrave's* Introduction to Gottfried Semper: The Four Elements of Architecture and Other Writings *(Cambridge: Cambridge University Press, 1989). See also Kenneth Frampton, "The Text-tile Tectonic: The Origin and Evolution of Wright's Woven Architecture," in Robert McCarter,* Frank Lloyd Wright, A Primer on Architectural Principles *(New York: Princeton Architectural Press, 1991): 124–149.*

Detail of structural intervention at light well

View of bridge to screened room

Freehand study of entry (right)
pencil on tracing paper

CALL
FLOOR
GUY

CAN IT
DO IT?

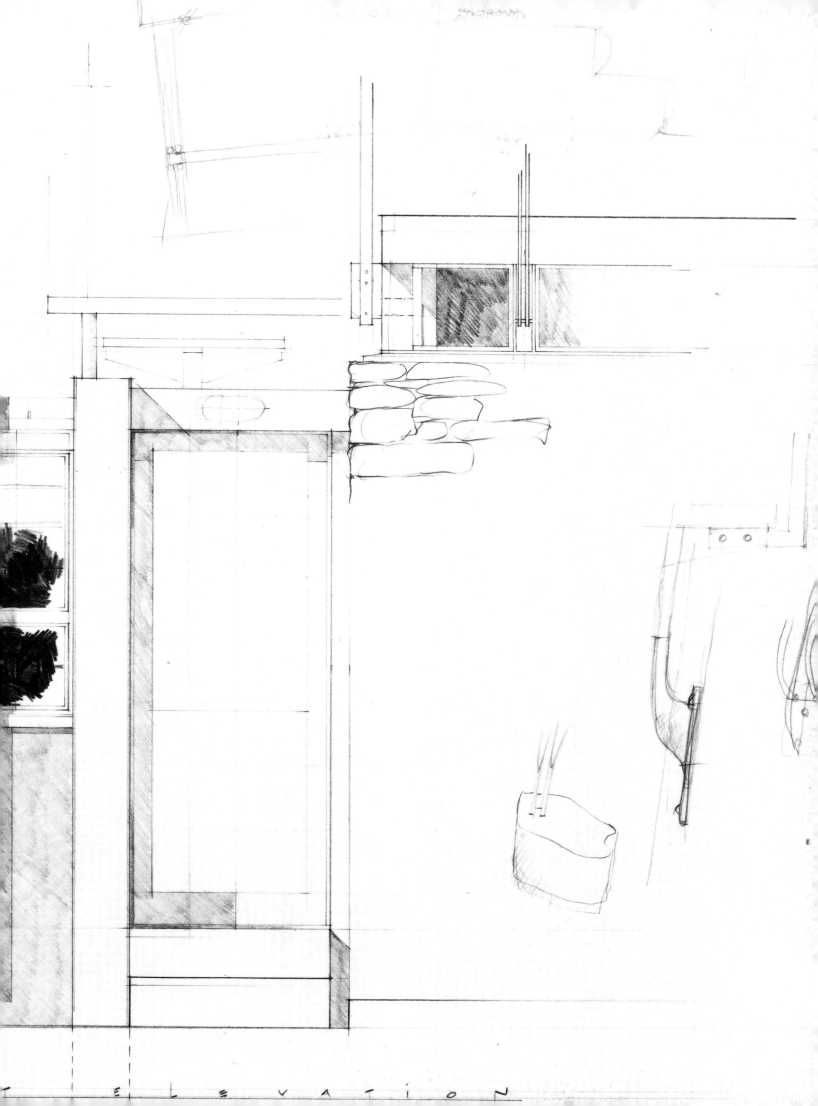

*Freehand study of bridge and
clerestory (left)
pencil on tracing paper*

Detail of bridge

Casino
Lambertville, New Jersey

The owners of a weekend country home wanted a place away from the main house where members of the family or guests could go to play pool, ping-pong, or cards, listen to music, dance, or read a book. They also wanted an outdoor room, screened-in, where they could go sit on summer nights. Within this program we saw the elements of the building type largely forgotten in the 20th century - the casino.

Not far from the main house and off the drive leading into the property are the walls of an 18th-century mill house which now enclose the main space of the Casino. Measuring approximately 22 x 30' and made of 2' thick masonry walls, the ruin is partially burrowed into a steep slope beside the mill stream.

Our intent was to leave the existing stone walls intact. Rather than making new openings into the structure, we wanted to preserve the walls and work with the few doors and windows present. Thus, to bring light into the Casino we created a clerestory which runs almost continuously around the building. A concrete slab becomes the roof of the Casino as well as the outdoor terrace above. On this terrace is the screened room, the roof of which is constructed of metal sheathing over a curved marine plywood sub-surface. From the outdoor room and the terrace one has a view of the surrounding property: a stream, a pond, an existing bridge and dam, a distant hill, and a swimming pool.

Inside, the Casino holds a small seating area, a pool table, which can be converted into a ping-pong table, bookshelves, and storage. A new construction is appended to the western edge of the mill house housing a water closet and a kitchenette and supporting the bridge that leads to the upper terrace.

Much of this project refers to the dialectic established between the "heavy" and the "light": heavy referring to the stone as material, to masonry as a method of construction, density, opacity, immobility, etc., and light referring to the frame construction, lightweight materials such as metal and glass, transparency, and spatial complexity.

John Keenen, Terence Riley

Detail of bridge and entry construction

*Detail of bridge support (right)
pencil on tracing paper*

KEENAN, John

Deborah Berke and Carey McWhorter

No. 71

No. 81

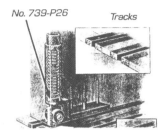

No. 739-P26   Tracks

Invisible Architecture
Peter Halley

The Projects of Berke and McWhorter are described by their supporters and even by the architects themselves as vernacular, even "banal" and "conventional." What kind of ideological persona does this work then offer to the client who wishes to identify with it? Does the client, too, wish to be defined as banal and conventional? Is the client seeking a conventional ideological mask?

In the classical era (to use Foucault's term), practically the sole role assumed by architecture, especially what is now called domestic architecture, was to impress and aggrandize. Large, orderly spaces and sumptuous materials created a theatre of monumental display, while a closed group of historical signifiers (particularly those associated with ancient cultures) gave a mythic transhistorical sense to the aspirations of the client.

Beginning with the Enlightenment in the Eighteenth Century, the signifying language of architecture loosened as the possession of power became less monolithic and more fluid. The meanings given to historical symbols began to shift, and historical reference became the language of subtle arguments about stasis and change, about order and freedom. Architecture also became the site of a debate about how the newly empowered, monied classes wished to represent themselves. The various issues of the capitalist era (embracing industrialism or rejecting it, embracing the historical past or denying it, etc.) are played out in the architecture of the Eighteenth and Nineteenth Centuries with ferocious intensity.

The Bauhaus is often seen as a break with this historical debate. Yet the architecture of the Bauhaus era, which defiantly embraced materialism, progressivism, and anti-historicism, can, in its intention to convey a polemic, also be seen as a culmination of this dialogue.

The work of Berke and McWhorter in many ways takes up where the Utopian impulses of the Bauhaus era ended. Their work does not mock the Utopian era as did so much "post-modernism." (This Oedipal struggle is no longer present in the architects of their generation.) Nor, significantly, does it sink into unconscious, reductivist "simulation" of the effects of the historical or the vernacular as did much architecture of the last decade.

Even though their work addresses the same kind of "enlightened elite" as did the experimentalist movements at the beginning of this century, a very different set of concerns is articulated for this same subclass at the century's end. First, their work is almost invisible as "architecture," except to the practiced eye. Rather than aggrandize, it makes invisible. Rather than provoke, it only lets the initiated in on its agenda. Here then we have an architecture for an intelligentsia that is no longer willing to challenge mass culture or deterministic power, but rather wants to hide its agenda from them. Here we have an architecture for a class that does not want to announce its own empowerment or prestige, but wants to blend in banally (the architectural equiva-

lent of William Burroughs' banker's suit).

Subtly and ideologically rather than as a simple visual strategy, this architecture then advances the program of the decentering of culture and power first proposed by Derridean thought a quarter-century ago. Here, cultural power recamps into a state of self-reflection and existential relativism. The possession of power no longer enables a bold or decisive challenge to the cultural status quo. Nor does power here any longer look to history for affirmation or substantiation. Rather, history becomes a subject for study and reflection; how history is defined itself becomes transformed. For Berke and McWhorter, history is no longer predicated on the "great themes" of western culture (as it still is in Moore or Tigerman, for example), but rather by a kind of Annaliste spirit, as a history of the everyday.

The everyday ... whether or not architecture itself can break its ideological shackles, thoughts in architecture can certainly try. I would propose to connect the work of Berke and McWhorter to a kind of pop American wonder in the everyday. This is a sensibility that has found expression in our era more in literature than in architecture: it ranges from transcendentalist (Emerson) to Zen (Cage); it finds wonder in a Greyhound bus station (Allen Ginsberg) or dawn on the deserted streets of Gentilly (Walker Percy).

Project: Halley Studio
Columbia County, New York

Standard door fixtures, typical (left)

View from southwest of studio and porch building

Detail of studio and porch building

Typical wall sections (right)

⊕ TOP PLATE

⊕ 11'-11½"
TOP PLATE of
2x4 FRAMING

⊕ 9'-10"
2nd FLOOR
DECKING

BATT INSUL
2x10 FL. JOISTS

2'-1½"

BATT INSUL

2x6 FRAMING

2x4 FRAMING

A9 2

3/4"

⅛"

Woo

SC

3 A9

SC
OI
3/4"
2x4
2x4
2x4
W/
DON
BT
CONC
BUI
ST

⊕ 0'-0"
CONC. SLAB
⊕ -0'-4"
FIN. GRADE

4" CONC. SLAB

⊕ -4'-8"
TOP of CONC. FOOTING

32 x 12 CONT. CONC. FOOTING

1 SECTION at PORCH
A.9   1" = 1'-0"

A9
5/8
3/
3/4
5/8
DOI
EX

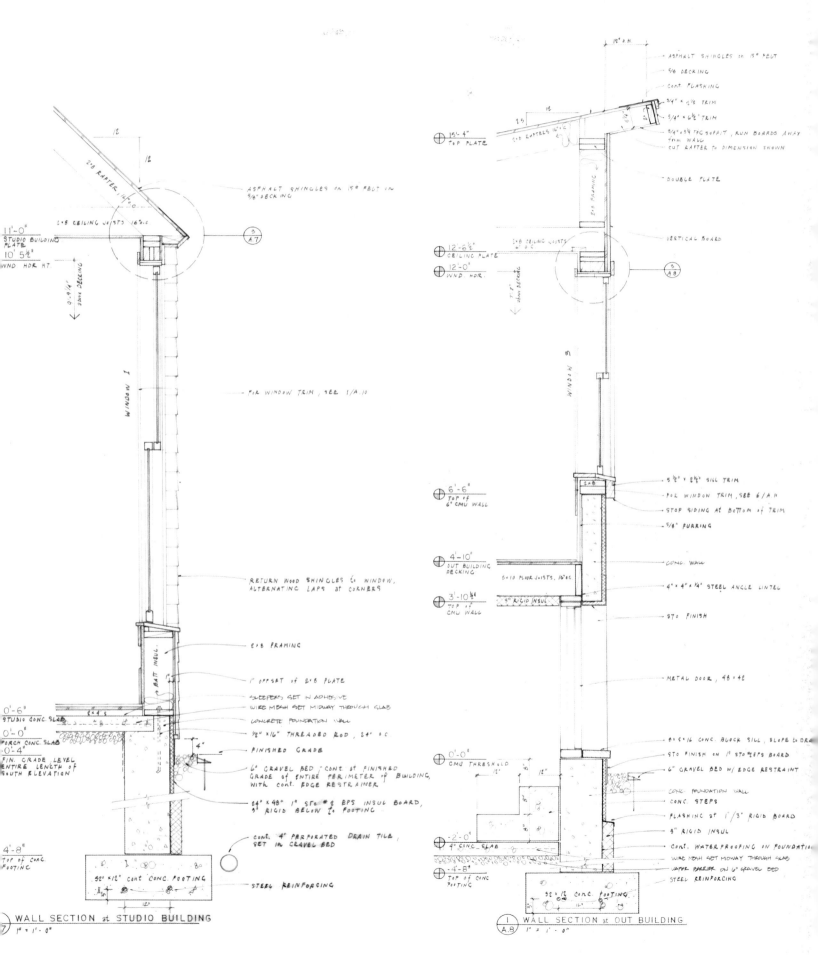

ASPHALT SHINGLES on 15# FELT in
5/8" DECKING

2×8 CEILING JOISTS 16"o.c.

11'-0"
STUDIO BUILDING
PLATE

10' 5½"
WND HDR. HT.

FOR WINDOW TRIM, SEE 1/A.10

RETURN WOOD SHINGLES to WINDOW,
ALTERNATING LAPS at CORNERS

2×8 FRAMING

1" OFFSET of 2×8 PLATE

SLEEPERS SET IN ADHESIVE

WIRE MESH SET MIDWAY THROUGH SLAB

0'-6"
STUDIO CONC. SLAB

0'-0"
PORCH CONC. SLAB

-0'-4"
FIN. GRADE LEVEL
ENTIRE LENGTH of
SOUTH ELEVATION

CONCRETE FOUNDATION WALL

½" ×16" THREADED ROD, 24" O.C.

FINISHED GRADE

6" GRAVEL BED, CONT. at FINISHED
GRADE of ENTIRE PERIMETER of BUILDING,
WITH CONT. EDGE RESTRAINER

24" × 48" 1" STO #2 EPS INSUL BOARD,
5" RIGID BELOW to FOOTING

CONT. 4" PERFORATED DRAIN TILE,
SET IN GRAVEL BED

4'-8"
TOP of CONC.
FOOTING

32"×12" CONT. CONC. FOOTING

STEEL REINFORCING

WALL SECTION at STUDIO BUILDING
7
A.7
1" = 1'-0"

12" O.H.

ASPHALT SHINGLES on 15# FELT

5/8" DECKING

CONT. FLASHING

3/4" × 6½" TRIM

5/4" × 6½" TRIM

3/4" × 3¾" TOC SOFFIT, RUN BOARDS AWAY
FROM WALL
CUT RAFTER to DIMENSION SHOWN

2×8 RAFTERS 16"o.c.

13'-4"
TOP PLATE

DOUBLE PLATE

VERTICAL BOARD

2×8 CEILING JOISTS
16"O.C.

12'-6½"
CEILING PLATE

12'-0"
WND. HDR.

WINDOW 3

5½" × 2½" SILL TRIM

FOR WINDOW TRIM, SEE 6/A.11

STOP SIDING at BOTTOM of TRIM

5/8" FURRING

6'-6"
TOP of
6" CMU WALL

CONC. WALL

4'-10"
OUT BUILDING
DECKING

2×10 FLOOR JOISTS, 16"o.c.

4" × 4" × ¼" STEEL ANGLE LINTEL

3'-10¼"
TOP of
CMU WALL

5" RIGID INSUL.

STO FINISH

METAL DOOR, 48×48

8"×8"×16" CONC. BLOCK SILL, SLOPE to DRAIN

0'-0"
CMU THRESHOLD

STO FINISH on 1" STO #2 EPS BOARD

6" GRAVEL BED W/ EDGE RESTRAINT

CONC. FOUNDATION WALL

CONC. STEPS

FLASHING at 1"/3" RIGID BOARD

3" RIGID INSUL

CONC. WATERPROOFING on FOUNDATION

WIRE MESH SET MIDWAY THROUGH SLAB

VAPOR BARRIER on 6" GRAVEL BED

STEEL REINFORCING

-2'-0"
4" CONC. SLAB

-4'-8"
TOP of CONC
FOOTING

32×12 CONC. FOOTING

WALL SECTION at OUT BUILDING
1
A.8
1" = 1'-0"

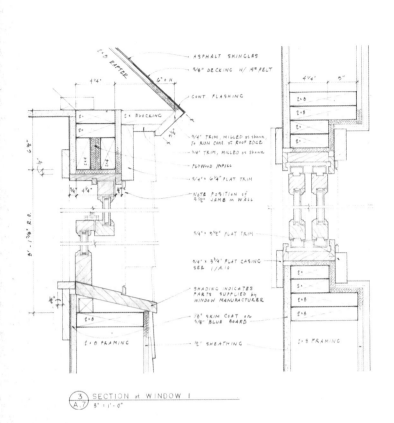

ASPHALT SHINGLES

3/8" DECKING w/ 15# FELT

CONT FLASHING

3/4" TRIM, MILLED as shown, to RUN CONT at ROOF EDGE

3/4" TRIM, MILLED as shown

PLYWOOD INFILL

5/4 x 6 1/4" FLAT TRIM

NOTE POSITION of 5 1/2" JAMB in WALL

5/4 x 3 1/2" FLAT TRIM

3/4 x 3 3/4" FLAT CASING SEE 1/A.10

SHADING INDICATES PARTS SUPPLIED by WINDOW MANUFACTURER

1/8" SKIM COAT on 5/8" BLUE BOARD

1/2" SHEATHING

③ SECTION at WINDOW 1
A.7   3" = 1'-0"

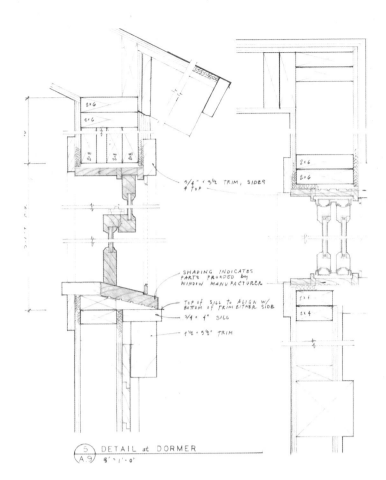

5/4" x 3 1/2" TRIM, SIDES & TOP

SHADING INDICATES PARTS PROVIDED by WINDOW MANUFACTURER

TOP of SILL to ALIGN w/ BOTTOM of TRIM EITHER SIDE

3/4 x 4" SILL

1 1/2 x 3 1/2" TRIM

⑤ DETAIL at DORMER
A.9   3" = 1'-0"

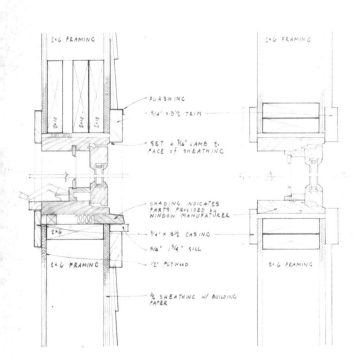

2 x 6 FRAMING

FLASHING

5/4 x 3 1/2" TRIM

SET 6 1/8" JAMB to FACE of SHEATHING

SHADING INDICATES PARTS PROVIDED by WINDOW MANUFACTURER

3/4 x 3 1/2 CASING

3/4 x 1 3/4" SILL

1/2" PLYWOOD

1/2" SHEATHING W/ BUILDING PAPER

④ DETAIL at WINDOW 2
A.9   3" = 1'-0"

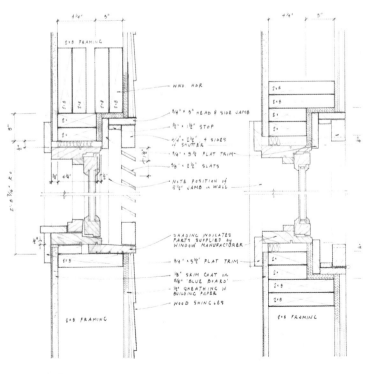

WND HDR

3/4" x 3" HEAD & SIDE JAMB

1/2" x 1 1/2" STOP

5/4 x 2 1/2" 4 SIDES of SHUTTER

3/4 x 3 1/2" FLAT TRIM

5/8 x 2 1/2" SLATS

NOTE POSITION of 5 1/2" JAMB in WALL

SHADING INDICATES PARTS SUPPLIED by WINDOW MANUFACTURER

3/4 x 3 1/2" FLAT TRIM

1/8" SKIM COAT on 5/8" BLUE BOARD

1/2" SHEATHING W BUILDING PAPER

WOOD SHINGLES

④ SECTION at WINDOW 5, 5A
A.7   3" = 1'-0"

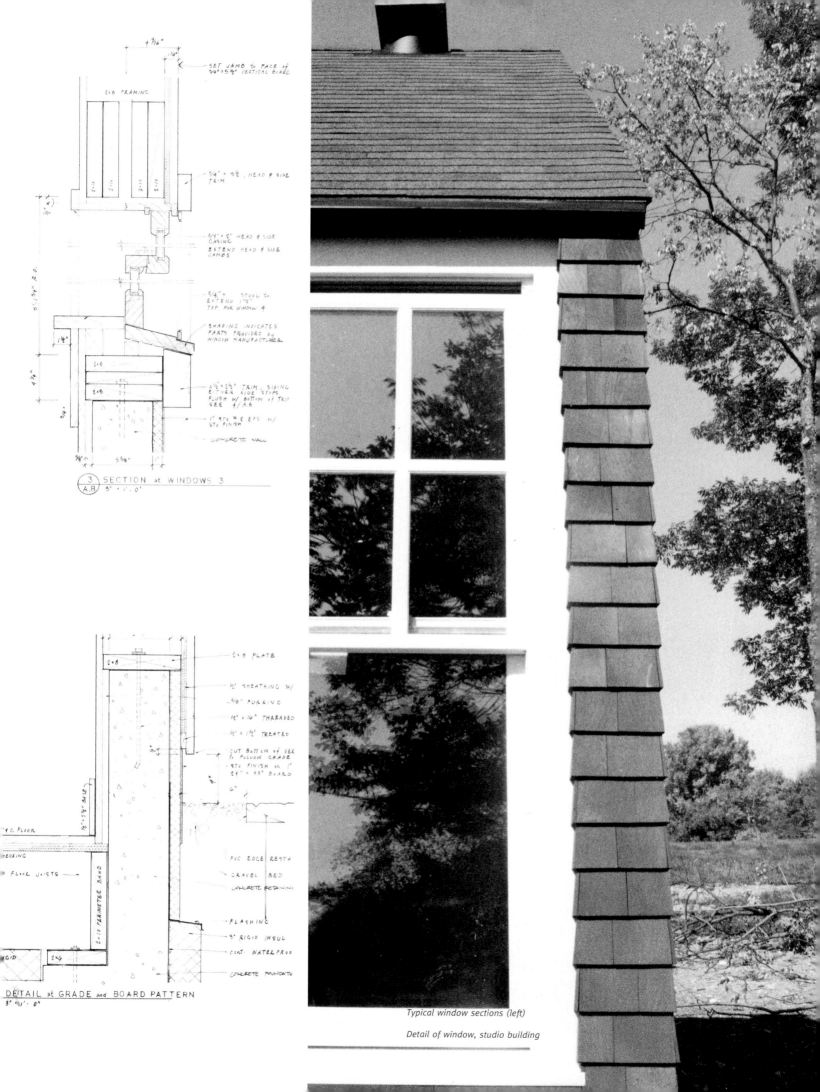

4 9/16"

1 1/4"

SET JAMB to FACE of
3/4" × 5 1/4" VERTICAL BOARD

2 × 8 FRAMING

5/4" × 5 1/2", HEAD & SIDE
TRIM

3/4" × 2" HEAD & SIDE
CASING
EXTEND HEAD & SIDE
JAMBS

5/4" × STOOL TO
EXTEND 1 1/2"
TYP FOR WINDOW 4

SHADING INDICATES
PARTS PROVIDED by
WINDOW MANUFACTURER

5 1/2" × 5 3/4" R.O.

5/4" × 5 1/2" TRIM, SIDING
EITHER SIDE STOPS
FLUSH W/ BOTTOM OF TRIM
SEE 4/A.8

1" STO & EPS W/
STO FINISH

CONCRETE WALL

3/8" 5 5/8" 1"

(3) SECTION at WINDOWS 3
A.8   3" = 1'-0"

2 × 8 PLATE

1/2" SHEATHING W/
5/8" FURRING

1/2" × 16" THREADED

1/2" × 1 1/2" TREATED

CUT BOTTOM of VER
to FOLLOW GRADE

STO FINISH on 1"
24" × 48" BOARD

PVC EDGE RESTR

GRAVEL BED

CONCRETE RETAINING

FLASHING

3" RIGID INSUL

CONT WATERPROO

CONCRETE FOUNDATI

C. FLOOR

DECKING

FLOOR JOISTS

2 × 10 PERIMETER BAND

RIGID   2 × 6

DETAIL at GRADE and BOARD PATTERN
3" = 1'-0"

Typical window sections (left)

Detail of window, studio building

Halley/Stewart Studio
Columbia County, New York

A New York City artist and his family have a week-end house in Columbia County, New York. The house is small, dates from the middle nineteenth century, and while not beautiful, has a certain integrity. However, it does not satisfy the needs of the artist and his family. Rather than add to the house directly, we decided to build another structure containing the spatial and functional components lacking in the main house.

The Halley/Stewart Studio is three building forms assembled on a hillside. The forms are evocative of, though not directly derivative of, the local rural vernacular. Each building form is intended to have a visual autonomy expressive of its distinct programmatic contents. The Studio Building, a single space structure, faces a view of the Berkshire Mountains. The Porch Building aligns itself with a stone wall that contains the meadow beyond. It is divided vertically into a common porch below and a children's attic above. The Out Building is divided horizontally into three chambers: a foyer, a bath, and a study. A wide staircase which follows the rise of the land is the spine connecting the three building forms internally.

The site for the studio was carefully selected. From the Main House, one moves past a garden shed and follows an existing row of trees toward a sloping grassy clearing to the Studio. The stone wall perpendicular to the slope defines the far edge of the site. There are three entrances to the composite structure: one directly into the Studio and another, (to ensure the artist's privacy), a half a level up off a small court created by the three masses, into the Out Building. The Porch Building opens to a sitting area defined by the stone wall and beyond to the meadow.

Deborah Berke

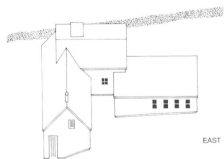

EAST

Interior of studio building

East elevation, axonometric (right)

167

Margaret Helfand and Marti Cowan

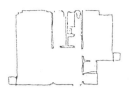

Reflection
Paola Iacucci

Reflection
Reflection becomes the logic of form and space.

The functional choice of materials

                and their inherent structure
        establish the essential.

Each element is isolated,

              examined and reduced
    to a fundamental form.

        Reflection becomes a method of building;
a way of casting form, of envisioning detail.

The continuity of reflection
        between constructed elements and space,

the sequence of echoes of materials

            in various tectonic states
creates a perceived rhythm,

        and intensity.

The logic of construction

            gives clarity and life
to the poetic idea of reflection,
        privileging the eye in glass fields,

mirrors and fleeting images of light.

The logic of duality in which reflection lives,
is grounded in an encounter

          of the two base geometries;

that of the existing enclosure,
      and that of the new forms within.

A spirit of Reflection inhabits this Apartment: space – projected, dislocated, extended; form – rotated, folded, and inverted; image – cast, mirrored, and illuminated in light. Born in the Architects, methods of envisioning form, transcribed into the materials of building, and transmitted through light, this spirit shapes one's experience.

The logic of duality in which reflection lives is established first as a way of determining space. We encounter the two base geometries – one that follows the existing walls, and that of the new architecture. In plan they are two figures that shift on a slight angle of rotation. Every element built anew at once follows this second orientation, and reflects itself in the existing plan. Elements fluctuate between the two forces. The central table of the study is made of two square planes of glass shifted to lock within the dual geometries inscribed on the ground below.

Reflection continues as a way of making form, of articulating the base geometry and accommodating program, through detail; in the way two folded steel plates, geometric inversions of one another, interlock and sustain the four mirror-image wooden panels of the dining table. This sort of elemental geometric connection between pieces clearly establishes a place for dining, study, and rest through the essential construction of table, chair, and bed.

Reflexive geometric operations, and the manner in which form comes together to determine objects, set up a logic of materials and connections – metal, wood, and glass. One notes the way the firm mellow surface of the purple cherry blocks acts to connect large fragile glass panels to the rigid metal frame. The glass is exposed or "suspended" in the frame, with simple wooden blocks transferring the weight of the transparent panels to the heavy, moving metal frame – light to glass, glass to wood, wood to metal, metal to motion.

Reflection lives in the material and light of these objects. The glass panels, six 5' x 9' *doors*, move to define the various zones one inhabits within the house. As the screens move, light is transmitted or alternately refracted by the dychronic surfaces of glass. These surfaces like parts of a giant moving lantern seem to produce or create light. Composed of several layers of hand-blown iridescent, translucent, and ribbed glass, this complex lens reflects and transmits various shades of light throughout the day and night. From pale greens to vivid magentas, the colors cast the space in an ever-changing opalescent palette.

Imbedded within this two-dimensional colored, crystalline matrix, one begins to trace and retrace pale shapes and lines searching to decipher a pattern. While the space one inhabits is literally or perspectively reflected in the surface of the glass panels, it is also figuratively reflected or represented by the patterns of colored glass, which evoke the plan and elevation of the surrounding space. The Architects have imbedded themselves and their process in the material; plane geometry projects to elevation, three-dimensional form condenses to pure pattern, and ideas dissolve in the material of light.

One discovers a continuous counterpoint; an echo between elements which construct, with extreme clarity of material and tectonic logic, the architecture which inhabits the house – echoing the vertical to the horizontal planes in the subtle tilting of surface. Through this echo, the physical geometry and color of materials, their density and quality of surface, become the primary force shaping space.

This is a work thought through the logic of building; from the simple care and pleasure of assembling form, to the connections between forms and the beauty of material.

Project: Adlersberg Apartment, New York City

Plan studies (left)

Detail of frosted glass door

Detail of brushed metal shelf

Exploded plan drawing (right)
ink on mylar

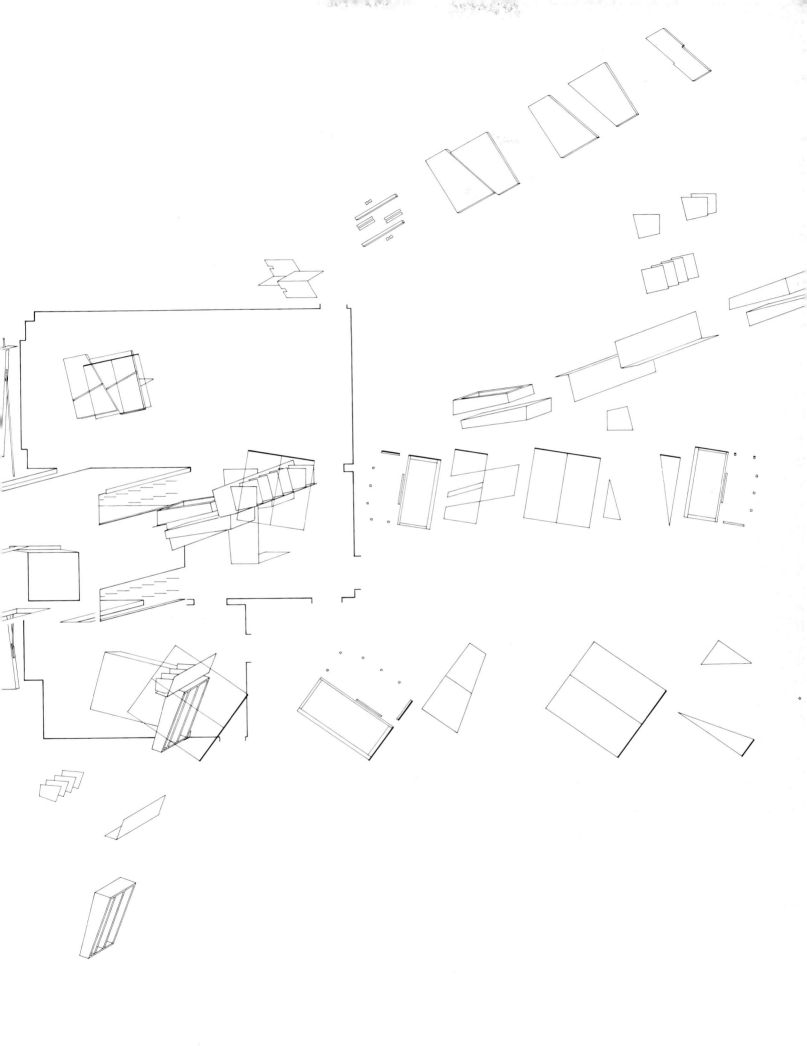

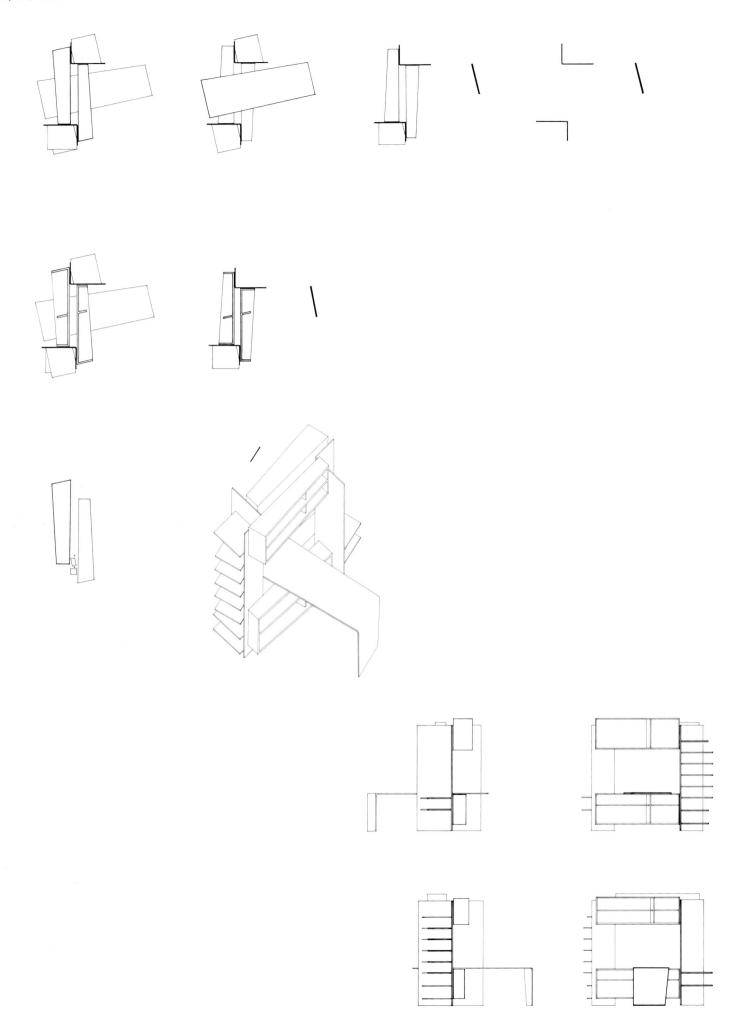

Plan, elevation and axonometric drawing of office unit (far left)
ink on mylar

Plan and elevation of side chair series (left)
ink on mylar

Detail of cherrywood dining table

Bachelor's Apartment
New York, New York

Site

One-bedroom apartment within a historic Art Deco building on Riverside Drive in Manhattan.

Program

Accommodate the Owner's specific requirements for home entertainment, working, and exercising in addition to the usual kitchen, bath, and bedroom needs.

Issues

While the Owner was enthusiastic about commissioning an adventurous design solution, he preferred to make a minimum of change to the existing shell of the apartment. Also, realizing that he may not remain in this space for a long term, it made sense to create a setting which could be transported.

Concept

The apartment is divided into four quadrants for living, dining, study, and kitchen/bath plus an adjacent fifth area for exercising, sleeping, and dressing. The kitchen/bath quadrant becomes the central core with two large openings on each face which serve both as doors and windows allowing natural light to penetrate to the interior. The openings are covered by rolling translucent panels constructed of three layers of different types of glass, each pattern based on the floor plan of the adjacent quadrant. The function of each quadrant is accommodated by independent elements constructed of woods, steel, and glass following a geometry which interrelates them.

Margaret Helfand, Marti Cowan

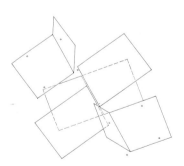

Detail of furniture and door

Exploded axonometric of dining chair (right)

HELFAND, Margaret

COWAN, Marti

Patricia and John Patkau

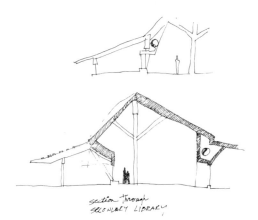

section through
SECONDARY LIBRARY

Tecto-Totemic Form: A Note on Patkau Associates
Kenneth Frampton

John and Patricia Patkau are two young Canadian architects whose achievements are all the more refreshing because of their discreetly tectonic character. The quality of this work suggests, once again, that we would do well to turn our attention to the periphery, if we wish to find our way back to more measured and sensitive forms of architectural practice. It is one of the paradoxes of the present that while the fashionable seems to be ever poised on the brink of a precipitous descent into self-indulgent artistry, the general level of architectural production grows more delicate and differentiated. One may claim that contemporary architecture has never been more vital even if this rigor is largely displayed in marginal, moderately scaled works. As one might expect, such work tends to be removed from the current modernist versus historicist debate: the reductio ad absurdum of neo avant garde versus neo nostalgic. Between these equally demagogic alternatives there still remains the possibility of continuing with the century-old tradition of modernity and the significance of the Patkau practice lies in its critical cultivation of this tradition at its best.

Nothing is a more striking demonstration of this tradition than the complex timber framework and sweeping roofs of the Seabird Island School, recently completed in Agassiz, British Columbia. The school building, like Patkau's earlier work, artfully creates an implicit urban space where none exists. However, the real power of the project derives from the remote building context and culture, the severity of the environment, and a particular building technology – from the simple habits of a small agricultural village; the traditions of an autochthonous Indian population; the coastal mountains of the forbidding, awe-inspiring Northwest; and the native form of timber-shingled shell construction.

Through these forces, the Seabird Island School infuses the tropes of modernity in Patkau's earlier work with a new energy, a force that derives from the urgency of the situation as well as from the directness of the client and the technical capacity of the society. Thus the most decisive point of departure is the base material itself, namely wood and the framing thereof, in relation to the resources of a self-build client for whom a framing model had to be made in order to complement the working drawings. All this surely reveals once again the tectonic commitment of the architects and their capacity to express themselves through revealed material and expressive joint. This is made most dramatically manifest in the suspension of a glulam timber superstructure over a reinforced concrete grade-beam and pile foundation. The fact that cylindrical piles rise up in places to form stub columns of varying heights only serves to emphasize the plastic dynamism of the overall fabric, its sense of being poised like a cat's cradle over an extended earthwork.

The totemic, mythic elements of the project emerge here at a more rooted level, where they express themselves in the form of a Semperian roof work, rising up as an alpine metaphor in response to the mountainous backdrop and then tapering out, in mid-distant silhouette so as to evoke by analogy the animistic imagery of the Pacific Northwest and to suggest, albeit discreetly, the great totemic houses of a lost oceanic culture. The roof work develops its full power along the internal spine of the building, running across the central common areas as a series of V-trusses and stacked, tree-like columns, soaring up into the darkness of the roof, occasionally pierced by top light. This mythic house space is clustered like an elongated labyrinth about a literal totem pole that stands like a sentinel over the entrance hall and reception desk.

Climatologically and socially the plan is laid out as a simple, rational organization, with all nine classrooms facing southwest towards the village green and its sparse surrounding settlement, while the back of the mammoth, housing the gymnasium, stands as a windowless wall, against the force of the northerly winds. Two reading rooms in the form of womb-like cylindrical furnishings are located left and right of the central axis serving the elementary and secondary wings of the school, while the prow of the kindergarten breaks out towards a play terrace. This sets itself forth as an alternative blaze of color in the form of new life, running due south into the summer sun under the most iconographically Pacific of all the large roofs from which the school is composed.

Under the Semperian roof work runs the woven wand of the spaces and teaching gardens. This straight line promenade terminates in the kindergarten at one end and in drying racks at the other, while the whole covered causeway is modulated by an inclined pergola built out of thin, undressed logs. This pergola cum brise soleil has its modular beat syncopated by the random application of clustered timber spears that both evoke and invite a half forgotten, yet still unforeseen history; a history of a modern normative life and culture that has yet to be fully experienced in the Pacific Northwest. This last is perhaps the most complex metaphor of all, for as in Aalto's Finnish Pavilion of 1937, it speaks of the fragile beauty of the forest and serves to remind us that we, in our turn, will stand or fall with its already threatened survival.

Project: Seabird Island School
Agaissiz, British Columbia

Sketch, section through secondary library (left)

Project construction

Project construction

Framing models, various views (right)
bass wood

*Framing model, detail
bass wood*

Project construction (right)

View of roofscape and the Coastal Range

Seabird Island School
Agassiz, British Columbia

Site

The Seabird Island Reserve is located on a large island of delta land in the Fraser River, approximately 120 kilometers east of Vancouver. Mountains of the Coastal Range of British Columbia tower over the river valley on all sides. The interior of the island consists of large open fields used for agricultural purposes. Individual houses ring the lightly wooded perimeter. Located at the down-stream end of the island, the community buildings are loosely organized around a grassed square in an incipient "U"-shaped configuration, open to the north.

Design

To strengthen and further define the emerging structure and character of the community center, the school was sited along the open northern edge of the existing grassed square. By making the school an integral part of the village common space, interaction between the school and the community is clearly encouraged. At the same time, the extreme winter winds which are funneled between the mountains down the river valley from the north are now mediated by the large mass of the school, allowing a more favorable microclimate to develop on the southern, community side of the school. Within this protected zone, outdoor play areas, teaching gardens, and other community facilities extend from the school edge to the village green. In mediating between the extreme winter from the north and the favorable exposure toward the village green on the south, the mass and scale of the school undergo a transformation. On the north, large sculptural volumes, vaguely zoomorphic in character, are closed, diverting the winds much like the mountains which surround the site. To the south the scale is small, the building open under generous eaves. A complex, more tectonic quality not present in the sculptural forms of the north is introduced through the use of a variety of struts, beams, and trellises which animate this edge, suggesting the potential richness of community life.

Construction

Heavy timber post and beam construction is the traditional building technique of the Indians of the Pacific Northwest. The structure of the Seabird Island School, a modern, "engineered" form of this technique, is comprised of glulam columns and beams with steel connections on a reinforced concrete grade-beam and pile foundation. (As much of this structure is to be erected by members of the band, who are experienced in large-scale construction methods, a detailed framing model was made to supplement conventional construction documents.) Walls and roofs are clad in cedar shingles, the traditional cladding material of the region. As they weather, these shingles will shade naturally, from a soft silver-grey to a deep red-brown depending upon orientation and exposure. In this way the sculptural volumes of the north will be enriched and subtly exaggerated. Under the broad eaves to the south and east, walls are clad in translucent white-stained plywood panels to increase luminosity and provide a contrast to the weathered character of the north much as the pearly interior of an oyster shell contrasts with the rugged grey tones of its exterior.

John and Patricia Patkau

PATKAU, Patricia

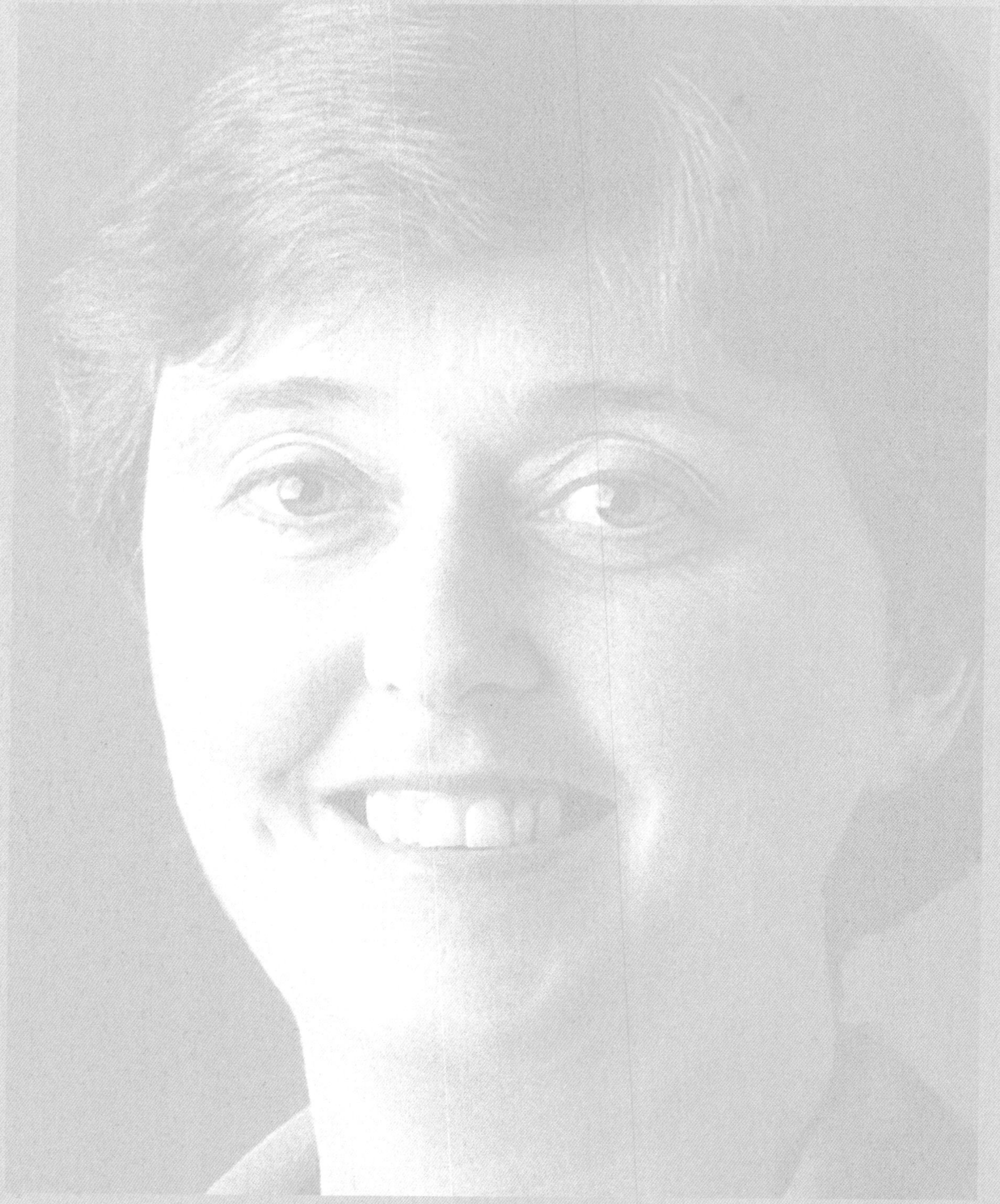

Thomas Leeser

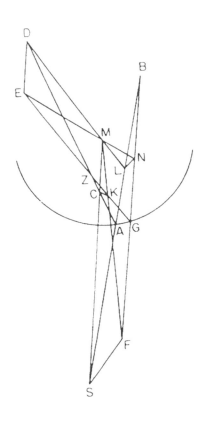

Twisting Strings
Hani Rashid

Doubt Double, dub, dubbing, dupe, duplicate, duplicity, duplex.

This house, set into a hillside, is deliberately precarious and unhinged. A structure that seems to be without a foundation, held tenuously by its own density and weight. Unlike the Villa Maleparte this house defies not the sea or the winds; rather it defies season. It purposely lingers in the woods as if it was itself a storm ready to break, or some strange creature about to take flight on the slightest impulse.

The twins that will occupy this house need to live as they always have, attached and yet autonomous, within and out of sight of each other. This then is the place for their own delirium. This is a house that accommodates the requisites of absence, avoidance, and disappearance. A double inhabitation contorted and intertwined, allowing for avoidance, cancellation, and the removal of anticipation.

The rooms, furnishings, appliances, fixtures, all meld together within these inclined walls to form cavernous entrails and creases. These residue spaces contain one another as if struggling to delete any sign of the surrounding territory and the ominous horizon-line (it too is a nuisance). Only occasional glimpses from within the structure evoke a sense of where this strange vessel is stationed, amidst and simultaneously outside of *nature*.

Yet the twins dislike nature for it resembles their own perplexing state of being. Each other's presence is a constant reminder of the inflictions of nature and its own reconcilability. This then is a place that not only shelters the twins from the natural but also from each other's natures. Here in these twisted rooms a *natural* amnesia is induced where two divergent paths eventually cancel each other out. Here an amnesiac delirium takes hold, where the distorted exterior is forever reconciled with the autonomous interior, revealing both the presence and absence of the other.

This architecture is ultimately an excerpted meander through the woods, a brief respite from the trail, where instead of a clearing, an obstruction in defiance of the picturesque is found. This taut convoluted architecture is bound to its own objecthood as if it were a skin that has undergone numerous reconstructions and foreign insertions. It is a landscape derived not from view control and perfection but rather from some less tangible and indiscreet technocratic origins. The seamless surfaces that enfold this work seem to be themselves delineating the encircling electromagnetic fields of the fax modems, computer terminals, and fleeting images of media that will relentlessly invade its interior and describe its internal programs and utility.

This architecture acknowledges that the twins of nature and technology today are intrinsically and problematically intertwined, for technology's onslaught affects our very notion of what constitutes nature while technology itself is a new *nature*.

Of Zweifalt and Doubts
Thomas Leeser

The Architectural League of New York Emerging Voices 1993
Lecture: Thomas Leeser, March 25, 1993

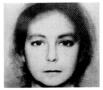

L: **Nancy Burson, *Androgyny* (six men and six women) Simulated photograph**
R: **(same, but mirrored)**

March 11, 1993, *The New York Times* Obituaries: London, March 11 (Reuters):
"Jennifer Gibbons, one of Britain's so-called Silent Twins, died on Tuesday. She was 29. No cause of death has been established. Miss Gibbons fell ill just hours after she and her sister, June, left Broadmoor hospital, where they had spent 11 years after a bizarre spree of arson, drug taking and burglary at their home in Wales. The twins, described by doctors as 'elective mutes,' had made a pact of silence at an early age and communicated with each other in an incomprehensible babble. At school they refused to read or write and retreated into their own world. After their arrest it emerged that they were prolific and secret writers who had taught themselves creative writing. In Broadmoor, the two kept obsessive diaries in tiny print that revealed a claustrophobic love-hate relationship. They were found to be schizophrenic."

Twins are the occupants as well as the program for this project I am going to show tonight. Twin brothers, an eye and a brain surgeon, whose twinning can be described as a mirroring or reflective duplication. The reflection, the mirror image, splits what it doubles, by adding itself to it. Because of the possibility of mirroring or reflective duplication, division must already be inherent or inscribed in that which is being reflected. This mirroring takes place not *through* a mirror, but within the Twins themselves as a mirrored image *in front of*, rather than *behind*, *the mirror*.[1] In other words, the condition of Twins is a condition of mirroring in *real*, rather than in *virtual* space. We know, for example, that in identical twins typically one twin is right handed, while the other one is left handed, or that the pattern of hair twists into a right-turning spiral, while that of the other's is turning to the left. Twinning, like mirroring, is therefore also a condition of inversion. Inversion not so much as the classical idea of opposites, but rather as the idea of opposing *difference*. The condition of Twins does not constitute a dialectic condition of "two-ness" or merely of *self and other*, but rather a simultaneous condition of self *within* the other, as well as the other within oneself. Twinning therefore always implies a third, an intermediate, or intersexual body. (I am using the term intersexual quite loosely not so much in its more precise meaning as "between the sexes or third sex," but rather implicitly as *outside* one's own sex or body.) In other words, a Twin is looking at his twinned body *from without*, therefore from the position of the Other,

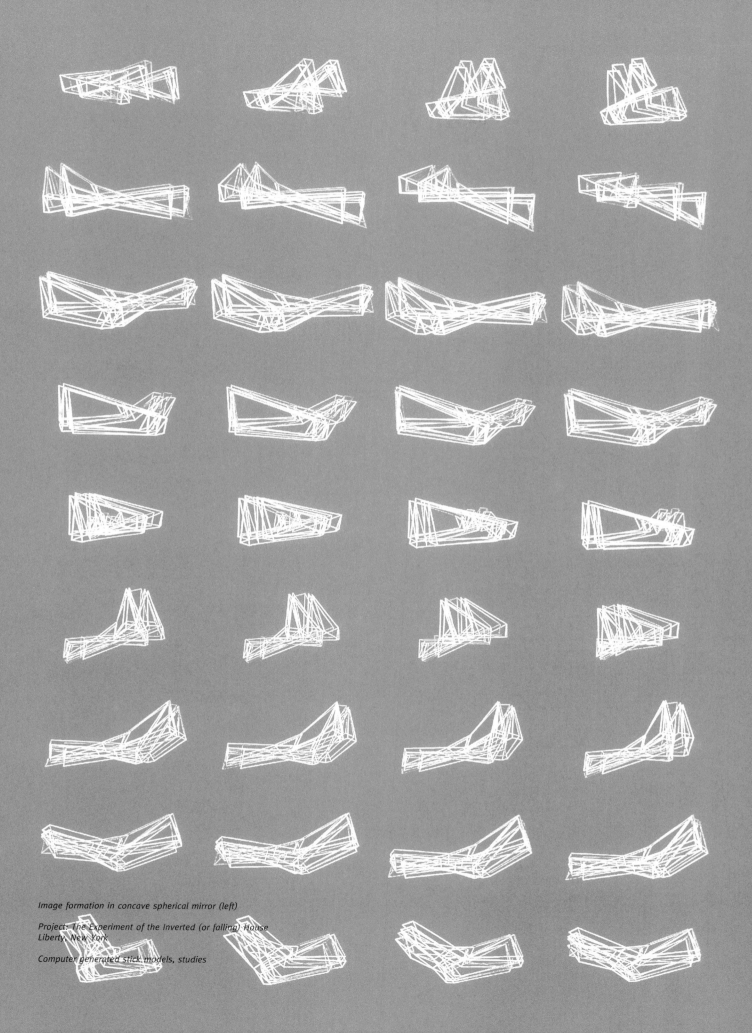

Image formation in concave spherical mirror (left)

Project: The Experiment of the Inverted (or falling) House
Liberty, New York

Computer generated stick models, studies

which places him or herself in a *simultaneous* condition of "Self" and "Other." This condition of *undecidable relationships* constructs a triangle of an "indeterminable geometry," which leads us into the question of geometry for one, as well as toward the question of simultaneous experience of the real and the imagined.[2]

L: **advance to black**
R: **Richard Torchia, *Not to Be Reproduced*, 1983; 11x17, Color Xerox, reproduced from René Magritte, *La reproduction interdite*, 1937, Oil on canvas**

The superposition of the *mirror-body* (the "Self") over the *mirrored body* (the "Other") allows for this blurring of the distinction of classical dialectic and questions the established duality of Self and Other. Parallel to the problem of twinning one has to look at the notion of *the double* and duplicity. The structure of duplicity, which doubles the relationship between the simple and its simulacra (or double), *always* refers to the other, its origin (or simple). In film for example, the double is deliberately assuming the role of an-other actor, who is made up to resemble, and whose acting is seamlessly cut into the action of the (other or) main actor. "Double" of course can also mean just *more* of something, to duplicate to make *an-other* copy.

L: **Anton Bragalia, *Double Print*, 1911**
R: **same**

The multiple, or multiplicity, implies an unspecified number of "copies" or "doubles." While the double refers to a duplication of an originating condition, the multiple is *without* any necessary reference to its origin. We could be looking at two of an unspecifiable number of multiples, without any knowledge, or even the possibility or need of the idea of origin. This non-hierarchical relationship - or *event*, as I would like to call it - again allows for the possibility of a *third determination, the undecidable.* There is no longer the duality of "yes vs. no" or "origin vs. its reproduction," but the "maybe" of the simulacrum or copy *without* an origin or ultimate referent.

Therefore, to summarize, if the double refers to an *originary duplication,* a *mold* or *model*, then the multiple refers to the *"event" of being multiplied*

without origin, and twinning is *indeterminable* inasmuch as it is "simultaneously referring to something it is not," namely being the origin and its double at the same time; one could say it consists out of *two* (mirrored or doubled) origins.

L: **Giulio Bragalia, *Image in Motion*, 1913**
R: **same**

Now, I *do not* want to pose these concepts as *clearly distinct* strategies, separate from each other, or *not even separable* from each other, but *rather* as a complex system of interweaving similarities and (dis)continuities, or "appearances reflexively *bent* upon themselves."[3] In other words, it is *not* the jarring and *fragmented* discontinuity of a well-known and overused formal *collision* of deconstructivism, but *rather* the search for this strategy of bending back onto itself or, one could say, a *blending together* or *blurring* of boundaries of similarity *within simultaneous events* through the employment of the concept of *continuous* surfaces.

L: **Giulio Bragalia, *The Slap*, 1913**
R: **same**

This idea of blurring allows us to understand the relationship between events as a complex system of flexible, continuous structures with a fluid connectivity among them as a more complex and multifaceted understanding or reading of cultural, urban, technological, and programmatic relationships, and *more importantly*, with the possibility for the construction of a *new* condition of *misreading*, a possibility for a kind of *deliberate accident.* A double-exposed photograph, where one seeks to separate one image from the other by tracing along the edges of one image, only to find that one has slipped unnoticed into the outline of the other image, is an example of a space folding back onto itself and producing just such an "accident" of *programmatic discontinuity* through a *spatial continuity* of a smooth, continuous turning inside out of surface and space.

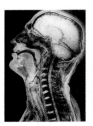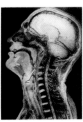

L: **Sectional Anatomy, Color Xerox, 1989**
R: **same**

Multiple or *double exposures, blurred* and *out-of-focus* images are phenomena usually associated with photography and certain textual qualities of that medium (like the lucidity of the silver particles within the emulsion), but can in fact be seen as the very image of a non-hierarchical blending of multiple parallel structures into a complex set of (dis)continuities. Whether the constantly rewritten choreography of self similar, doubled, and mirrored events of our daily lives that eventually amass to our social structures, or the constant influx of interrelated economic, cultural, technological, and social discontinuous currents, their relationship to each other *is that* of such an impossibly complex intertwined and inseparable *space of continuity*. In the geometry of space, the boundaries between the three-dimensional object (with its interiority) and the two-dimensional surface (with its exteriority) may be precisely the territory of that *undecidable relationship* - this "indeterminable geometry" I spoke of earlier. If one imagines a separation of that which defines the volume of an object, its geometric structure, from that which defines its surface, its planar structure, or its skin, and understands them as two physically *separate* elements *discontinuous* from each other, nonetheless *entirely dependent on* each other, therefore in a *relationship of continuity to* each other, one begins to liquefy and blur the boundaries of two-dimensional surface and three-dimensional space.

L: **W.W.I Battleship**
          (left half of double wide image)
R: **W.W.I Battleship**
          (right half of double wide image)

One such example might be the dazzle paintings found on World War I battleships, executed not for the purpose of total invisibility, but rather for the conspicuous and deliberate overlay of misleading figurative patterns, which were designed to *be* visible as new and indeterminable objects, completely re-configuring the geometrical properties of the battleship itself. The painted surface geometry assumed its own three-dimensional geometry by simultaneously adhering to the actual geometry of the ship itself.

I will show you later on how some of these ideas of surface, particularly of continuous surface and its relationship to three-dimensional volumetric geometry, are being explored, but let me now go to the question of geometry itself.

L: Diagram: *Image formation in concave spherical mirror*

R: **First stick model, Wood, 1991**

Medieval scholars of optical science were quite aware that they could not anticipate the future application of their most advanced principles and theories. Among the most sophisticated of these scientific theories was that of the image formation in a concave spherical mirror, a structure in which an erect and virtual image appears behind the mirror (in this diagram the image "S-F"), while in front appears an image that is inverted and real (image "L-N"). "D-E" is the real object positioned outside the center "M" of the spherical mirror, producing the inverted image "L-N" in real space, in front of the mirror. "C-K" is a second object placed between the center "M" and the spherical mirror, producing the erect image "S-F" in virtual space, behind the mirror. What we can see in this diagram is a complex doubling, twinning, and multiplying of parallel events similar to the ones I described earlier. Not only does the doubling appear through the very process of mirroring itself, but also the doubling of that which is being mirrored as two objects different in real space (D-E and C-K), yet identical (but not the same) in their mirrored images, one in virtual, the other in real space (S-F and L-N). But this diagram also points to something else: It foregrounds the *relationships* between elements, rather than the elements themselves. In doing so, it is a diagram of the parallel *events* of duplicity, multiplicity, mirroring, and splitting, de-emphasizing the object or objectness. My interest in this diagram lies in its inherent quality of this, what I want to call *event-structure*, over the static implication of platonic objects and their geometry. To inscribe this reading into the diagram, the projected images, in this case lines (e.g., D-E or L-N), have been turned into signifiers of the event of inversion. Triangles at each endpoint of the projections now turn this diagram into a three-dimensional construct of signs. (In optics, the principal structure of this diagram is called a circle of confusion, which describes a single lens with two different focal points.)

L: **1st solid model of diagram**

R: **Stick model of two parallel diagrams**

Again, in the stick model on the right you can see the triangulated frame structure, but this time, the diagram itself has been doubled. To quote Rodolpho

Gasché in "The Tain of the Mirror": "duplication questions precisely the possibility of distinguishing, in a clear and distinct manner, between appearing and what appears...." in other words, between object and event, which in turn, one could say, positions this "object" as Event. In the model on the left, surface has been introduced into the initial diagram, which now opens new possibilities of reading. No longer are we limited by the singularity of a linear structure. Surface is what allows us to move with more complexity across previously perceived boundaries.

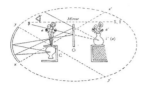

L: **Lacan,** *The Four Fundamental Concepts of Psycho-Analysis*

R: **Stick model of attempted triple mirroring**

In his discussions of the mirror stage in his book *The Four Fundamental Concepts of Psycho-Analysis*, Lacan would describe the use of literally the same diagram as follows: "Virtual images in some instances behave like objects, and real images can be made into virtual objects..... Here the imaginary space and the real space fuse; nonetheless, they have to be conceived of as different," and elsewhere: "For there to be an optics, for each given point in real space, there must be a corresponding point in the virtual, the imaginary space."

L: **Planar inversion/intersection analytic model**

R: **Planar, same as left side**

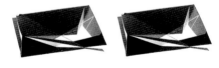

L: **Planar, but with diagram as void or absence**

R: **Planar, same as left side**

These diagrams are diagrams of precise, but flexible, relationships. They cannot be dimensioned in any outside of itself meaningful way. They do not rely on quantifiable measurements, dimensions, or even proportions. The connecting points are to be understood as flexible connections, their properties are solely properties of relationships. This irreducible, an exact geometry, as Edmund Husserl calls it (not to be confused with inexact, as in: not accurate), can be precisely described, yet it is not determinable

through fixed, quantifiable points or dimensions. It is dynamic in nature, fluid, yet rigorous. For precisely these properties, these diagrams are a possible basis for event-structures.

L/R **Figure doubling (experiment)**

Through at least two possible readings of the triangle at each end of the diagram model, namely up or down, a multiple splitting of the figure is made possible: in this experimental model triangles pointing up and down simultaneously, allowing for the two different figure separations shown here.

L/R **Figure doubling and splitting (experiment)**

L/R **Final stages of experimental models (about 50)**

These models are first experiments in the attempt to blur the figure of surface vs. volume geometry. Similar to the dazzle painting of the World War 1 battleships, the painted surfaces begin to change the reading of the volumetric figure. A displacement between three-dimensional form and two-dimensional surface starts to take place.

L: **First set of plans, roof plan**

R: **Axo from above and below**

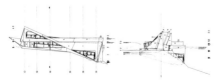

L: **Side elevation and section, surface displacements**

R: **End elevation and sections**

These drawings show the development of surface

displacements: The slippage of the bodies' surfaces around its edges shifts that which previously has been a bend, fold, or corner, onto a flat surface, and makes that which has been flat into an edge.

By developing these slipped surfaces as bands of glass (and incidentally glass being always also reflective like a mirror), and allowing them to become volumetric themselves, the surface, or skin, assumes properties of three dimensionality which previously solely belonged to the volume which it is inscribing.

Endnotes

1 *Rodolpho Gasché on Derrida's* Of Grammatology *in* The Tain of the Mirror: *"The reflection, the image, the double splits what it doubles, by adding itself to it, and the reflected or doubled is also split in itself. Because the possibility of reflective duplication (mirroring) must be inscribed within it, the reflected is divided by its reflection in itself."*

2 *Lacan shows this simultaneous experience of the real and the imagined through his "diagram of the inverted bouquet."*

3 *Edmund Husserl, "Philosophy as Rigorous Science," in R. Gasché,* The Tain of the Mirror, *p. 229.*

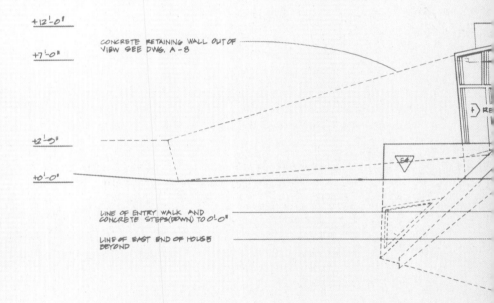

West elevation superimposed on section at column number 11
pencil on mylar

 WEST ELEVATION LOOKING EAST, AND SHOWING WINDOW TO SOUTH END #3

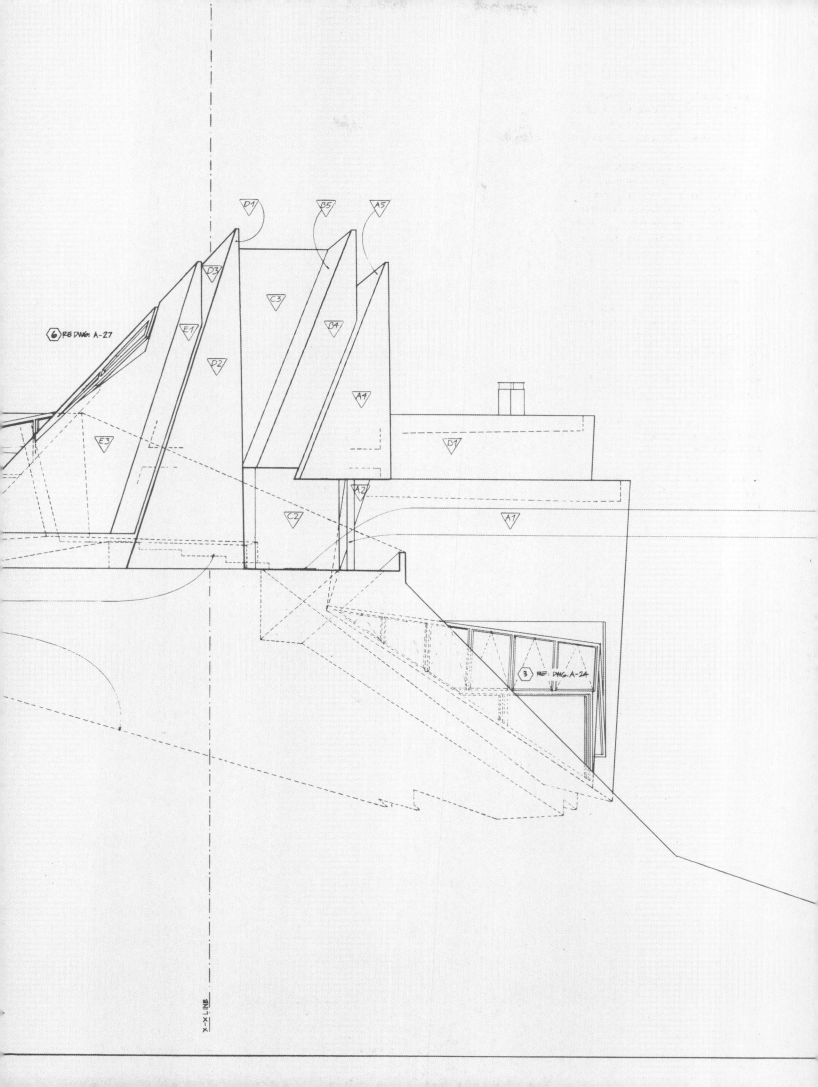

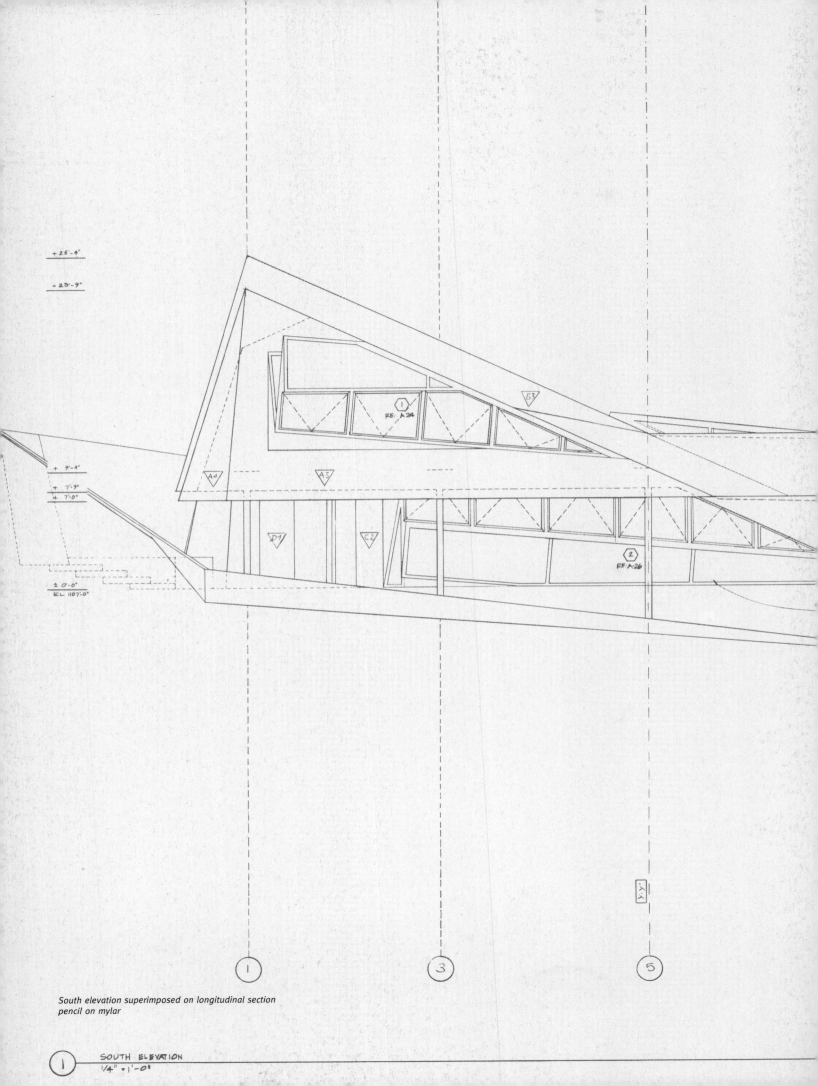

+ 26'-4"

+ 23'-9"

+ 9'-4"
+ 7'-9"
+ 7'-0"

± 0'-0"
EL 1107'-0"

① RE: A-24

△ B3

△ A4

△ A3

△ D1

△ C2

② RE: A-26

Y-Y

① ③ ⑤

South elevation superimposed on longitudinal section
pencil on mylar

① SOUTH ELEVATION
1/4" = 1'-0"

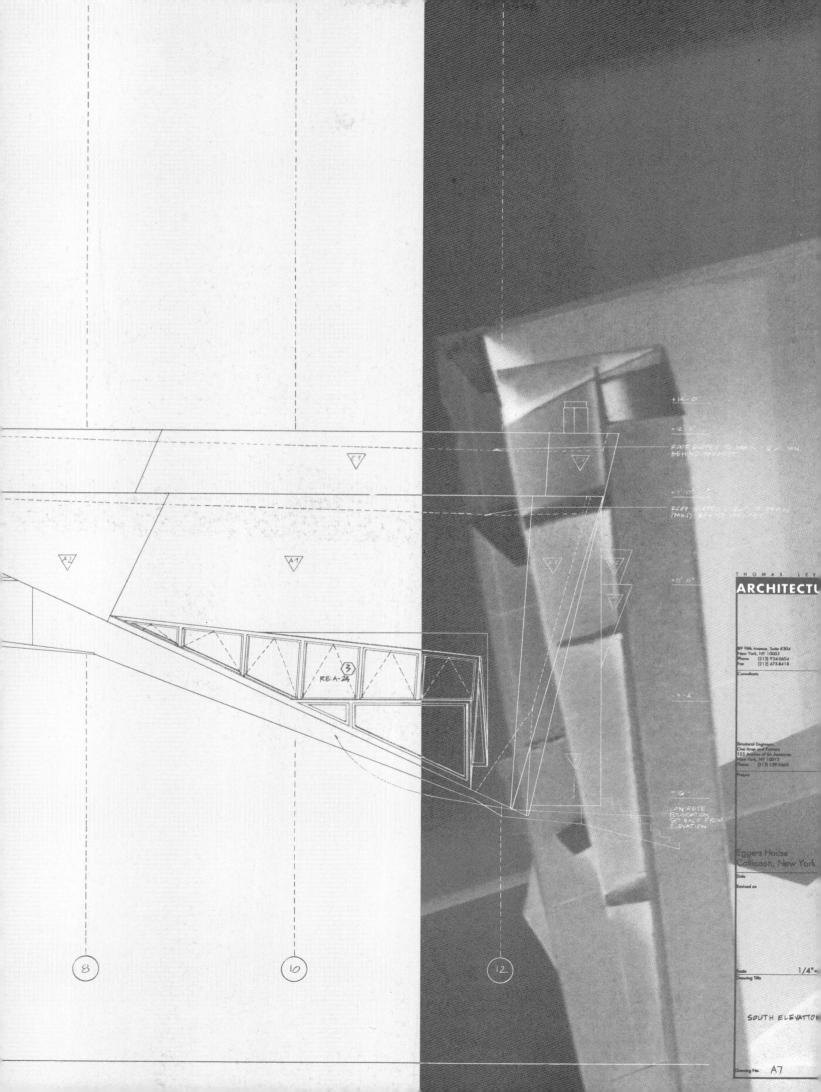

THOMAS LEE

ARCHITECTU

89 Fifth Avenue, Suite #304
New York, NY 10003
Phone   (212) 924-8604
Fax   (212) 475-8418

Consultants

Structural Engineer:
Ove Arup and Partners
155 Avenue of the Americas
New York, NY 10013
Phone   (212) 229-2669

Project

Eggers House
Callicoon, New York

Date

Revised on

Scale   1/4" =
Drawing Title

SOUTH ELEVATION

Drawing No.   A7

Detail of interior, model

Axinometric of interior (right)
ink on mylar

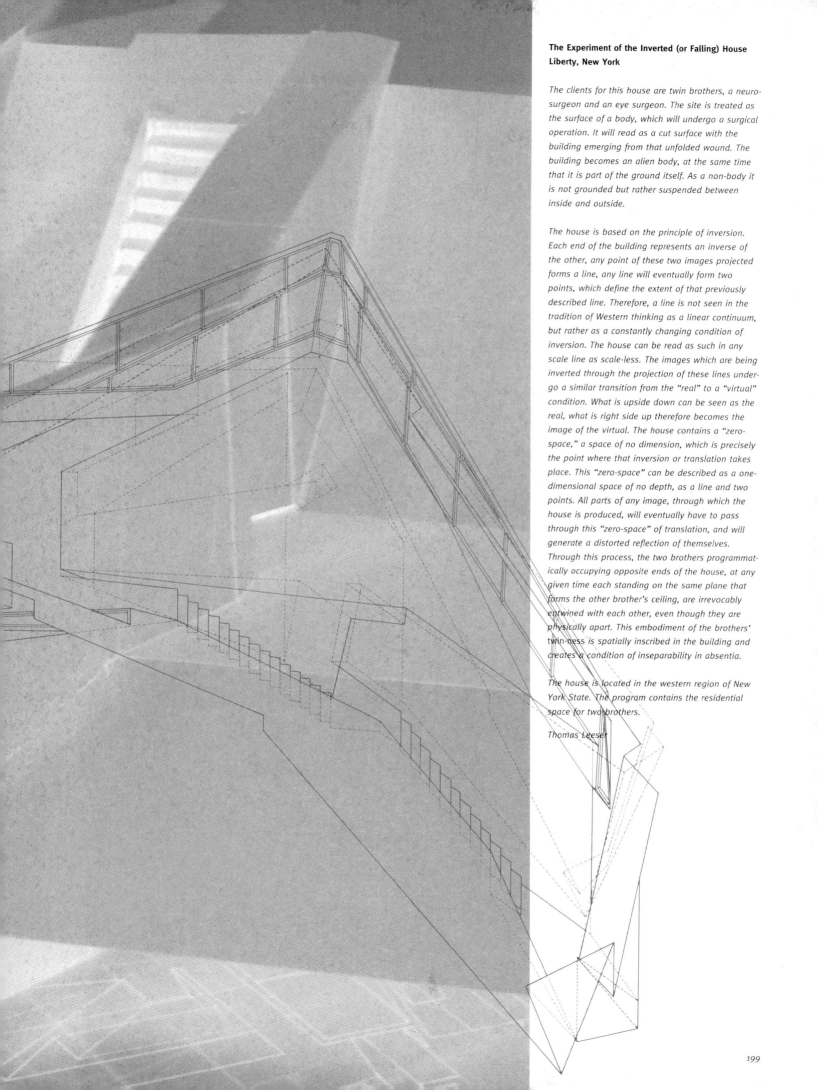

The Experiment of the Inverted (or Falling) House
Liberty, New York

The clients for this house are twin brothers, a neuro-surgeon and an eye surgeon. The site is treated as the surface of a body, which will undergo a surgical operation. It will read as a cut surface with the building emerging from that unfolded wound. The building becomes an alien body, at the same time that it is part of the ground itself. As a non-body it is not grounded but rather suspended between inside and outside.

The house is based on the principle of inversion. Each end of the building represents an inverse of the other, any point of these two images projected forms a line, any line will eventually form two points, which define the extent of that previously described line. Therefore, a line is not seen in the tradition of Western thinking as a linear continuum, but rather as a constantly changing condition of inversion. The house can be read as such in any scale line as scale-less. The images which are being inverted through the projection of these lines under-go a similar transition from the "real" to a "virtual" condition. What is upside down can be seen as the real, what is right side up therefore becomes the image of the virtual. The house contains a "zero-space," a space of no dimension, which is precisely the point where that inversion or translation takes place. This "zero-space" can be described as a one-dimensional space of no depth, as a line and two points. All parts of any image, through which the house is produced, will eventually have to pass through this "zero-space" of translation, and will generate a distorted reflection of themselves. Through this process, the two brothers programmat-ically occupying opposite ends of the house, at any given time each standing on the same plane that forms the other brother's ceiling, are irrevocably entwined with each other, even though they are physically apart. This embodiment of the brothers' twin-ness is spatially inscribed in the building and creates a condition of inseparability in absentia.

The house is located in the western region of New York State. The program contains the residential space for two brothers.

Thomas Leeser

learning, self

Deep within us, codes of conduct, powers of perception — ways of envisioning — are inscribed on our person. Our upbringing and instruction are instrumental in establishing these forces. *We are* — as the Hebrew saying *anahnu ha-limudim shelanu* goes — *what we learn*. And if our work can be seen as intensely "original" or "new," it can just as easily be seen as an extension of our personal history and the people, places and social contexts which shape us.

In this journal, we have focused on the individual and his or her creative vision. Yet our power, or *origin*-ality as individuals, is rooted in our *origin*, or place within a particular community. In this closing essay, Joseph Burton carefully situates the illusive poetic of Louis Kahn's thought within a turn-of-the-century community of creative, practicing artists and architects in Philadelphia. From his early studies in freehand drawing at the Public Industrial Art School to his architectural training at the University of Pennsylvania, Kahn's particular form of envisioning architecture sustained and transformed the ideas and energies of his youth in the academies of Philadelphia.

Contributing Artists and Architects:

J. Liberty Tadd, Instructor, The Public Industrial Art School; William F. Gray, Professor of Art History, Central High School;

Paul Philippe Cret, Professor of Architecture, University of Pennsylvania

Philadelphia, Pennsylvania

A member of Kahn's studio, Marshall Meyers, notes that Kahn was unsure of the origins of his ideas, and hoped that his thoughts on architecture would eventually be placed within a broader historical context.[1] On this point, Kahn said:

I speak very little about it, because I don't know how to extend things, because I don't have any historical knowledge, nor any research tendencies. I can't look up and find other literature, I just can't do it. And so it's left, in a way, in a very undeveloped state, as though it were just an offering for someone else, you know, to extend. It doesn't happen, because I really say too little to make it completely understandable. That's why I like to talk about it, because I talk about it more freely, because writing is very difficult for me, though I've done some....[2]

Although intensely personal, and at times difficult to decipher, Louis Kahn's vision of architecture can be traced to the people, places, and intellectual currents which shaped his childhood in Philadelphia. From 1910 to 1924 Kahn studied drawing, the visual arts, and architecture within an intimate community of teachers and institutions in Philadelphia: J. Liberty Tadd, drawing instructor, the Public Industrial Art School; William Gray, Professor of Art History, Central High School; and Paul Cret, Professor of Architecture, the University of Pennsylvania.

1900–1917
The Progressive Era

This period of Kahn's training took place during a time of great political and aesthetic Romanticism in America – known today as the Progressive Era, circa 1900–1917. Named after the late 19th-century reform-minded *Progressive Movement,* this community of young intellectuals and professionals was associated with political, social, and aesthetic reform. Progressivists' philosophy was a particular cross of Romanticism and pragmatism, firmly rooted in the expansive Transcendentalism of Ralph Waldo Emerson. Presented in his book *Nature*[3] of 1836, Emerson's spiritual dualities of Immanence and Transcendence were used to justify and guarantee the democratic ideals of equality and liberty. The immanence of divinity throughout nature ensures that all humankind, in their spiritual patrimony, are equal. Each child of God transcends physical limitations into freedom when he or she depends upon his or her creative genius. Humankind, when it draws upon its inner divine nature, serves as a co-creator with God in the phenomenal world. Of this divine mediator, Emerson proclaimed: "Man is here to be a reformer."

The Progressives strongly championed public art education with special schools and programs in fine art and industrial art. As a community, they firmly believed that art and art education played a fundamental role in the moral perfectibility of the citizen and thus the state. The art of the Progressive Era simultaneously looked backward to a primeval, Jeffersonian arcadia and forward in time to a scientific and industrialized utopia. America was understood to be unfettered by the past and its rigid traditions, yet heir to the evolutionary achievements of history.

The artist, as with all Progressives, was to pragmatically choose and adapt freely from yesterday in order to move with imagination and invention into tomorrow. This alchemical "melting pot" of American democratic art, harmonizing the primitive and the evolved, produced diverse and ironic shades of gray. Its inherent ambiguities polarized into numerous hybrids of conservative and radical aesthetic preferences which ran between academic figurative art and avant-garde non-objective art. This duality is best seen in the period's most popular painting style, Neoclassicism or "American Renaissance," and its most radical one, Post-Impressionism – each style emphasized, in its own way, both an archaic primitivism and a scientific abstraction.

In architecture one also notes such stylistic diversity within a Progressive sensibility. The Beaux-Arts Imperialism of McKim, Mead and White with its ancient Greco-Roman details was associated with the Progressives' *City Beautiful Movement*. Similarly, one also notes Cram's medievalism, the orientalism and organicism of Sullivan and Wright, and the modernist abstraction of Goodhue's late work. Each of these aesthetic visions shared in the complex Romanticism of the Progressive era.

To our collective benefit, Kahn's ideas are grounded in this idealistic, visionary, and reform-minded time – and if we wish to understand Kahn's person we should first turn to the ideas and attitudes of Kahn's teachers.

1912–1914
J. Liberty Tadd, drawing instructor
Public Industrial Art School

Of the three teachers from this period that Kahn credited as influential upon his thought, Liberty Tadd was the most closely associated with the Progressive Movement. The educational ideals of the Progressives honored the individuality of the student yet struggled to harmonize this uniqueness within a collective context. Tadd spoke on this subject:

To be a good teacher requires essentially the inspiration that the art of teaching is divine. It is a mission to teach children having souls. The teacher must especially realize that each mind or soul is an immortal part of the future heaven he or she is helping to build.[4]

For Progressives, education was organic and tailored to each student. It unveiled the expressive uniqueness of the individual from the inside out. Tadd elaborated:

In educating the young ... there is no reason why we should not give them ... a knowledge of their own character and the possibilities of which they are capable.[5]

Tadd was a graduate of the Pennsylvania Academy of Fine Arts and his time at this institution, 1876, 1879, 1880, and 1881, exactly corresponds with Thomas Eakins' greatest influence as a teacher and a director of the institution.[6] Tadd was trained by Eakins to work, "as the ancient Greeks," directly from nature. He learned that authentic art derives its vitality from direct observation of living nature, not the precedents and academic cliches of other artists. Study from life was complemented by the use of scientific discoveries and methods. Photography and anatomical dissection furthered the students' factual understanding of nature. Following Eakins, Tadd turned his back on the traditional methods of academic training and promoted in his art classes an individual interpretation based upon the student's own "self-reliant" thought process. Tadd's pedagogy in his courses given at the Public Industrial Art School continued Eakins' Romantic Realism, a style associated with the "American Renaissance."[7] Tadd intellectually supported his teaching methods with Emersonian Transcendentalism, contemporary scientific psychology, as well as Spencer, and Progressive interpretations of Hegel. Tadd's instruction encouraged animism, organicism, automatic, subconscious expression, and symbolism. Tadd's method of teaching drawing, called "natural education," was made an integral part of Philadelphia's system of public schools.[8]

In the fall of 1910, Kahn was personally introduced to Tadd by his fourth-grade teacher. At this time any boy or girl with talent in art in the Philadelphia School System was permitted to go to the Public Industrial Art School directed by Tadd. Tadd developed the pedagogy and trained the teachers for the school. Tadd's

Progressive program was a local success story. By 1891, he had expanded from a responsibility of 120 children to 1700. In the beginning, children attended two afternoons a week for two hours and during Kahn's education for 1/2 day per week.

Tadd attained national and international prominence as a visionary in art instruction for elementary, middle, high, and normal schools. His book, *New Methods in Education: Art, Real Manual Training, and Nature Study,* was first published in 1899 and was translated into German and published the following year as *Neuewege zur Kunstlerischen Erziehung der Jugend.* Tadd's prominence was aided by his professional association with another Progressive educator, William N. Hailman. Author of many books and articles concerning education in English and German, Hailman wrote the introduction to Tadd's book. He pronounced its pedagogy to be the fulfillment of "Froebel's educational prophecy" and to be the definitive example of such instruction in America. Hailman had discovered Tadd's work in 1893 in the educational exhibits of the Chicago Columbian Exposition. Tadd had achieved in practice Froebel's educational vision better than Hailman himself and Froebel's other American and international disciples. Hailman elaborated how Froebel's educational principles were best realized in Tadd's work.

Elsewhere, I had seen the child weighted down with cubes and balls, with cylinders and cones, with lines straight and curved, parallel and diverging, loading himself with wearisome definitions of these things or investing them with an unhealthy mysticism in accordance with a sadly perverted reading of Froebel's thought; here I found practical comprehension and free control of these things, attained without weariness and suppressed sorrow, a loving application of Froebel's living thought; cubes and cylinders, squares and circles becoming familiar friends through the service they gave in the expression of thoughts and in the achievement of purpose. Here I saw the so-called principles of parallelism and perpendicularity, of radiation and balance, of circle and involute, of perspective and shadow, discovered by the children in the needs of their own souls, clearly put forth and thoughtfully applied in spontaneous work, shining in the lucidity of native, not of borrowed, light.[9]

Tadd's pedagogy was three part and is summarized in the secondary title of his book: *Art, Real Manual Training, and Nature Study.* However, his emphasis upon nature study was the fundamental, romantic foundation of this tripartite approach. According to Tadd, nature is the great teacher. A student taught to love and closely observe the "Book of Nature" is given the golden key to unlock all knowledge both physical and spiritual. This is because nature is a divine expression, a kind of sacred script.

If God speaks at all (and who doubts it?), He speaks through His works, "There are tongues in trees, books in the running brook, sermons in stones, and good in everything" (Shakespeare). Ought we not to understand these tongues, read these books and understand these sermons?[10]

Therefore, nature study leads to an appreciation of true beauty and teaches one the fundamental process of creation. This divine model is the prime means to all art or human creation.[11] Tadd's romantic theory of education parallels that of Plato and his process of *anamnesis* initiated by *eros.* The human love of natural, physical beauty, a mesmer-like, telluric force, transforms and awakens one gradually to a higher, abstract awareness.

The inspiration is in the natural forms, as it should be, and the mere contemplation of the forms seems to influence the pupils to action. It is inspiring to the true teacher to realize the moving force and power of nature. Bring something into the class room like a new bird form, or fish form, all of the children follow it with their eyes, which seem to almost stick out; there is no lack of attention here, the magnetic influence is at work, the divine energy is flowing. We should flow with it instead of trying to thwart it, as is too often done. This magnetic and energizing power of nature has a splendid influence on the physical, mental and moral development of the young. It also fills the children with interest, imbues them with vigor, inspires them to think and work, while at the same time giving them an appreciation of beauty that adds vastly to the ability of the young to enjoy life.... It is thus distinctly practical, and commends itself to the most materially inclined, as well as satisfying the more ethical aspirations of our nature. "The emotion accompanying every generous act adds an atom to the fabric of the ideal man."[12]

Hence, Tadd argued that the young student must begin with the study of objects from nature, i.e., shells, plants, fish, birds, and animals, before studying in class the geometric, ideal forms underlying nature — cubes, pyramids, and spheres. Abstract theory presented before direct sensual experience of natural phenomena appears meaningless, purposeless, boring, and too difficult to the student. Tadd said that students are always more interested in drawing natural objects. Only later do students begin to see the intellectual ideal of the universal geometries which underlie all natural morphology. Figure 1. The senses must be stimulated before the intellect in order to promote firsthand discovery and original insight. Then, the student's natural motivation and confidence established upon personal success and achievement are not undermined. As much as possible, Tadd's students worked directly from nature. In the Philadelphia Public Industrial Art School, he used stuffed birds, fish, and animals, as well as photographs and plaster casts of these, to present nature to students. In private lessons, for example, students were taken on field trips to the zoo to study and draw live animals. In his private summer school classes in the Adirondacks at Sarana Lake, students worked directly in nature, outdoors "en plein air," and did studies of farm animals from life. Figures 1–2.

Art and real manual training are the two tools which allow one to study nature best. Tadd's method was learning by doing, summed up in the aphorism, "Every deed is a prayer." The student is educated autodidactically by self-initiated study. Tadd said that this process of self-teaching is:

The art of building ideas by using most of the channels of impression and most of the means of expression.[13]

Tadd demonstrated how drawing could aid study in many branches of knowledge, such as language, mathematics, technical subjects — construction and mechanical drawing — and the sciences of zoology, biology, botany, chemistry, entomology, and mineralogy. He elaborated upon the empirical richness of drawing:

All must admit that a picture presents a subject capable of illustration far more forcibly than mere words. One who accurately draws a bird, or a skeleton, or a flower, or a mathematical problem, has a more complete mastery of that special topic than could be gained in almost any other way.[14]

Tadd's exercises were geared to the development of physical strength, control, and dexterity. Ambidextrous exercise was one of his unique developments and contributions to art education. Figures 3–4.

His ambidextrous blackboard drills, for example, drawing overscaled ornaments, developed the ability to maintain correct proportions at different scales and the physical flexibility necessary for employment in many crafts. Similar ambidextrous

exercises not only in two dimensions but in 3D clay and wood carving at different scales continued this process. The students methodically rotated between these exercises in drawing, modeling in clay, and woodcarving. Figures 5–6.

Tadd said that only through working in 3D could the student improve his or her abilities to see critically and draw with precision in two dimensions. The physical sense of touch working on soft clay and hard wood trained the eye to see even more subtly than when working only in two-dimensional mediums.[15] He called three-dimensional modeling "speaking through the finger tips." Tadd argued that the best delineators are also sculptors, citing Michelangelo among several others. The result of learning to speak through the fingertips is an automatic and expressive drawing ability where hand, eye, and mind are synthesized into one instrument.

... when we have actually, through the sense of touch, made the form in soft material and then actually by hard struggling made the same form in tough wood, it is a very easy matter to draw it on paper or the blackboard with the hand as firm and with a line as clean as though it were being made by a steel bar.[16]

Tadd used "memory drills" to help impress through repetitive drawings the objective image upon the mind. Similar mnemonic training was also used by Eakins, Tadd's teacher. With "the power of being able to mentally photograph the object," Tadd explained, the student will automatically begin to idealize and universalize nature in his/her work through unconscious and conscious simplification.[17] Tadd's memory drills were repeated over and over again, as a musician practices scales, until drawing and 3D sculpting became completely automatic and instinctive for the student. The physical body and hand became an expressive instrument for the mind of the artist. Tadd believed that his technique freed the inner genius of the student to express ideas and feelings spontaneously.

The pupil should learn to draw as automatically as he learns to write.[18]

Drawing and manual training, properly taught ... are modes of thought expression, just as speech and writing are modes of thought expression. Drawing is a universal tongue.[19]

With perceptual knowledge automatically embodied in the artist through memory work, one is free to use, reinterpret, and express these facts in personal and subjective ways.

As I have repeatedly quoted, "accurate perception and exact memory are the fundamental bases of sound reasoning and imagination."[20]

One must imitate nature first before one can express. Mimesis is sketching from nature. Design is expression.

I like my pupils and teachers to understand the distinction there is between sketching from nature and designing. In the one case we put down facts, and in the other, ideas. There is a tendency for many students to sketch only from nature. We get our ideas by thinking as well. More time should be given, then, to dwelling on our impressions and to systematic mental reproduction, and to giving expression to these ideas constantly by designing and creative work.[21]

Tadd's Progressive pedagogy was a "natural" process taking the student from imitation to symbolization of inner experience — from "Impressionism" to "Expressionism." Art expresses human thought and feeling best. Drawing in two dimensions and modeling in three dimensions are a form of expressive writing revealing the underlying spiritual character and soul nature of the author. Art thus mirrors the formative process of the Divine Creator who writes Its character in nature. Art for Tadd then becomes the truest form of self-expression, the highest goal of education.[22]

Besides the romantic-based aesthetic theory, it is Kahn's drawing method that evokes Tadd most clearly. Kahn portrayed his 1959 delineations of the medieval city of Carcassonne as a kind of writing — a mnemonic method going from *mimesis* to creative expression. Figures 7–8.

A few years ago I visited Carcassonne. From the moment I entered the gates, I began to write with drawing, the images which I learned about now presenting themselves to me like realized dreams. I began studiously to memorize in line the proportions and the living details of these great buildings. I spent the whole day in the courts, on the ramparts, and in the towers, diminishing my care about the proper proportions and exact details. At the close of the day I was inventing shapes and placing buildings in different relationships than they were.[23]

Kahn drew buildings from the ground up, reflecting the physical forces of gravity moving through them. This tectonic sensibility is akin to Auguste Choisy's "worm's-eye view" illustrations of architecture. It also captures the essence of Tadd's teaching endeavor: the synthesis of mind, eye, hand, and touch while drawing. Tadd said of such psychosomatic integration:

the hand will very soon grasp the feeling that it is delineating something tangible and concrete, not simply making pencil and chalk lines.[24]

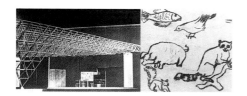

Fifty years after studying with Tadd, Kahn was still able to demonstrate ambidextrous drawing. Figure 4. His greatest tribute to Tadd's teaching is symbolized in the use of the chalkboard. Whether intended for a child's room as shown in a painting circa 1930, an elementary school design by Anne G. Tyng of the early 1950's with children's illustrations by Kahn, or for the unplanned intuitions of Nobel Prize winners walking under the porticos of the Salk Institute, designed 1959–1965, he provided the graphic medium of his early education to further human speculation. Figures 9–10.

It was also Tadd speaking behind Kahn's words when the architect discussed the goal of education and its agencies.

School is a place which has this unique ability to serve the talent of the individual. Not just to impart knowledge but to serve the talent of the individual.

No person should be examined where his talents don't lie. I know, I studied physics. I took notes in physics. I took notes so arduously that I didn't hear what was said. Had I listened to the teacher and not taken notes, I would have learned something about physics. I took notes to pass examinations. And even then I had to copy somebody's notes which were more accurate because my mind wasn't in that direction.

Had I been asked after the physics to draw physics, I could do it.
I could express through drawing what I learned in physics class. This
would be my way of expressing physics.[25]

In his built constructions, Kahn did draw physics, delineating the nature of materials
and the forces of gravity.

1912–1920
Willian F.Gray
Professor of Art History
Central High School

William F. Gray, the professor who lectured in art history and architectural history at
Central High School, was responsible for stimulating the direction of Kahn's later pro-
fessional studies. As head of the Art Department at this elite Philadelphia institution,
Gray established an integrated approach toward the history of art and architecture.
This more inclusive understanding of the arts began with his studies at the
Pennsylvania Academy of Fine Arts from 1889 to 1891, a time when Thomas P.
Anshutz, a student of Thomas Eakins, was the leading force of the school.[26] As an
educator, Anshutz was even more open-minded than his teacher and is credited with
conveying Eakins' most Progressive ideas into the 20th century.[27] He rejected
academic conventions and encouraged his students to find their own expressive
voice. He actively promoted among his students European modern art and its
theories of Impressionism and Post-Impressionism.

Tutored by Anshutz in this tradition of Expressionism, Gray, like Tadd, propagated a
Progressive vision through his teaching. Perhaps more importantly for Kahn, however,
he addressed the discipline of architecture from this distinctly American position. He
was an outspoken advocate of Philadelphia's *City Beautiful Movement* and an active
member in the artistic community of the city. Being head of the Art Department at
Central High School, he exercised his power to further the quality of architecture in
Philadelphia. One of his students at Central, John Harbeson, remembered Gray's
important influence upon fellow students:

William F. Gray ... used his position as head of the Art Department of this
school to give his students an opportunity to learn something about the history
of architecture, about its styles and its beauties. To him, many men who have
made brilliant records in architecture owe their start, their desire to do
something worthwhile in a noble art. This quiet, dignified, sensitive man did
much to inspire young Sternfeld; it was from Professor Gray that he learned
about Paul Cret and what he was teaching at the Architectural School at the
University of Pennsylvania, and what college training would do for him. And it
was Gray who made it possible for him to get a scholarship to Penn.[28]

Gray's ideas on architecture during the first decades of this century may be surmised
from a lecture he gave in 1910 and later published in 1915 entitled *Philadelphia's
Architecture,* in which Gray, influenced by Ruskin, argued that materials in architecture
be expressed honestly, in a straightforward manner.

Although grounding his architectural principles in Ruskin's Romanticism, Gray, like
many Progressives, was not overly enthusiastic about the Gothic style, although he
appreciated reserved versions of it as well as of other medieval revivals, such as
Romanesque and Byzantine. Gray may have been the first to interest Kahn in the
campaniles and towered fortifications of Italian medieval cities. Figures 11–12.

He would also have introduced Kahn to the architecture of the late 18th and early
19th centuries. Gray's personal preferences favored the spare detail and simple form

of a restrained Neoclassical architecture known as Greek Revival. He celebrated the ancient Choragic Monument of Lysicrates as a prototypical example of the style. More modern examples extolled were the work of Inigo Jones, William Chambers, and U. Walters. His interest in an architecture of unpretentious simplicity and rational clarity is consistent with that of many contemporary taste-makers in America. This classical movement during the first decades of the century was associated with the Progressive values of Jeffersonian republicanism and democracy. Its foremost apologist was Fiske Kimball, who later became the director of Philadelphia's Museum of Fine Art in 1925. Gray did not approve of England's 17th-century Baroque architecture, an aristocratic style. He was also not fond of American examples of the French neo-Baroque style, such as Philadelphia's City Hall, associated with the Second Empire of Napoleon III. Of City Hall, Gray wrote:

```
The French scheme of central and terminal pavilions, with intermediate wings or
curtains, and the superimposed orders, which have come down from Roman times,
are here the dominant features of the design, but lacking in that finer sense
of form and proportion, without which the often narrow gap between the sublime
and the ridiculous is so easily crossed. The most conspicuous feature of all,
the tower, is least successful. Its manifold subdivisions and broken lines
eliminate the finest element in tower design – the simple, upward sweep, seen
at its best in the Italian Campanile.... The detail throughout is coarse and
exuberant and the iron cornice is a most egregious error.[29]
```

Gray's ideal for a more simplified tower design was ultimately realized in the brick, Sullivanesque skyscrapers of Chicago.

```
The modern business building, particularly the skyscraper or cloud scratcher,
with its rapid increase in height due to the enormous recent development in
steel construction, presented a problem that has taken a considerable time in
its solution, if, indeed, it may be considered solved....
```

```
The first of the utilitarian tall buildings of Chicago, with an absolutely
plain brick skin on the steel skeleton, pointed the way to the solution – the
treatment of the whole structure as a mass of plinth to be provided with a base
and terminal treatment dependent on the nature of the building. All the impres-
siveness of the mass is thereby accentuated and the problem brought back to
first principles, easier of solution.[30]
```

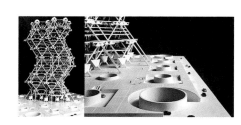

In 1919, Gray publicly recommended that the City Hall be torn down and the site be restored to a public square as William Penn had originally intended.[31] He suggested that on the perimeter of the square two restrained Neoclassical buildings to house the needs of the city be built, modeled after those of Gabriel on the Place de la Concorde in Paris. The later Free Library of Philadelphia recalls Gray's vision transplanted to Logan Circle. This campaign to tear down City Hall in 1919, the year that Kahn was enrolled in Gray's course at Central High, may have in part prompted Kahn's later proposals for Philadelphia's City Hall. Some of these schemes included demolition of the building and replacing it with a dramatic design done in collaboration with Anne G. Tyng. The new project, called "Tomorrow's City Hall," was both public square and tower. Figures 13–14.

Like Philadelphia's Second Empire style, Gray also harshly criticized the excesses of the Aesthetic Movement in Philadelphia during the late 19th century. He condemned the overly "original" architecture of Frank Furness with the morally charged words:

```
Any architectural feature which is not self-explanatory is wrong.[32]
```

Gray referred Furness and other followers of structural mannerism to the doctrines of Ruskin.

In the 1950's, Gray noted that five of his former students later won the Paris Prize after studying with Cret at Penn. The two most celebrated of these students were John Harbeson and Harry Sternfeld. Sternfeld also went on to receive the Prix de Rome, while Harbeson became a partner with Cret. Gray often referred to these students as "Cret worshippers." This was due in part to his promoting at Central High the talents of Cret as an internationally recognized Philadelphia architect and teacher. Unfortunately, however these students were never fully accepted or encouraged by Cret precisely because of their radical tastes – tastes which Gray had fostered. Gray in typical Progressive fashion would have engendered an independent attitude and revolutionary spirit in his students at Central High – a spirit unfamiliar to Cret.

Gray died in 1956 before he could name Kahn as his most luminous and successful protégé. Although Kahn would never be completely approved by Cret, the probable reason Cret rejected such a major talent was Kahn's romantic sympathies and Progressive taste. This American vision taught by many of the teachers of Philadelphia's institutions was never endorsed by Cret himself.

1923–1924
Paul Philippe Cret
Professor of Architecture
University of Pennsylvania

Paul Philippe Cret was Kahn's design professor during his final year of architectural study at the University of Pennsylvania, 1923–24. Cret, born, raised, and educated in France, was a third-generation Néo-Grec, the student of Pascal and Guadet at the Ecole des Beaux-Arts in Paris. His view of human history, unlike that of the Progressives, was seen through the concrete objectivity of French rationalism and late 19th-century materialist science. Philosophically based in the positivist and deterministic theories of Hippolyte Taine and Herbert Spencer, Cret opposed American Romanticism with its subjectivism, idealism, and emphasis upon revolutionary reform. Cret battled the schizoid Romanticism of the Progressives on their two fronts, conservative and radical. These were, respectively, the primitivism of American Neoclassicism with its historic detailing and the utopianism of modernist architecture. The modern style was typified by the late work of Bertram Grosvenor Goodhue and the Art Deco skyscrapers of New York City, an American school of design led by Harvey Wiley Corbet and Hugh Ferriss. The titles of several of Cret's published essays bear witness to his debate with the Progressives: "The Question of Education: Evolution Vs. Revolution," "Modernist and Conservative," "The Classic Versus the Modernist," and "'The Architectural See-Saw' or 'The Law of Eternal Return.'"

According to David Brownlee in *Building the City Beautiful,* both Progressive styles of Neoclassicism and Modernism were influenced by Post-Impressionism.[33] The name for this revolutionary, abstract art pioneered by Cézanne and his followers was coined by English critic Roger Fry circa 1911.[34] For the next decade in the United States, all of modern painting was subsumed under Fry's label, including Fauvism, Cubism, and Futurism. Fry's nomenclature is, however, only chronological and not descriptive. It is more revealing to remember that Post-Impressionism's founders, especially Matisse, describe this subjective, anti-mimetic art as "Expressionism" or "Self-Expression." The influence of Post-Impressionism's neo-romantic theories upon American Neoclassicists and Modernists is in their mutual dependence upon abstraction, a metaphor for science and utopia; and primitivism, a metaphor for nature and arcadia.[35] Similarly, both styles were associated with contemporary theories of synesthesia which argued for a correspondence between color, form, and sound.

In contradiction to Progressive expressionist theory, Cret believed in mimesis. He said that architecture was an "imitative art."[36] Ostensibly, he was not referring to Plato and the imitation of ideas but to Aristotle and the imitation of universal principles abstracted from nature. Cret's scientific and objective imitative art was to follow evolution as interpreted by Darwin, not the Progressives. With cultural Darwinism, Cret skeptically opposed Progressive millennial excesses. His rational positivism did not allow for the incongruities of an American vision paradoxically fusing arcadia with utopia.

The history of architecture as well as that of the Ecole des Beaux-Art in France was analyzed by Cret as a lengthy dialectic between conflicting views which periodically evolved to a new synthesis. He generalized the fundamental polarities of this dynamic process as either an impetus toward evolution or one toward revolution — slow, organic-like development across generations or the sudden overthrow of the status quo by antithesis. Cret shared Herbert Spencer's agnostic attitude as well as his all-encompassing exposition of evolution, concisely phrased as the movement from "incoherent homogeneity to coherent heterogeneity." Cret, however, shortened the maxim to "homogeneity moving to heterogeneity," limiting its breadth of interpretation.[37] He thus saw architecture slowly and imperceptibly evolving across centuries. Revolution plays a necessary but illusionary role in this process of change. Its influence upon the ultimate outcome — how a radical position is synthesized into its conservative opposite — is unknown and unpredictable and in the long run barely noticeable.

For Cret, it is foolhardy to think that a single individual in one lifetime could significantly contribute to the progress of evolution. The chimera of revolution to affect drastic change is summed up in the Darwinist aphorism, "nature does not skip steps." Therefore, Cret took a conservative stance against the reform-minded individual in contemporary architecture. He believed this to be too romantic, unnatural, and unrealistic — in the end impossible. In an essay of 1909, "Truth and Tradition," Cret referred to the Darwinian parallel in counterpoint to the romantic notion of the revolutionary, creative genius proposed by American Progressives. The average architect, epitomized by a certain J.W. Brownie, is incapable of formulating an original architecture — a one-man revolution. In an extended caricature, Cret, following Santayana, attacked the Hegelian academic idealism of the Progressives. Writing, tongue in cheek, he used Bernard Shaw's satire on British reform, *Man and Superman,* to drive home his point:

Brownie was dumbfounded. "Our only hope, then, is in evolution." Evolution is a slow process, and the prospect of knowing that superman, forty thousand years from now, will perhaps build truthful architecture, is a rather comfortless contingency. Meanwhile, as he had to build, being an architect, he set himself again to the task of designing churches, residences, bank buildings and the rest as well as he could, though still hindered by the tastes of the clients which were not always the same as his own, by the meagre funds put at his disposal, by unfavorable sites, and, above all, by his own talent, of which he was the first to recognize the limitations. Everybody cannot be a genius.[38]

In the context of his Darwinist perspective, Cret's sense of modern architecture, compared to that of his modernist peers, was a much broader and inclusive panorama. Modern architecture, according to Cret, begins with the Christian epoch around AD 500. During this period two great architectural styles emerged and evolved across the ages, the gothic and, more recently, the renaissance style, an instauration of Greco-Roman antiquity. Despite other stylistic revivals such as a superficial gothic one, the true and dominant style of the 19th century was classicism which continued the development from the 1500's. Classicism or "modified renaissance" is modern architecture. Its maturation during the last 400 years has witnessed a movement from simplicity to greater complexity. The classical tradition with its non-personal evolution across millennia exemplifies architectural progress best, being a "survival of the fittest" style. Cret used the terms "modern" for "modified renaissance" or present-day classicism, and "modernist" to portray the revolutionary dialectic found within contemporary architecture. Classicism must evolve according to natural law. In its modern, more complex state, there is no place for backsliding to a more primitive and simple, archaeologically correct, classicism. This, Cret said, was as embarrassing and unseemly as an elderly person using baby talk to express himself. In line with earlier Néo-Grecs, he opposed the romantic primitivism of any period exhibiting a regression to an archaic state of development, especially late 18th- and early 19th-century Neoclassicism with its simple, absolutely symmetrical geometries and its authentic details taken from ancient Greece, Paestum, Herculaneum, and Pompeii. Cret opposed the 20th-century American taste for Neoclassicism as an anathema, unsuitable for a complex, present-day society and untrue to natural principles of evolution.

Capable of designing in many styles including a modernist version of Art Deco for the 1933 Chicago Century of Progress, Cret always pragmatically accepted the stylistic dictates of his clientele. However, as much as possible, Cret practiced as he thought and physically articulated a classicism in evolution according to the circumstances of the first part of the 20th century. This is known best in America as "modernized classicism" or "stripped classicism."[39] Applying Darwinian evolutionary principles to architecture, his plan designs are less simple, more baroque in their elaboration, appropriate to the complicated, heterogeneous nature of contemporary life. Cret's planning strategies contrast with the simplified footprints of Progressive Neoclassical buildings. Cret reasoned:

Modern architecture can then no longer aspire to the simplicity of the Antique or the Mediaeval. A modern plan provides a multitude of rooms for various uses distributed generally over several floors, and the external and internal appearance of the building faithfully renders this complexity by the number of openings, of stories, of reduplications of apartments on each floor, etc.

We may say that the more modern a program is, the more complicated it is; and we cannot speak of this complexity as a fault chargeable to the architect, when it is only the expression of our use and custom.[40]

The stripped classicism of the facades that he designed in the mid-1920's may also be considered evolutionary in their formal aspect. The abstract imagery of these elevations apparently draws upon the Post-Impressionists' association of science with such an aesthetic. Cret, apparently, was willing to ignore the primitivism simultaneously associated with Post-Impressionism for a technical, scientific reason. His stripped classicism was also a simplification reflecting the fact of modern steel construction, not an atavistic regression similar to Neoclassical primitivism. Elizabeth Grossman in *Paul Philippe Cret: Rationalism and Imagery in American Architecture* argues that he reduced the details of traditional masonry classicism, a dead-load corbeled structure exemplified by moldings and capitals, to characterize modern steel construction in a monumental manner.[41] The metal assembly frame of horizontal and vertical members tied together and acting as a unit does not need corbeled elements: moldings and capitals. She also suggests that this depiction of the steel frame, which functions structurally similarly to that of wood, reinforced the tradition, authoritatively pronounced by Vitruvius, that the classical orders were originally timber and not stone. In such ways, Cret evolved the renaissance tradition to express the technical complexity and sophistication of a 20th-century culture.

Cret's scientific position on evolution was in contrast to the popular romantic one of the Progressives. Historians of evolution contend that romantic dialectic theory (usually attributed to Hegel), not Darwin's biological theory, is a more accurate model for cultural evolution. Cret's grievous miscalculation would cost him a more celebrated and honored position in American architectural histories. Because of his ambivalence to Yankee tastes and his anti-Progressive stance, Cret was never really accepted as an American architect.[42] Although naturalized and a recipient of an AIA gold medal in 1928, Cret was still known as a "French" architect long after other European émigrés, such as the more romantic Eliel Saarinen, were accepted as authentic American architects. Cret's tragedy was that he arrived in his adopted land fully mature in a European skepticism of revolution, a doubt fostered by the Continental debacles of 1848. Unlike his student Kahn, Cret never was to experience personally the American myth held high by the Progressives. Cret's faithful disciples also suffered the same peer rejection as Cret. One of his top students, regarding his own stunted career, complained that Cret's teaching and theory did not prepare him professionally for the revolutionary apotheosis of the International Style in the U.S. after World War II.[43] Kahn, however, benefiting in America from the largess of Progressive institutions and their philosophy, was intellectually prepared to break with tradition.

Although grounded in American Romanticism, Louis Kahn's sensibility is obviously in debt to Cret's more objective French Rationalism. Kenneth Frampton was the first scholar to document the Gallic influence upon the younger architect's thought in his important article "Louis I. Kahn and the French Connection."[44] This French subtlety is manifest in his search for structural images of simultaneous rational and aesthetic worth as well as his concern for finding the right *parti* for a project, one with "character" — expressing the essence of contemporary needs, psychological and physical. Like the Néo-Grecs, Kahn was devoted to creating a Progressive, legible architecture, one that could be read by the rational mind discursively, almost left to right, through the logic of its physiognomy. Like Cret, he supported a non-personal ideal expressed by the term "commonness," and he recognized the validity of architectural precedents. However, Kahn's romantic bent led him simultaneously to pursue, against the warnings of Cret, a primitive modernism. His geometrically simplified architectural imagery with its modern structural innovations escapes the limits of scientific history into the irrational, poetic experience of mythical time. The contradictory result of this synthesis was a Hi-Tech Primitivism. Here Kahn was in debt to both Progressive camps, Neoclassicists and Modernists. The following statements made in 1959 and 1962, respectively, exhibit Kahn's careful synthesis of Cret's French ideals and those more American.

... modern space is really not different from Renaissance space. In many ways it is not. We still want domes, we still want walls, we still want arches, arcades, and loggias of all kinds.[45]

Think of the wonderful discoveries of science today, and think of how much our architecture is at a standstill. I believe our architecture looks like Renaissance buildings, simply in new materials. I do not think it looks like modern buildings to me.[46]

Speaking of his own experiences as a young student in Philadelphia, Kahn said:

This is the city of availabilities. When I was a kid, one could avail oneself of places where one could learn without having the money to do so – it was all free. I went to several art schools in this city and I felt that was a wonderful thing to have these availabilities.... Now I think about the city in the same terms of availabilities. A city is measured by its institutions – not by its traffic systems, not by certain mechanical services, but by the way a man can find the places where he can develop his expression.[47]

I realized in India and Pakistan that a great majority of the people are without ambition because there is no way in which they are able to elevate themselves beyond living from hand to mouth, and what is worse, talents have no outlets.[48]

... In these countries where commonality is rarely expressed in the institutions available, I might not have had such aspirations.[49]

In time, the romantic pedagogical principles of the Progressives grew to become Kahn's own. He stated:

I believe in schools of natural talent.... School should be the center of freedom.... There should be no judgement, there should be no comparing one person with another.... If you have a classroom of thirty students in which freedom reigns, you would have thirty teachers.[50]

These educational ideals, encouraged by personal experience, inspired Kahn's making of architecture. He conveyed this Progressive sensibility as a nonverbal, expressive language rooted in the spirit of nature and humankind:

For me, architecture is not a business but a religion, devotion and dedication for human enjoyment.[51]

Endnotes

1 *Marshall D. Meyers, Conversations with author (Philadelphia: 1979–1981). Marshall Meyers was a member of Louis Kahn's office circa 1957 to the time of Kahn's death in 1974. In Kahn's office, he served as project architect for the Kimbell Museum.*

2 *Alessandra Latour, editor and introduction,* Louis I. Kahn, Writings, Lectures, Interviews *(New York: Rizzoli, 1991): 309.*

3 *Louis Kahn in his personal library kept at his office possessed the following copy concerning* Emerson: Ralph Waldo Emerson, *Selected Essays, (London (?): T. Nelson and Sons, Ltd., no date). The book had the name of Kahn's daughter, "Sue Kahn," written inside. I catalogued Kahn's personal library between 1978 and 1981 as part of the research for my University of Pennsylvania dissertation, 1983. This collection of books is currently housed in the home of Kahn's widow, Mrs. Esther I. Kahn.*

4 *J. Liberty Tadd,* New Methods of Education: Art, Real Manual Training, Nature Study *(Springfield: Orange Judd Company, 1899): 15.*

5 *Ibid., 359.*

6 *Marietta P. Boyer, Librarian at the Pennsylvania Academy of the Fine Arts, Telephone conversation with the author (Philadelphia: March 20, 1991). Ms. Boyer kindly researched the dates of J. Liberty Tadd's and William F. Gray's attendance for me in the closed archives of the Academy. Lloyd Goodrich,* Thomas Eakins *(Washington: National Gallery of Art, 1982). Wilford Wildes Scott,* The Artistic Vanguard in Philadelphia, 1905–1920 *(Ph.D. dissertation, University of Delaware, 1983).*

7 The American Renaissance, 1876–1917, *exh. cat. (New York: The Brooklyn Museum, Pantheon Books, 1979).*

8 *Sally Lorensen Gross,* American Manuals for Art Instruction in the Public Schools: Progress, Prophecy, and Art for the Millennium *(Ph.D. dissertation, Bryn Mawr College, 1987): 256–277.*

9 *Tadd, xxi.*
10 *Ibid., 62.*
11 *Ibid., 155.*
12 *Ibid., xii, 253–254.*
13 *Ibid., 24–25.*
14 *Ibid., 339–340.*
15 *Ibid., 188.*
16 *Ibid., 233.*
17 *Ibid., 162–163.*
18 *Ibid., 76–77.*
19 *Ibid., 32–33.*
20 *Ibid., 208.*
21 *Ibid., 57.*
22 *Ibid., 32–33.*

23 Louis I. Kahn: Drawings, *exh. cat. (New York: Max Protech Gallery; Los Angeles: Access Press Inc., 1981): 3.*

24 *Tadd, 128.*

25 *Richard Saul Wurman, editor,* What Will Be Has Always Been, The Words of Louis I. Kahn *(New York: Access Press Ltd. and Rizzoli, 1986): 76.*

26 *Boyer.*
27 *Scott, 52–57.*

28 *Willard G. Myers, "William F. Gray," Obituary in Sketch Club files (Philadelphia: Sketch Club, 1956).*

29 *William F. Gray,* Philadelphia's Architecture *(Philadelphia: City History Society of Philadelphia, 1915): 339–343.*

30 *Gray,* Philadelphia's Architecture, *361–363.*

31 *"City Hall? Awful Cry 'Tear It Down,'"* Bulletin *(Philadelphia: January 25, 1919).*

32 *Gray,* Philadelphi'a Architecture, *357.*

33 *David B. Brownlee,* Building the City Beautiful, *exh. cat. (Philadelphia: Philadelphia Museum of Art, 1989): 1–12.*

34 *Donald E. Gordon, "On the Origin of the Word 'Expressionism,'"* Journal of the Warburg and Courtauld Institutes, *29 (London: Warburg Institute, University of London, 1966): 368-385;* Expressionism, Art and Idea *(New Haven: Yale University Press, 1887): 174–176. Richard Shiff,* Cezanne and the End of Impressionism *(Chicago: The University of Chicago Press, 1984): 155–157.*

35 *Howard Anthony Risatti,* American Critical Reaction to European Modernism, 1908 to 1917 *(Ph.D. dissertation, University of Illinois at Urbana-Champaign, 1978).*

36 *Paul P. Cret, "The Architect as Collaborator of the Engineer,"* Architectural Forum, *49 (1929): 97–104.*

37 *Ibid.*

38 *Paul P. Cret, "Truth and Tradition,"* Architectural Record, *25 (1909): 107–110.*

39 *Craig Zabel and Susan Scott Munshower, editors,* American Public Architecture, European Roots and Native Expressions *(University Park, Pennsylvania: The Pennsylvania State University, 1989): 272-303.*

40 *Paul P. Cret, "Modern Architecture,"* Significance of the Fine Arts *(Boston: Marshall Jones Company, 1923): 181–243.*

41 *Elizabeth Green Grossman,* Paul Philippe Cret: Rationalism and Imagery in American Architecture *(Ph.D. dissertation, Brown University, 1980): 122–134.*

42 *Ibid., 2–3, 37–92.*

43 *John Lane Evans, Telephone conversation with author (Philadelphia: March 1991).*

44 *Kenneth Frampton, "Louis I. Kahn and the French Connection,"* Oppositions, *22 (Cambridge: MIT Press, Fall 1980).*

45 *Latour, 90.*
46 *Latour, 149.*
47 *Wurman, 122.*
48 *Latour, 267.*
49 *Ibid., 344.*
50 *Wurman, 153.*

51 *August E. Komendant,* Eighteen Years with Architect Louis I. Kahn *(Englewood Cliffs, New Jersey: Aloray Publishers, 1975).*

Credits

All texts, drawings and photographs have been supplied by the authors and/or contributors unless otherwise noted.

Louis Kahn: The Berkeley Lecture, 1966

photo credits:
pgs. 12 – 17, 24 – 27. Louis I Kahn Collection, University of Pennsylvania and Pennsylvania Historical and Museum Commission. All images are referenced by drawing number.

pg. 12 – 13. 540.60

pg. 14 – 15. 540.74

pg. 16 – 17. 540.104

pg. 18. redrawn by R. Joyce

pg. 24. 650-196

pg. 25. 650-195

pg. 26. 650-205

pg. 27. 650-234

pg. 28. redrawn by R. Joyce

pg. 34. photograph by R. Joyce

pg. 49. Beverly Pabst

Jean Nouvel
Doctrines and Uncertainties; Toward a Number of Architectures; Extracts from a Lecture at the Centre George Pompidou

All text courtesy of the author and Jean Nouvel Architects. Original text published in Spanish: "Jean Nouvel", catalogue for an exhibition, The Association of Catalon Architects, Barcelona 1990.

translation: Stephen Mercado

photocredits:
pg. 52, 54, 56, 58, 60. video images [Georges Fessy]

pg. 63 Arnoud Baumann / Sipa Press

Gunther Behnisch
For an Open Architecture; Finding Form; Techniques and Materials; Diversity

All text courtesy of the author and Behnisch and Partner. Original text published in German: "Behnisch and Partner", catalogue for an exhibition, Stuttgart 1992.

photocredits:
pg. 64, 69, 70 Behnisch and Partner

pg. 73, 74, 75. Christian Kandzia

pg. 77. Behnisch and Partner

Adele Naude-Santos
Excerpts from a conversation

photocredits:
pg. 78. Tomio Ohashi

pg. 79. Antonio DeSouza Santos

pg. 82. Mariko Matsunura

pg. 83. Barry Halkin

pg. 84, 85. Hiro Sakaguchi, Studio A to Z

pg. 93. Kevin Walsh

Aldo Rossi
Architecture, furniture and some of my dogs; A Conversation: Aldo Rossi and Bernard Huet

All text courtesy of Bernard Huet and Studio d' Architectura. Original text published in German: "Aldo Rossi Architekt", catalogue for an exhibition, Martin-Gropius-Bau, Berlin 1993.

translation: Katerine May

photocredits:
pg. 97. SDA Italia

pg. 98. Ned Matura

pg. 99. SDA Italia

pg. 100. SDA Italia

pg. 101. Menchem Adelman

pg. 102. SDA Italia

pg. 103. SDA Italia

pg. 104. SDA Italia

pg. 113. SDA Italia

W.G. Clark
Lost Colony

photocredits:
114 – 123. W.G. Clark
pg. 125. Clark and Menefee Architects

Robert Venturi/Denise Scott Brown
Interview with Denise Scott Brown and Robert Venturi Phillipe Barriere and Sylvia Lavin

All text courtesy of Phillipe Barriere and Venturi, Scott Brown Architects. Original text published in French: "L' Architecture d' Aujord'hui", February 1991.

photocredits:
pg. 126. Matt Wargo

pg. 131, 132. Matt Wargo

pg. 137, 138. Matt Wargo

pg. 140. Matt Wargo

pg. 142 – 143 Matt Wargo

pg. 144 – 145. John T. Miller

John Keenan Terrance Riley
Tectonic Collage:

photocredits:
pg. 148. John Keenan

pg. 149, 151, 152. Eduard Hueber

pg. 152 – 153. John Keenan

pg. 154 – 155. John Keenan

pg. 155, 156 – 157. Eduard Hueber

pg. 157. John Keenan

pg. 158, 159. Peter Musebrink

Deborah Berke and Carey McWhorter
Invisible Architecture

photocredits:
pg. 161. Catherine Bogert

pg. 162. Catherine Bogert

pg. 162, 163, 164, 165. Berke and McWhorter Architects

pg. 165. Catherine Bogert

pg. 166. Catherine Bogert

pg 167. Berke McWhorter Architects

pg. 168. Jack Deutsch

pg. 169. Andy Bergman

Margaret Helfand and Marti Cohen
Reflection

photocredits:
pg. 170, 175. Marti Cohen

pg. 177. Margaret Helfand

pg. 178. Dorothy Alexander

pg. 179. William Whitehurst

Patricia and John Patkau
Tecto-Totemic Form: A Note on Patkau Associates

photocredits:
pg. 180. Patkau Architects

pg. 181. Patkau Architects

pg. 182. Patkau Architects

pg. 182 – 183. James Dow

pg. 184. James Dow

pg. 184 – 185. Patkau Architects

pg. 186-187. Patkau Architects

pg. 188-189. Raymond Lum

Thomas Leeser
Twisting Strings
Of Zweifalt and Doubts

photocredits:
pg. 190, 193. David C. Lindberg, Studies in the History of Medieval Optics (London: Variorium Reprints, 1983).

190 - 192. 'Androgyny' and 'Not to Be Reproduced'. Margot Lovejoy, Postmodern Currents, Art and Artists in the Age of Electronic Media, (UMI Research Press, Ann Arbor, Michigan, 1989).

192. 'Double Print', 'Image in Motion', 'The Slap', 'Sectional Anatomy'. Supplied by the author.

192. 'W.W.1 Battleship'. Bernard Fitzsimons. Warships of the First World War (London: BPC Publishing Ltd., 1973).

193. 'The Four Fundamental Concepts of Psycho-Analysis'. The Seminar of Jacques Lacan, Book 1. Freud's Papers on Technique, 1953-1954. (New York: Norton, 1978).

pg. 202. Erica Lennard

The Aesthetic Education of Louis I. Kahn, 1912-1924
Joseph A. Burton

Research for this paper was partially funded by a 1989 grant from the Graham Foundation for Advanced Studies in the Fine Arts, a 1989 University of Minnesota grant, and a 1990 Clemson University grant. I am indebted to Dr. Sally Lorenson Gross for her generous help in introducing me to the subject of art education during the Progressive Era. See: Sally Lorensen Gross, American Manuals for Art Instruction in the Public Schools: Progress, Prophecy, and Art for the Millennium (Ph.D. disserta-

tion, Bryn Mawr College, 1987). The title of the paper recognizes the influence of German literary thought upon Louis I. Kahn largely through his mother. Bertha Mendelssohn Kahn's favorite German authors were Goethe and Schiller. Johann Christoph Friedrich Schiller was the author of The Aesthetic Education of Man in a Series of Letters.

photocredits:
pg. 207. Elementary Forms in Clay: Geometric Forms and Bird Forms. J. Liberty Tadd, New Methods of Education: Art, Real Manual Training, Nature Study (Springfield: Orange Judd Company, 1899): 191.

pg. 207. Drawing from Life. J. Liberty Tadd, New Methods of Education: Art, Real Manual Training, Nature Study (Springfield: Orange Judd Company, 1899): 414.

pg. 207. First Ambidextrous Exercises: African-American Youth in Philadelphia Primary School. J. Liberty Tadd, New Methods of Education: Art, Real Manual Training, Nature Study (Springfield: Orange Judd Company, 1899): 72.

pg. 207. Louis I. Kahn Exhibiting Ambidextrous Drawing Courtesy of Martin Rich. Photograph by Martin Rich

pg. 208. Modeling a Head. J. Liberty Tadd, New Methods of Education: Art, Real Manual Training, Nature Study (Springfield: Orange Judd Company, 1899): 225.

pg. 208. Wood Carving. J. Liberty Tadd, New Methods of Education: Art, Real Manual Training, Nature Study (Springfield: Orange Judd Company, 1899): 19.

pg. 209. Louis I. Kahn: Citadel Gate, Carcassonne, France, 1959. Louis I. Kahn Collection, University of Pennsylvania. Gift of Richard Saul Wurman.

pg. 209. Louis I. Kahn, Architect : Citadel Gate, Capitol Building, Dacca, Bangladesh Photograph by Joseph A. Burton.

pg. 209. Anne G. Tyng. Project for an Elementary School, 1949-51.

pg. 209. Animal Illustrations by Louis I. Kahn. Philadelphia AIA Year Book 1952. Photograph by Edward Gallob.

pg. 210. Louis I. Kahn. Assisi, Italy, ca. 1929. Courtesy of the Pennsylvania Academy of the Fine Arts, Philadelphia. Gift of Mrs. Louis I. Kahn.

pg. 210. Louis I. Kahn. Market Street East Studies: Bird's eye perspective of Civic Center, looking west, ca. 1957. Louis I. Kahn Collection, University of Pennsylvania. Gift of Richard Saul Wurman.

pg.211. Louis I. Kahn and Anne G. Tyng. City Tower. Louis I. Kahn Collection, University of Pennsylvania and Pennsylvania Historical and Museum Commission. Photograph by Robert Damora.

pg.211. Detail of the City Tower and Plaza Square. Louis I. Kahn Collection, University of Pennsylvania and Pennsylvania Historical and Museum Commission. Photograph by Robert Damora.

Foreward; Vision, Intention; Inspiration and Making; Learning, Self

All text selections and introductory statements by Robert Joyce, co-editor.

Colophon

Perspecta 28 was designed and produced digitally during 1993-1994 in Montréal, Quebec and at Connecticut College in New London, Connecticut.

Hardware.
Apple Macintosh Quadra 800™ computer; APS SyQuest drive; ApplePro 630 Laser Printer; and Ethernet and LocalTalk networking.

Software.
The text was composed in QuarkXpress; image development was created in Adobe Illustrator and Photoshop.

Typography.
Perspecta 28 was set in Meta, Times Roman, Univers and Courier. Meta, a digital typeface designed by Erik Spiekermann in Germany was introduced in 1990. Times Roman, a typeface designed by Stanely Morison was introduced in The London Times on October 3, 1932. Times Roman is based on Robert Granjon's Gros Cicero, produced in Paris in 1569 and modified for Plantin. Univers, a typeface designed by Adrian Frutiger in Switzerland, was first distributed in 1957. It was designed to simplify typographic nomenclature by introducing a system of twenty-one variations based on stroke and weight. Courier, a typeface developed from the typewriter, has been carried over to wide-spread use in desktop publishing.

Electronic Prepress by Typogram Inc., New York City. Color transparencies and black and white images were scanned into the 10-track Scitex system and converted to black and white images files. Preliminary image tone and contrast correction was proofed on black match prints and 2540 linotronic paper. Final film negative is 2540 dpi L560 film 175 line at 18 x 24". Printed on a sheet fed press at South China Printing in Hong Kong.

Perspecta 28 is an edition of 3000 copies.

They are inspired, you see, by just the same ... feelings ... about existence.

Selection from "Louis I. Kahn: Berkeley Lecture, 1966" page 8, line 6